FOLKLORE
HAMPSHIRE

FOLKL*of*ORE
HAMPSHIRE

PENNY LEGG

The
History
Press

For Joe, with love.

First published 2010

Reprinted 2015, 2019

The History Press
97 St George's Place,
Cheltenham, Gloucestershire, GL50 3QB
www.thehistorypress.co.uk

© Penny Legg, 2010, 2015

British Library Cataloguing in Publication Data.
A catalogue record for this book is available from the British Library.

ISBN 978 0 7524 5179 4

Typesetting and origination by The History Press
Printed in Great Britain by TJ International Ltd, Padstow, Cornwall

CONTENTS

ACKNOWLEDGEMENTS

I hope I have remembered everyone who has helped me with the research of this book. If I have forgotten to add your name, please accept my apologies and my sincere gratitude for your assistance.

My thanks to:
Joe Legg, my husband; Nicola Guy, my Commissioning Editor at The History Press; Sylvia Kent; Richard Gordon; Anthony Loudon, Tichborne Dole; Suzanne Foster, Winchester College; Bitterne Historical Society; Ros Cooper, Federation Secretary of Hampshire County Federation of Women's Institutes; 'Sir' Graham Hart, Sue Pheasant, 'Sir' David Priestly and the members of the Southampton Old Bowling Green; Paul Marsh, Otterbourne Mummers, Roud/Marsh Collection; Jimmy Marsh; Chris Buswell, QARANC; the late Eric Geden-Tysoe and Hannah Geden-Tysoe; David and Nicky Basson; Phil Yates, Historian for the Theatre Royal, Winchester; Catherine Aitchison Hull; Paul Stickler and Derek Stevens, Hampshire Constabulary History Society; Julie Forest; Albert Wilkins, Bagman of the Winchester Morris Men; Mike Slocombe; Jean Cook; the late Sarah Morgan; Derek Schofield, Editor of *English Song and Dance*; Bob Askew; Craig, Morgan, Robson; the Askew sisters; Deborah Mitchell, Joan Wood and the Southampton Philharmonic Choir; Chris Hayles, Southern Life; John Hurst, Eling Tide Mill; Alex Wylie; Nigel Wood and Lynn Daudel, Lingwood Netley Hospital Archive; Tim Taylor, Secretary of the Abbotts Ann Parochial Church Council; Peter Goff; the late John Melody, former Southampton Town Crier; Paul Potter; Patrick Kirkby; Pam Whittington; Simon Whalley; Kit Hayward; the helpful staff at the Hampshire Records Office; Dr John Maher, Web Editor and Ring Overseas Bagman, themorrisring.org; Sue Hill, Archivist for the Southampton City Council; Dr Andy Russel, Southhampton's Archaeology Unit Manager; Dick Brooker and Steve Roud.

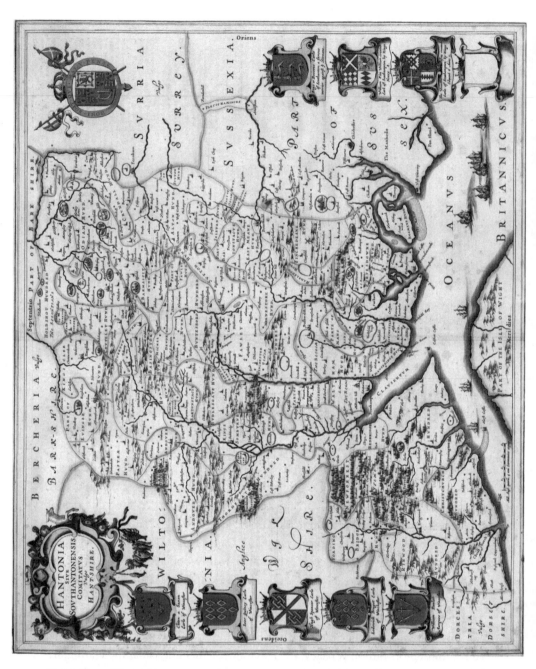

Blaeu's Map of Hampshire, 1645

PREFACE TO
FOLKLORE OF HAMPSHIRE

All over the country our old customs are dying and have been doing so for centuries. The Puritans did their best to eradicate superstition. The Ages of Reason and Enlightenment in the eighteenth and nineteenth centuries saw no room for traditions going back hundreds of years and whose origins were forgotten in the passage of time, especially if they were boisterous, rowdy or rude.

Hampshire, the ninth largest county in England, is situated in the extreme south of the country and covers an area of 3,769 square kilometres, which is 1,455 square miles. It stretches to the borders of Dorset, Wiltshire, Berkshire, West Sussex and Surrey. Its acres include the New Forest and part of the South Downs, and it has two unitary authorities, Portsmouth and Southampton. Since 2002 the Hampshire county flower has been the dog rose, while Hampshire cricket has been played at the Rose Bowl since 2001.

This book attempts to give an insight into the folklore of this proud county. I have looked at traditions, superstitions and old customs, some of which have died out and others which continue. I have sought out music and verse and things that go bump in the night. I have talked to local people and have tried to convey their thoughts on the happenings in their county. Of course, there is always too much information to go into a book this size and so I hope I will be forgiven for my editorial decisions; not everything I found made it into the published book.

I must thank Nicola Guy, my Commissioning Editor at The History Press, for her unfailing assistance and Sylvia Kent, for introducing me to Nicola. I must also thank all the people who have helped me with the research for this book.

Their names and organisations are listed in the Acknowledgements section earlier in the book. Finally, I must thank my long-suffering husband, Joe, who kept me going with his cheerful enthusiasm, and his enjoyment of being dragged about Hampshire when I wanted to see for myself what I was writing about.

I have thoroughly enjoyed researching the folklore of Hampshire and I hope you enjoy reading about it.

Penny Legg

July 2010

PREFACE TO THE 2015 EDITION

I am delighted to be given the chance to update this, my first book. When it came out in 2010, I received several e-mails telling me how readers had enjoyed it. That information was gratifying and I thank all those who contacted me. What was surprising though, was the fact that the book was being used as a guide book to the county. Fantastic!

To all my readers, I hope you have fun with this book and I thank you for reading it.

Penny Legg

August 2015

ONE

ANNUAL CUSTOMS

Come lasses and lads, get leave of your dads,
And away to the Maypole hie,
For every he has got him a she,
And the fiddler's standing by.
For Willie shall dance with Jane,
And Johnny has got his Joan,
To trip it, trip it, trip it, trip it, trip it up and down.

Anon
'Come Lads and Lasses', *c.* 1670, *Oxford Song Book*

All over the county, Hampshire folk have evolved customs and traditions since time began, for reasons sometimes shrouded in the mists of history. This chapter takes a snapshot look at Hampshire's annual customs, some of which are very old indeed.

Wassailing

Twelfth Night apple wassailing was considered an essential part of ensuring a good apple harvest. To guarantee a good crop the apple orchards were blessed. This involved the villagers forming a circle about the largest apple tree in the orchard, pouring cider around the tree's roots and placing cider-soaked bread or cake up into the branches. These were for the robins, which were thought to be good spirits in the orchard. The villagers then chanted songs to support growth and guns were fired to ward off evil spirits.

Although apple wassailing was a custom in many parts of the country, during the nineteenth century in Hampshire the folk would sometimes take their was-sailing bowls, filled with hot spiced wine and roasted apples, around the village at New Year, knocking on doors and treating the householders to a song and a sip of wine in return for a small sum. This continued an earlier custom of sitting with the householder and passing the wassailing bowl around those present, whilst offering the old Saxon toast 'Waeshael', meaning 'good health'.

Twelfth Night

Writing in 1832, William Hone relates a Twelfth Night ritual that was then a 'disused custom among the people'. He quotes Barnaby Googe (1540-1594), the early pastoral poet, who describes the 'censing of a loaf and themselves as a preservative against sickness and witchcraft throughout the year'.

The family would assemble in the living room on the evening of Twelfth Night and the master of the house would burn frankincense and place a loaf of bread on the table in front of him. He would then breathe in the smoke. His wife would follow him and then each of their children and the rest of the household. This was to:

> ... preserve they say their teeth,
> and nose and eye and eare,
> From every kind of maladie
> and sickness all the yeare.

The pan burning the frankincense was then taken, along with the loaf of bread, in procession around the house. The smoke was allowed to fragrance all the rooms so:

> That neither bread nor meat do want
> nor witch with dreadful charme,
> Have power to hurt their children, or
> do their cattell harme.

Plough Monday

Traditionally the first Monday after Twelfth Night was Plough Monday. This was the day that men would return to their work after the Christmas holidays. The festival was handed down from the Roman Compitalia festival in January which Tarquinius Priscus, the fifth King of Rome who reigned from 616 BC to 579 BC, was thought to have inaugurated.

On the Sunday before Plough Monday, farm labourers took ploughs to church to be blessed. In pre-Reformation England, the Plough Light, a church candle that was kept lit all year, was ceremonially paraded during the service.

The following day ploughing would begin for the new season, but it was not a day for serious work and so the labour would end early. There would then be a race, which consisted of the ploughmen getting home to their master and calling 'cock in the pot' before the dairymaids finished their duties and called 'cock on the dunghill'. The winner would be given their prize, a cockerel.

The ploughs were then decorated with horse brasses, bells and ribbons and the plough boy, called the Plough Bullock or Plough Stot, would drag the decorated ploughs from door to door asking for 'plough money'. This was partly to keep the Plough Light burning in the church and the rest was spent on a party known as a 'frolic'. Anyone not contributing to the ploughman collector, dressed as a woman and called 'Bessy', who accompanied the Plough Stot, would find his front garden ploughed up. Bessy became the queen of the frolic and presided over the Plough Monday banquet.

The banquet itself was traditionally of a root vegetables and meat stock pottage or soup, followed by 'plough pudding', a suet pudding filled with meat and onions. This was followed by plum pottage, the forerunner of what we know today as plum pudding.

The ploughs were known as 'Fond', 'Fool' or 'White' Ploughs; 'Fond' or 'Fool' because the plough procession was not meant to be serious, while 'White' refers to the Mummers who customarily dressed in white clothing, gaily embellished with flowers and ribbons. The ploughs were also decorated in a similar fashion on Plough Monday. At the banquet there was frequently a performance of a Mummers play and folk dancing.

The term 'Speed the plough' or 'God speed the plough' comes from a song sung by ploughmen on Plough Monday in hope for success in future plantings.

Lady Mabella Gets Her Way

The Tichborne Dole was born of a colourful history. So the legend goes, in the twelfth century during the reign of Henry II of England (1133-1189, reigned from 1154-1189), Lady Mabella (Mabel) de Tichborne lay on her deathbed. She was the gently born daughter of Ralph de Lymerston and the wife of a soldier, the Lord of the Manor of Tichborne, Roger de Tichborne, of the ancient family of the same name. The name derives from the nearby River Itchen, with the suffix 'bourn' meaning 'a stream'.

Lady Mabella was known for her humanity and kindness. As her last wish she asked her husband to establish an annual dole for the poor from the Tichborne estates. Sir Roger, not being a particularly charitably minded individual, replied that he would give as much as the value of land that she was able to walk around while holding a lighted torch in her hand.

Lady Mabella was a determined woman. Although suffering from an unnamed wasting disease, she managed to drag herself around twenty-three acres of farmland before the torch went out. To the present day this field is known as 'the Crawls'. Knowing her husband well, she added a curse to her request to ensure future compliance. Should the dole not be distributed, there would be seven sons born to the house, followed immediately by a generation of seven daughters. The Tichborne name would die out and the house would fall down. This was a curse not to be taken lightly!

It is said that the dole was distributed annually in the form of bread, or the sum of tuppence (under 5p in today's money) if 1,400 loaves proved to be insufficient. In 1794 however, magistrates, disturbed by the numbers of paupers and vagabonds the dole was attracting, decreed that it must stop.

Although it was not the family that had stopped distributing the dole, Lady Mabella's curse soon made itself felt. Sir Henry Tichborne was the resident at Tichborne House at the time and he had seven sons. Eight years after the dole ceased, in 1802, thirteen-year-old George, the sixth son, died and later in the same year part of the old house fell down. Four years later, in 1806, the fifth son, John, died unmarried in the East Indies. Benjamin, the second son, who was also unmarried, died in 1810 in China. Roger, the seventh son, died without issue a few years later. Henry was the eldest and the father of a hopeful family of seven daughters. The third son, Edward, in an effort to cheat the curse, changed his name to Doughty, after which the area in Holloway, London, is named, and had one son, Henry. He died, aged six, in 1835. Soon after this Edward Doughty reinstituted the dole and it has continued ever since.

In the meantime, the fourth son, James, had married in 1827 and had a son born before the dole was restored, Roger Charles Tichborne, and a second son, Alfred Joseph, who was born afterwards. Roger Charles was lost at sea in 1845 and was impersonated many years later by Arthur Orton in the infamous case of the Tichborne Claimant, which cost the family £100,000 to defend in court. Alfred Joseph, born after the dole was restored, survived. He was the great-grandfather of the late Sir Anthony Doughty Tichborne, 14th Baronet, the grandfather of the current owner of Tichborne House, Anthony Loudon.

Stockbroker Anthony is married to a New Zealander, Catherine, and they have two children. The present-day ceremony of the Tichborne Dole is very much a family affair. Anthony says:

> When you have grown up with the legend it feels almost normal. But of course to others it is completely different, strange and unique. So I am very proud of it and I think it's fantastic to have a history that goes back that far and to be able to do something charitable every year and to do something that has been going on for so long.

The dole distributed now is plain flour and, according to local resident Karen Bushnell, 'It's really good flour, the best!' Mina Crockford agrees, saying, 'It makes lovely scones!' Mina has been coming to the dole every year since 1955 and used to bring her daughter, Sarah, to the event in her pram. Peter Dickinson, Cheriton resident since 1947, says, 'Originally the dole was to be the produce from a field down the road. It is an agricultural impossibility to grow wheat every year for nearly a thousand years'.

Anthony Loudon explains what goes on behind the scenes before Lady Day, 25 March, the day of the Tichborne Dole:

> First we order flour on a sale or return basis. You never know if you will have quite enough, although there is a set amount that we are supposed to give out, a gallon for each adult and half a gallon for each child, and not everyone comes to collect it. Then we have to make sure that the priest is invited to lunch, as we bless the flour, and that we are here on the day.

Canon Alan Griffiths from the Winchester Diocese blesses the flour and says a prayer for the repose of the soul of Lady Mabella Tichborne. The residents of the parishes of Tichborne and Cheriton are called up in house order to receive their allotted amount. They come bearing suitable receptacles, pillowcases and carrier bags, and there is a general buzz of excitement in the air. The Loudon's young family help out and all are soon covered in a film of white. Anthony Loudon says of the children, 'They love it!'

About two tonnes of flour are doled out each year. Dave Fullick, whose family moved to Cheriton in 1949, remembers when he was a lad:

> As children at school we used to take the day off on this day to borrow the local cart and push people's flour home for half a crown. We used to make a bit of pocket money. It's a lovely tradition and I hope it goes on for many, many years.

With Lady Mabella's curse in the background and a steely determination by the family to continue with the tradition, it seems that the Tichborne Dole is set to be a feature of village life in the area for many years to come.

Our Game

If you are an Old Wykehamist, you will know what 'Our Game' refers to and will probably either read on to ensure that the details given here are correct, or will turn the page on the assumption that you know all there is to be known about it and therefore do not need to read anything else. If you are not now, and never have been, a pupil at Winchester College and are therefore not a Wykehamist, you are probably wondering what this is all about.

Winchester College Football, or WinCoFo, is affectionately known by Wykehamists young and old as 'Our Game'. The younger Wykehamists also use the slightly more informal nickname 'Winkies', an appellation much frowned upon by the older generation.

This complicated mixture of elements of traditional football and rugby, played with an over-inflated round ball, was first contested along the length of Winchester's Kingsgate Street in the sixteenth century. It was literally a battle to get the ball from one end of the street to the other and there were no rules.

It was later moved to St Catherine's Hill as the college owned the hill and it was a safer place for a fiercely fought game to take place. Here it was more difficult to keep the ball in play as the pitch, a flat rectangle, was at the apex of the sloping hillsides. As the Winchester College website points out, the game was 'little more than a free-for-all', with the object being to try to send the ball over the opponent's marker line, a cut in the turf known as 'worms', to score a point.

To stop the ball from careering down the hill, junior boys were lined up along the edges of the pitch and were used as human walls to contain the ball and the players. These were known, somewhat unimaginatively, as 'kickers in'. Their position was dangerous as they faced injury from fast-moving, hard-kicked footballs and from out of control players careering into them.

The first rules came into existence in about 1790 and it is about this time that play began at Meads, although it was not until the 1860s that play on St Catherine's Hill ceased. By 1825, not only were matches being regularly played between the College and Commoners, but also the kickers in were replaced as walls by poles and ropes, effectively enclosing the play in a non-encroaching manner. It was not until 1844, however, that they were relieved of their ball-stopping duties, when canvas screens were introduced. The poles and ropes remained. The pitch was then known as a 'canvas'. In 1866 netting was invented and the canvas was taken down. Spectators breathed a collective sigh of relief at being able to see the game properly for the first time in over twenty years.

The game is played by two teams, with two referees, on a canvas that is 73m long and 24.5m wide. The netting around it is 2.5m high to stop the ball from leaving the canvas. The teams can comprise either fifteen, ten or six men. House competitions between the smaller teams last twenty minutes each way, while the larger senior teams play for thirty minutes each way. The standard fifteen-man team has eight forwards, called 'Men of the Hot'. A 'hot' is a scrum. Four half-backs, or 'Hotwatches', try to get the ball past the 'hot' and defend their 'worms'. There are three full-backs, known as 'kicks'. What is known in conventional football as 'dribbling' is not allowed in Winchester College Football. The ball cannot be kicked higher than 5ft above the ground, unless it bounces off an opponent. The 'hot' starts and restarts the play, except when a goal has been scored. The game proceeds on the principle that each team can only kick the ball once before the other team touches it. It is therefore in each team's best interest to kick the ball as hard and as far as possible. There are many rules and they are still evolving as play is refined. There have been thirteen different rulebooks since 1790.

The game was traditionally played in the autumn term, but is now played in Common Time between January and March. It is played by all members of the school and at the senior level there are three teams: College, who play in blue and white; Old Tutor's Houses (known as OTH or Houses), who wear brown and white; and Commoners, who wear red and white.

The game is currently thought to be exclusive to Winchester College. From 1866 to 1873 it was played at the Parks in Oxford and it was also played in South Africa until rugby was invented. It is thought possible that a similar street game may be played in Bolivia, but this has not been confirmed.

The Easter Fair at Portsdown Hill

Victorian Portsmouth looked forward to Easter, when the fair would arrive and for a few days some fun could be had. On Easter Monday vast crowds would make their way from the town out into the country, for much of the suburbs we know now had not been built then and rural Hampshire was much nearer the built-up town centre than it is now. Most would walk, particularly youngsters intent on spending what little they had at the fair, not on getting there. Others would go by donkey-drawn cart or by horse-drawn wagon and Cosham High Street was said to resemble 'Epsom town on Derby morning' (Esmond and Triggs).

They were drawn to the myriad attractions that, to Victorian folk, seemed so different and exciting, but which perhaps seem old fashioned and slow to twenty-first century tastes, used to sophisticated electronic entertainment. Fat ladies and gypsies telling fortunes, coconut shies and skeleton men, horses and swing boats, hoopla and boxing, all thrown together with music from steam organs, cries of delight, calls of stall holders and much laughter, combined to offer distractions aplenty for Portsmouth's populace. Indeed, the glow from the fair in the evening was bright enough to be seen from Portsdown Hill to Hilsea and beyond.

A donkey derby would draw crowds of excited spectators as sailors, facing swishing tails, urged their beasts forward, often in the wrong direction! If you were a young gentleman, to show how strong you were was desirable, particularly if there were admiring ladies present, so the 'test your strength' barometers, towering up to 15ft in the air with a bell on the top, were popular. It looked so easy as the stallholder, who rang the bell every time, struck the machine with a large mallet-like hammer. The gentlemen who tried their strength soon found out that this was an illusion.

The boxers, stripped down to the waist to show their impressive muscles, added to the din by challenging all and sundry to a bout for a monetary prize. Each had no shortage of contenders, who usually came off the worst.

To eat there were oranges, apples and nuts in addition to the exotic coconuts. Lemonade was sold from great glass bowls.

Easter Monday was a day to look forward to on Portsdown Hill, which now has Sites of Nature Conservation Interest, and is a haven for butterflies, orchid species and spiders.

May Day, or Garland Day

The coming of spring and the renewal of the soil was a joyous event in days gone by, when central heating, supermarkets and the mass transportation of food had not been invented. The pagan Romans celebrated the Feast of Floralia between 28 April and 3 May, where they worshipped the goddess Flora and the coming of the spring flowers. This festival, which is believed to have begun in about 238 BC, involved much drinking and promiscuity. It also led to the forerunner of the Maypole we know today as, in response to whole trees being uprooted and left in front of girlfriends' front doors by overeager young swains, the authorities built tall poles in an effort to save local trees. The idea caught on and spread. The Celts celebrated Beltane, the coming of spring and the beginning of new life. For centuries May Day, or Garland Day as it is also known, has been a joyous observation of fertility.

In medieval times dancing around a Maypole on the village green on May Day was popular. The brightly coloured ribbons were said to be the colours of the rainbow, reinforcing the natural nature of the ritual. These were attached to the top of the pole, which had been cut that morning. Going into the woods to look for a suitable tree was a much-anticipated part of the celebrations for young people, bent on escaping the watchful eyes of chaperones at home. The May Garland proceeded from house to house and then on to the Maypole, led by the May Queen in her hawthorn crown and, sometimes, the May King, dressed in green as a symbol of nature and abundance. The dancers were all young men and women and as they danced, the ribbons intertwined and wound round the central pole.

The dew was thought to be an aid to a young lady's complexion and many a girl slipped outside to bathe her face in dew at dawn on May Day.

The Christian Church looked benignly at these revels, which came to include games and contests, but later, the Puritans in the seventeenth century were outraged. The bad behaviour associated with the May Day revels, drunkenness and dancing offended their sensibilities and the Maypole was banned by statute in 1644.

Anthony Brode found that in the parish records for Brockenhurst in the New Forest in 1670, there is a record of the prosecution of Henry Browne, who was fined and had his horse and cart confiscated for felling a tree to make into a Maypole. The objection was that the tree was erected as a Maypole, not that it had been felled in the first place!

Banned they may have been, but that did not stop Maypoles being erected to celebrate the return of Charles II to the throne, although the day was changed to 29 May and the name changed to Royal Oak Day. However, by the nineteenth century Maypole dancing was firmly back on the May Day agenda, albeit now danced by children and with much of the origin of the day forgotten.

The Hampshire Federation of Women's Institute's book, *It Happened in Hampshire*, first published in 1936, tells of some of the May Day customs that were still in living memory at that time. Children across the county gathered flowers and tied them to the end of a stick. They then went around their village hoping for a May Day penny, singing as they went.

The children of Marchwood sang:

A branch of May we have brought you,
And at your door it stands.
It's a very fine sprout,
And well spread about,
It's the work of our Lord's hands.

In Chilbolton they sang:

Please to see a fine garland,
Made early in the morning.
The 1st May is Garland Day,
Please see a fine garland.

In Bursledon the garland was covered until the penny was paid. The reward for this largesse was to see the flowers. Here the children sang a slightly different version:

The first of May is Garland Day,
A penny to see my garland.

In a village near Crookham the girls wore blue-striped cotton frocks and white tippet scarves, with white straw bonnets as they came around with their garlands.

Maypoles were recorded by the ladies of the Women's Institute as being erected in Twyford, Kingsclere, Bishops Waltham, Overton, Hurstbourne Tarrant, Old Basing and Greywell. The Bitterne Historical Society has a photograph from the turn of the twentieth century of a Maypole in Bitterne.

Milkmaids were singled out for comment in Hampshire, although they were noted as dancers all over the south of England. A milkmaid dancing was said to be 'exciting herself' about the Maypole but were also noted for the garlands placed about their milk pails, which they balanced on their heads when they

went to their customers delivering the milk, where they received a small sum
for their dancing.

Churches and houses were decorated for May Day, bedecked with hawthorn called the 'May-Bush' or 'May-Tree' by Hampshire folk. Chimney
sweeps danced in May-Houses made of green boughs on St Mary Bourne's
Summerhaugh, known later as the Square. Here the sweeps came, bringing with
them the tools of their trade which they clashed as they danced around the
Jack-in-the-Green, a man dressed as a tree, symbolising spring.

As Hampshire has become more sophisticated these customs have declined
and we have largely forgotten the basis of them. Nowadays when we see a
Maypole, we are more inclined to enjoy seeing the fun children have weav-
ing around it as they dance than to reflect on the original meanings involved.
The choir of King Edward VI School in Southampton, which sang beside the
Bargate on May Day mornings for many years after reviving the old custom in
1957, has also now ceased the practice, as the school has difficulty persuading
the choristers to turn up at six in the morning to sing the day in. Much of the
joyous nature of the celebration of the coming of spring has disappeared. One
ray of hope though is that the county's morris men are active on May Day. In
Southampton, the King John Morris Men 'dance in the May' at the Bargate at
five o'clock in the morning each May Day. On Southsea seafront the Victory
Morris Men greet the day as they have every year for the last thirty years, while
at Wyndham's Pond on Yateley Common the Yateley Morris Men 'dance up the
sun'. Long may these traditions continue.

Merry Fairs

The word 'merry' is taken from the French for 'cherry' (merise). Merry trees are
full of sweet, juicy, black cherries, their large stones out of proportion to their skins.
On Merry Sundays people would come for miles around to pay 3d per lb and eat
their fill. There were Merry Fairs at Woodgreen, Chandlers Ford and Fawley.

Merry Fairs at Woodgreen were a victim of their own success. They attracted
so many people, who proceeded to eat, drink and generally make riotous merry
with cock fighting, wrestling and other sports supplementing the feasting, that
a local clergyman, scandalised at such goings-on on the Sabbath, purchased the
Merry Garden and stopped the tradition.

In Chandler's Ford, Merrileas Road is a lasting reminder of the cherry
orchards in the area. The Merry Fair in Chandlers Ford was held at Ramalley, a
name which is thought to be a corruption of 'Merrilea'. Near the New Forest,

Woodgreen Village Hall has murals covering its interior walls. These depict village people and life. One of them features the apple harvest, which has now replaced the merry picking.

The Harvest

From back into the mists of time the harvest has been celebrated. It was a time for thanksgiving, and for gathering and storing food for the coming winter.

Lammas Day, from sundown on 1 August to sundown on 2 August, marked the quarter year since Beltane, or May Day, the spring festival, and was celebrated as the beginning of the Harvest Festival.

The Anglo-Saxon name Lammas, or Loaf-Mass, was known to the Celts as Lughnasadh. Lugh was the god of light. It was his beneficence that brought the long days of summer, which allowed the crops to ripen and be harvested.

It was believed that a harvest spirit lived in the cornfields and, as the fields were reaped, it had to retreat into the last corner of uncut land. The spirit was known in Hampshire as the 'Corn' or 'Kern Baby'. No one wanted the unenviable task of cutting down the last of the harvest and so the sickles were thrown from a distance, so that none could be accused of being the one who had cut the last corn standing and, by so doing, making the 'Kern Baby' homeless. The last sheaf was plaited into the shape of a corn dolly and this became the 'Kern Baby', which was carried home on the last load. She was either ploughed back into the field, thereby returning her to the soil, or was ceremonially burnt and was replaced by the following year's dolly. To this day, corn dolly images can still be seen in churches at harvest time.

Maggie Black, in her informative *WI Calendar of Feasts*, notes the importance of looking after the casual labourers, known as 'faggers', who came to bring in the harvest. They had to be fed and housed and were often booked months in advance. Sometimes the workers would come back to the same area year after year. It was not just men, but their wives, children and, often, the extended family of grandparents, who would turn up expecting to be fed and sheltered in return for work.

The farmer would appoint a Harvest Lord, one of his own workers, whose job it was to regulate hours and reaping rates for each team of harvesters. He would regularly switch men around to prevent them tiring at heavy tasks too quickly. He would also be in charge of the women rakers and stackers. He would provide food and drink during the working day and dictated when the fifteen-minute rest periods would be taken.

The farmer's wife would be kept busy during the harvest. It would fall to her to provide good quality 'vittles' for the workers. Often the farmer was judged on how good the food provided was, and this dictated the quality of harvester the farmer would be able to hire the following year.

Harvest Suppers, also known as Mell Suppers – 'mell' being the old Norse word for 'corn' – used to be sumptuous feasts with roasted meat, flowing ale and much celebration. Both Wendy Boase in her book *Folklore of Hampshire and the Isle of Wight* and the ladies of the Women's Institute in their book, *It Happened in Hampshire*, tell of the Harvest Home Supper in the 1860s on the Marlshanger estate near Oakley and Deane, outside Basingstoke. The male employees were presented with button holes made of oak, wheat, barley and rye, tied with a red ribbon. After the harvest thanksgiving service at the church they returned to the Rectory Barn for a feast, with singing, speeches and toasts. It was a joyous occasion.

In Bursledon the horses were decorated with scarlet rosettes and their collars had scarlet-fringed canopies which held four bells. These jingled when they tossed their heads as they took the wheat to the mill. These decorations were similar to those recorded on May Day horses in the photographic archive of the Bitterne Historical Society.

As time went by, the importance of celebrating the harvest has declined. In an age where supermarkets supply all our needs and seasonal produce is available all year around, the Harvest Festival has become a declining tradition, observed in church services where the altar is covered with the bounty of the harvest such as vegetables, fruit and bread. The wonder and heartfelt thanks we once felt at the bounteous nature of the harvest has sadly disappeared.

Southampton's Knights

The Knighthood of the Old Green Bowling Club Competition is a special event in the club's diary. Not only is it an event which brings with it much pomp and circumstance, it also ensures the continuity of a long tradition that spans centuries.

Graham Hart, or rather, 'Sir' Graham as he has been known since he won the competition in 2003 and acquired the honorary title, has been with the club for ten years. 'I primarily came here because of the traditions of the Green and I came to see for myself. I was lucky enough to win the competition the first time I entered it. You can't play in it after that'.

Tradition is something that the club holds dear. The club claims the Green to be the oldest bowling green in the world, being established 'prior to 1299'

according to the club's research. The lawns were originally laid in 1187 as a
close for the Warden of God's House Hospital nearby in this oldest part of
Southampton, which became known as Saltmarsh. What is certain is that the
site on which the Green now stands has continuously been host to bowling for
many generations. 'Sir' Graham says:

> We know that on an old Southampton map, dated 1611, there are people play-
> ing bowls, or boule or petanque. I should imagine that that was the first game
> that was played on the field and it developed into bowls as we know it. The
> chap who looked after the Green was called the 'Master of the Green'. That is
> why we still have a Master of the Green today. We don't have a President, he is
> known as Master of the Green. That is another tradition.

Much of the early history of the Southampton Old Bowling Green was not
recorded, as noted by 'Sir' Bert Baker and his team who compiled the history of the Green, *The First 700 Years*, in 1999. This, they noted, may have
been because of the severe penalties for playing the game if you were one
of the 'inferior people', who were prohibited from playing in 1541. Fines
of up to 20s were payable by miscreants caught enjoying bowling and the
lucrative statute was rigorously enforced. By 1637 the Green was a ground
'where many gentlemen, with the gentile merchants of this town, take their
recreation'.

As 'Sir' Graham comments, 'A chap came over from Florida and worked out
that we had been bowling here for thirty-four generations. If you think about it,
all the people who bowl here are local to the area, so thirty-four generations of
local Southampton people have bowled at the old Green'.

The Knighthood Competition, started in 1776, is the second oldest sporting
competition in the world, after the Society of Archers' Antient Silver Arrow
archery event, which began in 1673 in Yorkshire. Nothing has ever stopped the
competition. When a Second World War bomb dropped on the top left-hand
corner of the Green on 13 August 1940, leaving a 6ft-deep crater which was
18ft across, the tournament still went ahead. In 1945 there was a record number
of entrants, all of them eager to win the tournament in the year the war ended.
'Sir' Bert Pascoe was the victor and his winner's medal was inscribed with the
words, 'Total Surrender'. Originally known as Mr Miller's Silver Medal Contest,
it was renamed in 1815 as the Knight's Competition.

In 2009, the 235th Knighthood of the Southampton Old Bowling Green
Competition began in a steady pouring rain. The Knights, resplendent in their
top hats and tails and all wearing their coveted medals on sky blue ribbons,

had umbrellas to hand. The players, known as the 'Gentleman Commoners', wearing the regulation white playing uniform, looked distinctly soggy but not a word of complaint was heard.

'Sir' Graham explained:

> It is a bit different to normal bowls. We usually play up and down the Green but with this game the wood, the Jack, is put anywhere on the Green and the mat is put anywhere on the Green. You have to bowl corner to corner, diagonally, straight up and down, it makes it much more difficult because you can't read the Green every time. Whoever is bowling can't see where the wood ends up. At the other end the Knights take the measurement and the one who ends up nearest gets the point for that end and then we start all over again. The first one to seven shots is the winner. The different Green and conditions mean it goes on for an average of ten days. It's been known to go to three weeks before the competition has been won. Another time someone comes along and wins it on the first day. When I won it, it took ten days, playing every day.

David Priestly won the 2009 tournament, which he described as being 'Brilliant!' He was invested 'Sir' David by Knight in Charge 'Sir' Fred Rolfe, in the presence of the Sheriff of Southampton, Councillor Carol Cuneo; the Town Crier, John Melody; and the Master of the Green, Alan Pickett.

Tradition lives on.

The Old Green Song

We are the Old Green Bowlers and far has spread our fame,
We try to win but if we loose, to us it's just the same.
Out on the Green we have a goal, we tell you so for all to know,
We are the Old Green Bowlers, since 1299 we've played.

If the Number Ones fail then perhaps the Twos,
If the Threes were of song, we never get the blues.
We leave it to the Skips to draw a shot or take a pot and smash the lot,
We are the Old Green Bowlers, since 1299 we've played.

Now at last we've come to the most important end,
That's the 22nd, when we go round the bend,

Drinking with the friends we have made today, we light the way to the game
we play.
We are the Old Green Bowlers, since 1299 we've played.

Weyhill Fair

Fairs were either chartered trading markets or 'wakes', those that grew up in
the wake of a church festival. Some of the more important fairs attracted traders
from all over the country and from Europe.

In medieval England, the guilds decreed who could trade and charged merchants for the privilege. Often this permission was only granted for the annual
fairs. If a wooden hand or glove was displayed on the Guildhall roof, traders
could set up their stalls and the Town Crier would announce that 'The glove is
up!' Taking the glove down signified the end of the market.

Weyhill Charter Fair, near Andover, was one of the oldest and most important
fairs in the country. It was the setting for the wife-sale in Hardy's *The Mayor of
Casterbridge* and at one time had a turnover in sheep worth £300,000. It was
held annually, beginning on Old Michaelmas Day (10 October) and stretching
to three weeks, on the same site since at least the eleventh century.

The site was significant. It lay on the crossroads of the Gold Road, which
brought Irish gold from the port at Holyhead to the port of Dover, the gate-
way to European markets, and the Tin Road from the mines in Cornwall to
Southampton. It was also on the Drove Road, which for generations had been
the route taken by herdsmen and their flocks. Weyhill Fair drew bargain hunters
from near and far.

It is thought to have been an area for pagan ritual, as excavations there have
found evidence such as ox teeth that suggest this. The local custom of 'Horning
the Colt' also gives weight to this idea.

On the night before the fair the Horn Supper was held at the Star Inn at
Weyhill. Any newcomer to the fair was ceremonially crowned with a hat decorated with a pair of ram's horns and he was given a metal cup full of ale. On
drinking the ale it was expected that the initiate would buy half a gallon of
alcohol for those present. The horn cap can still be seen in the Star Inn.

In the seventeenth century, traders were often robbed on their way from the
fair. There were rich pickings for those interested in the colour of money and
not bothered if they used fair means or foul to obtain it. Eventually a group
of farmers got together, calling themselves 'Farnham Gentlemen'. They armed
themselves and acted as protectors for those leaving the fair. Eventually they

were asked to look after the money itself. This was the basis of the Lloyds banking empire.

Trafalgar Night

Few of us will be unaware of Vice Admiral Horatio Nelson, 1st Viscount Nelson, 1st Duke of Bronté, KB (29 September 1758–21 October 1805) and the Battle of Trafalgar. Although Nelson hailed from Norfolk, it is with Portsmouth that he will ever be linked in Hampshire. More than 200 years since his death, he is still as popular as he was when the entire country mourned his death. His ship, the aptly named *Victory*, stands as a shrine to his memory in Portsmouth dockyard and welcomes over 500,000 visitors each year.

A frail looking man, he suffered from malaria for most of his life and had yellow fever in his twenties. He was blind in his right eye after being hit in the face at the Siege of Corsica in 1794 and carried a hernia after being hit in the stomach at the Battle of Cape St Vincent in 1797. He lost his right arm in 1797 while fighting in the Canary Islands. Nevertheless, he was a brave man and a born leader. He had what he called 'the Nelson Touch', the ability to inspire and bring out the best in his men. He respected those under him and was a devout Christian. He was heaped with honours for the battles and prestige he won for his country.

He entered the Royal Navy as a midshipman in 1770 and learnt his craft as he progressed, most notably in the American War of Independence. War with the French brought him fame and respect. By 1797 he was a Rear Admiral and had been made a Knight of the Bath (KB). In 1798 he was created Baron Nelson of the Nile. For four months in 1799 he commanded the Mediterranean Fleet and was made Duke of Bronté. When he landed in Yarmouth in 1800 he was given not just a hero's welcome but the Freedom of the Borough too. The following year he was promoted to Vice-Admiral. After the Armistice of October 1801, Nelson had time to take his seat in the House of Lords. However, when Britain and France went to war again in 1803, he was appointed Commander-in-Chief of the Mediterranean Fleet and joined HMS *Victory*. The Spanish joined the war in 1804 and Nelson found his fleet battling two determined enemy countries.

The Battle of Trafalgar took place on 21 October 1805 off the coast of Cape Trafalgar. Despite being outnumbered, with thirty-three enemy ships to his twenty-seven, Nelson was confident of victory. In the early morning Nelson wrote his will and a prayer and then asked Signal Lieutenant John Pasco to send a message to the fleet. It read, 'England confides that every man will do his duty'.

As the word 'expects' could be flown using only one flag, Nelson agreed to substitute this word for 'confides' and the message that is now seared into the history books was hoisted. He was also advised to remove his decorations from his coat to make him less of a target for sharpshooters. He declined this advice, stating that he was not afraid to show them to the enemy.

Fierce fighting ensued. At 1 p.m., Captain Hardy, the *Victory's* captain and Nelson's friend, found Nelson on his knees on the quarterdeck. A sniper had hit him from the seventy-four-gun ship *Redoubtable*, 50ft away. Mortally wounded, Nelson was carried below. He lived long enough to hear that several of the enemy ships had surrendered. He died at 4.30 p.m.

The battle was a complete success for the British forces. The French and Spanish fleets were destroyed. Britain celebrated the victory while mourning the loss of their hero. Nelson's body was returned to Britain and given a state funeral, when he was laid to rest in St Paul's Cathedral.

Each year on Trafalgar Night, 21 October, the Royal Navy remembers Nelson and the famous victory he brought Britain. A ceremony of remembrance is held in Portsmouth on board HMS *Victory* and a wreath is laid on the spot at which the great man fell. Commissioned officers hold a dinner in the wardroom. Traditionally there are five courses, which usually features Beef Wellington or roast beef as the main course. Port is served and is passed 'to the left, by the left'. Toasts are made; the Loyal Toast is to the sovereign, while the Immortal Memory Toast is drunk standing and in silence. The words of this toast are as follows: 'The Immortal Memory of Lord Nelson and those who fell with him'.

Nelson's flagship now rests in Portsmouth Naval Shipyard. She is still in service, the flagship of the Commander-in-Chief Naval Home Command. She is also a Georgian Navy museum. She was launched at Chatham dockyard in 1765 and commissioned in 1778. She was retired from active service after thirty-four years and took up mooring in Portsmouth harbour, where she stayed for over 100 years. In 1922 she was moved to dry dock and restoration has continued ever since. Today, visitors can tour her and see this great ship for themselves.

The Portsmouth Naval Dockyard Barracks opened in 1903 and were known as HMS *Victory*. This caused confusion when Nelson's flagship came to the dockyard, as there were then two HMS *Victory's* at Portsmouth. On 1 August 1974, the barracks were officially renamed HMS *Nelson*. It would seem that Portsmouth and the great commander are destined to be inextricably linked.

Mumming Plays at Christmas

Once, most villages in Hampshire had their own gang of Mummers. Now, although not as numerous as they were, the tradition survives in pockets of the county.

The folk tale told in the Mummers' hero/combat play involves themes of death and resurrection and was traditionally enacted in the winter, particularly at Christmas and most often on Boxing Day. By its very nature Mumming was a 'visiting' custom, and most gangs covered a lot of ground each season. Although most gangs had their particular territory, some overlapping was inevitable. The same play would be performed at different points, often pubs or private houses, for a small fee. Paul Marsh, the late-leader of the Otterbourne Mummers, with which his family was involved for many years, said:

> Often what happened was that people moved around and they took their play with them, as it was an important part of their life. It was performed by men of the labouring class in wintertime, when there was little or no money coming in. As new people arrived, or circumstances changed, the play became different to the one performed previously.
>
> Some of the plays were literally minutes long, whilst others lasted quite a long time. A lot of them had two lengths, the 'going-in-the-pub-for-a-quick-round-and-get-out-before-the-trouble-starts' length, and an extended version which they would do in the big houses. They often started with a few verses of a carol. The longer they performed, the more, theoretically, they would earn. They would act out the play upstairs in the big room for all the nobility and gentry and then they would go downstairs to the servants' quarters and sing and do all sorts of things that they would never do upstairs.

Minor characters, such as Little Johnnie Jack who carried the collecting box, appeared to augment those of Father Christmas, who opened the play, King George, originally Saint George, the Turkish Knight, who was sometimes called the Turkey Snipe, and the Doctor.

In 1936 the ladies of the Women's Institute spoke to Mr Walker, who was a member of the Woodhay Mummers between 1879 and 1884, when the group ceased. He recalled how a Mrs Bastin taught the seven actors and one concertina player in a shed in the garden of an old cottage near the green at East End.

This is the play as he remembered it, courtesy of the Hampshire Federation of Women's Institutes:

Mummering

'I hope, the Master of the house, I hope he is within,
And if he is, pray tell us so, and soon we will begin,
With a down a down derry! A down a down derry!
For we are come this Christmas time on purpose to be merry.'

'See, in come I, poor old Father Christmas.
Welcome or welcome not.
I hope poor old Father Christmas
Will never be forgot.'

'There's roast beef, plum pudding, mince pies: who likes that better than we!
Give room, give room, my gallant souls, give me and my men room to rhyme.
We will show you a bit of bolactivity, this merry Christmas time.'

'In come I, King George the Bold,
If anyone's blood is hot,
I'll quickly drain it cold.'

'Hush, hush, King George don't make thyself too large a squall.'

'In comes I, a Turkish Knight
From Turkish land I come to fight.
Me and seven more
Fought and beat seven score
Finer men and men of war.
Come to take from thee they throne
And cut King George's glory down.'

'Wish my long sword and spike on my shoulder, so will I clear my way,
One, two, by three, you dare not make me stay.'

'Speak plainly though, bold fellow, give better terms unto me,
My recollect and thy speckolect will make a better man than I.'

'Is there a doctor to be found,
To cure this man that lies bleeding on the ground?'

'Yes, there is a doctor to be found.
In comes I, old Dr. Brown,
The first doctor in the town.'

'I've a medicine in my pocket which will cure all ills and even bring the dead
to life again.'

'What do you give for a doctor?'

'Ten guineas is my fee.'

'But twenty I'll give to thee.'

'Here, Jack, take one of my knick knacks
And swallow down a tick-tack.
Rise up and sing a merry song,
March, march away.
The trumpets sound, and cymbals play,
March, march away.
To the jolly old fife and drum.'

'See in comes I, little saucy Jack,
My wife and family on my back.
Out of nine I've got but five,
All the rest I starved alive,
Times being hard.'

'See, in comes I, the man that's not been hit,
With my big head and little wit.
Cure more than you, than any other man.'

'What can you cure?'

'Cure a pig with a murrain.'

'Is that all you can do?'

'No, that is not all that I can do; I can cure a magpie with a stick.'

'How do you do that?'

'Cut his head off and throw him in a ditch.'

The story was remarkably similar wherever the play was performed, although local colour was added to make each unique. Paul Marsh said:

> The Mummers took their plays seriously and performed them with dignity. When there were funny lines they were delivered straight, letting the lines speak for themselves. Many revival gangs act out the parts and ham up the jokes, often to such an extent that they lose the point of the play.
>
> In the Otterbourne Mummers I take the part of Old Father Christmas (and have done for thirty-four years), and we put in a couple of topical references each year, but we don't lose our respect for the play. One resident said, 'It's always fresh, yet always the same'.
>
> Often the joke is on the politicians. I recall in 1988 the Doctor, as well as all his usual claims, claiming to be able to cure illnesses caused by eating curried eggs!

This was, of course, a reference to Edwina Currie, who resigned as Health Minister after saying that most of Britain's egg production was infected by salmonella. More recently it has been missing data discs or cash for peerages. In 2009, it was duck houses and MPs' expenses.

Costumes frequently concealed the actor's face as it was considered unlucky to be recognised. In some areas the faces were blacked and there was little other effort at disguise. Alford and Gallop, commenting on seeing the Overton Mummers perform in the snow at Freefolk, mention:

> Their paper streamers lashed about them in the wintry wind… the ten pound Doctor, in a high hat wreathed with paper ribbons… and the old leader, whose sons are all in the play, and who claims three hundred years of family participation, carefully covered his face with his streamers, remarking, 'They mustn't know who I be'.

Jack had dolls sewn on to his costume, which Wendy Boase speculated could represent the Virgin Mary and Child, and may have been a tradition handed down from a medieval mystery play. Some gangs dressed more in character, but costumes frequently consisted of wallpaper cut up into strips, like streamers. The Mummers would walk miles in a day, trudging from venue to venue in all weathers. 'One of the things with the Mummers was that as they progressed around they would look like plucked chickens at the end – out in the elements they would have to keep patching,' says Marsh.

From 1976 until 1982 Paul Marsh and Steve Roud actively researched Hampshire Mummers, when they could still obtain first-hand information from oral sources; people who took part in, or remembered seeing, the Mummers. They identified the leader in the Overton Mummers play as Mr Burgess (d. 1935) whose son, Bill (b. 1909), was one of the sons mentioned by Alford and Gallop.

Paul Marsh said:

> In the 1930s Mummers could still be seen tramping the lanes from pub to pub and house to house, at least in north Hampshire: Overton, North Waltham, Longparish, Andover, Crookham and Kingsclere, which all had active 'gangs', but to meet their southern counterparts one would have had to go back at least to the early 1920s, if not to before the Great War.

The First World War finished many of the Mummers' gangs in Hampshire. So many men were lost that it had a devastating effect on the tradition. 'It is pretty certain that virtually every village in Hampshire had its own Mummers gang at one time – each with its version of the play, and its own way of making the costumes,' says Marsh.

The Roud/Marsh collection has ninety-five play locations (almost doubling the amount previously known, collected by Edwin Christopher Cawte, Alex Helm and Norman Peacock for the Folklore Society in 1967) with texts from oral and written sources, interviews with participants and eyewitnesses, audio recordings and 125 photos, many of them taken by George Long (b. 1882).

The Roud/Marsh collection is unpublished, apart from a source list in Winchester Local Studies Library, and is with the authors.

Times have changed, as have Christmas customs, but there are currently eleven Hampshire Mummers gangs listed on the mastermummers.org website, including Overton and Crookham, with another two dance groups listed as also performing Mummers plays in addition to their folk dancing. Many of these gangs are revivals but they have become an established part of modern-day Christmas in their locale, though nowadays the collection usually goes to charity.

Today, the Mummers in Otterbourne perform at three o'clock on just one occasion – the Sunday before Christmas – when the local population turns out to witness the event. The sword fight between the gaily coloured actors, their outfits of fluttering paper and full-face tall helmets, making them resemble something out of a *Dr Who* episode, is a high point of the performance. Long may this tradition, which has brought such pleasure at Christmas, survive in Hampshire.

TWO

OMENS, GHOSTLY TALES

AND THINGS THAT GO BUMP IN THE NIGHT

From ghoulies and ghosties and long-leggety beasties
And things that go bump in the night,
Good Lord, deliver us!

Anon
Cornish

The *Concise Oxford Dictionary* states that a ghost is 'the supposed apparition of a dead person or animal; a disembodied spirit'. For many of us, the thought that a restless spirit is walking the world sends a shiver down our spine. Why is the spirit walking still? What has happened in a property to lead to its haunting? Why are we so fascinated by the supernatural? Is it that secretly we long for the thrill of the hair rising on the back of our necks as we listen for the telltale angry bumps and rattles associated with much ghostly activity? Or do we have sympathy for the spirit trapped between two worlds, doomed to walk corridors for eternity in penance for some earthly act, sometimes committed centuries before?

Whatever it is, Hampshire folk are fascinated. A quick look on the Internet under a search for 'ghost walks in Hampshire UK' offers over 30,000 hits, although not all of these are for this county when you look closely. If you fancy it you can join guided walking tours around Portsmouth, Gosport and Fareham, or team up with investigators looking into reported paranormal activity in Hampshire sites such as ancient Wymering Manor, near Portsmouth, recorded in the Domesday

Book and which is now a youth hostel. This is reported to have 'a staggering amount' of paranormal activity according to the Paranormal Tours website. Even the Hampshire County Council website lists guided ghost walks in Netley and Winchester on its no-nonsense, information packed site, www3.hants.gov.uk.

This chapter looks at just a tiny proportion of the rich variety of Hampshire's ghostly sightings, unearthly bumps and rattles, and tells some of the stories behind the sad histories of a selection of Hampshire's haunted places.

Jack the Painter

During the American War of Independence the threat of terrorism was as high as it has been during later conflicts, and certainly through the twenty-first century's 'war on terror'.

When boats were made of wood and associated sailing paraphernalia, such as ropes and sails, were highly flammable, the threat of fire in Britain's dockyards was a constant menace.

One man, known variously as James Hill, James Hind and John or James Atkins or Aitkins, was a Scotsman born in 1752. He had been apprenticed to a house painter in Edinburgh, but had risen above his roots and had learned to read and write. He lived in the American colonies for two years and sympathised with the American independence movement. He came back to England determined to do what he could to hinder British hopes of winning the War of Independence. He joined the Army under the name James Boswell, according to Hone writing in 1832 (The Year Book). Later sources say he joined the Royal Navy. All agree that he deserted and rejoined the military, re-enlisting under a new name each time. Thus he was able to learn the layout of the various dockyards and he filed away this information for future use.

On 7 December 1776 a fire started in the Rope House at Portsmouth Dockyard, which caused £60,000 of damage, a vast sum for the time, and was only put out with a huge amount of manpower. The fire was thought to have started accidentally but, on 15 January 1777, an incendiary device was discovered, which Hone describes as 'a tin box, peculiarly constructed, with matches partly burnt, and spirits of wine at the bottom'. This threw doubt on the accidental nature of the Rope House blaze.

James Hill was the suspected arsonist. He had fled the scene not knowing a tinsmith, who later testified at his trial, had seen him. It emerged that on 6 December Hill had tried to set the Rope House alight but his matches were wet. He had therefore delayed until the following day in order to buy dry matches. He went on to successfully set three ships, residences, and warehouses in the dockyard at Bristol ablaze, but failed in a similar attempt in Plymouth.

When he fled he left some vital documents behind. He had contacted an American agent in Paris and offered his services to the independence movement. He had been given cash, a false French passport and instructions on how to make the incendiary device, which he had tried to use later. It was the passport and the incriminating instructions that were found in his lodgings. A £50 reward was issued for 'Jack the Painter's' capture. Hill was stopped in Odiham on suspicion of breaking and entering and his similar appearance to that of the man on the 'wanted' poster was noticed. At his trial in Winchester, Hill was identified by the tinsmith and by the lady who sold him the dry matches. His fate sealed, he confessed.

Sentenced to hang on 10 March 1777, his gallows was the 64ft-high main mast of HMS *Arethusa*, which was hauled to the entrance gates of the Portsmouth dockyard for the purpose. From this vantage point, before he died he could see that the destruction he had caused had not crippled the dockyard, which was meant to be a lesson to him. Hone tells us that at the last he 'behaved with decency, seemed penitent, acknowledged the justice of his sentence and advised the government to vigilance'. His corpse was taken down and hung on a gibbet in chains on the beach at Fort Blockhouse at the mouth of Portsmouth harbour as a warning to other would-be terrorists.

Years later he was taken down by sailors and his bones were used to pay a debt at a local inn. One wonders how much the bones were worth! Since that time, there have been persistent reports of Jack the Painter's ghost being seen dragging chains in various parts of Old Portsmouth.

Beaulieu Abbey

Beaulieu is a beautiful village in the New Forest. Home to the National Automobile Museum and Beaulieu Abbey, the village draws visitors from all over the world eager to experience all that this fascinating place offers.

Beaulieu Abbey is home to a host of ghostly monks who wander amongst the stately ruins, witnessed by many over the years. Allegedly the sound of chanting, identified as Gregorian but this has been debated, is heard on the air and the smell of incense lingers after they have gone. The abbey is reputed to be one of the most haunted places in Britain. The monks have been described as wearing white habits with black scapular cloths over their shoulders, in the Cistercian manner.

The abbey, with its magnificent gatehouse, the Palace House, was established in the thirteenth century. It is said that in 1201 monks appealed to King John for exemption from his taxes. For this outrageous behaviour they were thrown into the nearest dungeon and told that they would be put to death the next day by being trampled by horses. Overnight the king had a bad dream. He dreamt he was being whipped as punishment for the treatment he had meted out to the monks. When he awoke he was covered in weals. So great was his regret at his treatment of the monks that he released them and gave them the land at Beaulieu to establish an abbey.

The Cistercian abbey, or *Bellus Locus Regis*, 'The Beautiful Place of the King' in Latin, was built in 1204. Thirty monks from Citeaux in France joined it, and they founded four daughter abbeys: Netley Abbey in 1239, Hailes Abbey in 1246, Newenham Abbey in 1247, and St Mary Graces Abbey in 1350.

During the Dissolution of the Monasteries, Beaulieu was given to Thomas Wriothesley, 1st Earl of Southampton (1505-1550), who converted Palace House to become his private residence. Today Wriothesley's descendant Edward, the 3rd Baron Montagu of Beaulieu, and his wife, Lady Fiona, reside at Beaulieu. They share Palace House with a Grey Lady, said to be Lady Isabella, an eighteenth-century inhabitant.

Hayling Island Ghosts

In her book *The Haunted South*, Joan Forman recounts the tale of Old Fleet Manor House on Hayling Island. Owned between 1943 and 1960 by Colonel L.E. Sheppard, the house was built near the site of a priory at the end of the fifteenth century. Reports of a man dressed in black appearing to family, staff and visitors alike persisted for many years. The colonel's dogs behaved as if they could see someone invisible to their owners, apparently moving aside to let them pass or jumping out of windows to avoid them. The colonel himself reported feeling someone stroking his head. This had been reported by others too and led to the belief that the ghost was a benign monk from the priory, the black clothing possibly being that of his habit and the stroking being a blessing bestowed.

Meanwhile, the church at Northney is supposed to be haunted by the ghost of a sailor who walks in the area. Evidence of this is sketchy, although it is reported both by Joan Forman and on the Paranormal Database on the Internet.

Railway Ghosts

Surprisingly, there are not that many reports of ghosts on the railways of Hampshire. Other counties seem to have the monopoly on haunted railway stations, signal boxes, lines and tunnels!

The informative Paranormal Database lists only two reports in the county. One, at Hayling Island's disused station, which was closed down in the 1960s, is of a haunting manifestation. A man in a faded uniform appears regularly. It is thought that he was a guard on the line there.

The other report is of what the site calls a 'post-mortem manifestation'. In 1971 a lady wept inconsolably on the platform at Swanwick Station, just outside Southampton. She kept repeating the phrase, 'I can't go back'. The man sitting next to her tried to console her but his train came in and he left her to catch it. He later called the police to see if she was all right, as he felt guilty about leaving her in such a distressed state. He was assured that the matter would be looked into. He then saw a local newspaper and recognised the crying lady he had been attempting to console as the same person who had been hit by a train the day before. She had at that time been dead for twenty-four hours...

The Eastleigh Railway Works celebrated its centenary in 2009 by putting on a display of steam, diesel and electric engines and opening up the site to the public. The nostalgia caused by this event was immense and thousands came through its gates to remember and wonder at a bygone age.

The Eastleigh Works is a huge site. In its heyday it was lit brightly at night near the main entrance but the light gradually diminished as the staff ventured further away from the entrance. This caused many a shiver to run up the spine of night workers who were shunting the engines and getting them ready for the next day's running.

Jimmy Marsh was a fireman in the Motive Power Department based at Eastleigh, who worked on the Southern Region trains between 1960 and 1965. He recalls that tales of ghostly, unexplained happenings abounded amongst the men working there:

We were on twenty-four hour call. When you were driving the engine up the yard to bring it back down into the shed from the coaling yard, you went out into darkness and you were on your own. Often to turn the engine you had to get down to pull the points and get back up again. When I did it I just concentrated on where I had to go and what I had to do, because there was a ghost story. A man had had an accident there and his ghost haunted that loop.

Two of Jimmy's friends had got into trouble with the railway authorities for walking through cement and then making 'ghostly' footprints across the footplate of an engine cab when a new recruit had got out in order to change the points:

> They went up across the footplate and down the other side and the poor lad came back and climbed up onto the footplate and there they were, two lines of white footprints that certainly were not there when he got down! He panicked and left. He ran back down the track to the lights and someone asked him to go and get the engine, but he wasn't going to do it! They were ghostly footprints; the ghost of the loop had crossed the footplate he thought. No way was he going back there.

That this light-hearted fooling was based on reported sightings of an apparition at the works is uncertain, but what is better known is the chuckling ghost at Winchester Station. Jimmy Marsh takes up the tale again:

> Winchester Station was one of the few stations that the fast trains to London stopped at during my time on the railway. Southampton Parkway wasn't there then, but most of the express trains stopped at Eastleigh, Winchester, Basingstoke and Waterloo. During the day Winchester Station hummed with life. After eleven at night though nothing at all happened. Most of the lights went out, it was dark and behind it, right behind it out of the way, was a titchy little engine shed. It was very small indeed and housed in there was what we all called the Winchester Bug. It was a tiny tank engine that didn't even have a steam brake. The fireman who was working on it had to wind on the hand brake each time the driver needed to stop. The man who drove it on a regular basis had been crippled in an accident, so this duty was the only one he did. He came down at eight o'clock each morning, got in to the engine, drove it all day as he shunted the yard and then went home at night. Because there was no one there after six at night the fire had to be thrown out. If it were left it would continue to keep up the steam and this could lead to disaster. The water in the boiler would be used up and if that happened and nothing was done about it, then the plugs underneath the top part of the boiler, which are filled with lead, would melt and allow steam and water to rush through into the firebox. The injectors must be put on at once if this happens, to put more water in the boiler and the fire must be thrown out straight away or the boiler would blow up.
>
> The day shift fireman had to throw the fire out each night before he could go home. At one o'clock in the morning, another fireman had to go along and

light it up again. It may have been just a small engine, but it still had a large volume of water in the boiler. It takes many hours to heat up and all the time the steam gauge and water level tubes on the footplate have to be watched. On this duty it was all done on your own. I was always nervous when I was there. I used to wait until I got the little oil lamp going, so I could see what I was doing before I even went inside that little shed. Once inside I was so conscious that at the top of the bank, behind the engine shed, was a church and, of course, a churchyard. You could see some of the gravestones in the moonlight.

I was twenty-one or twenty-two at the time and once when I did this job I heard something as I worked. I remember as I heard it that I was convinced it was a human chuckle and I thought, 'Oh, my God!' The story of one lad who was here before me came flashing into my mind. The Winchester Bug had such a small cab you couldn't use a full-sized shovel because there wasn't room to swing it around, as it was too big. So it was easier to pick the coal up and throw it into the firebox by hand, then turn round again for more, in a side-to-side motion. This lad turned towards the coalbunker and had a piece of coal placed into his hand. He turned and threw it into the firebox before realising he was supposed to be the only one there. Who had given him that piece of coal? A frantic search produced no results; he was the only one there. I heard this story just after I started the job and the boy himself told me that piece of coal was definitely placed into his hand by someone else. When he could find no one else around he heard a ghostly chuckle that gradually got fainter until it died away altogether. That is just what I heard, the same ghostly chuckle that sent prickles of fear up my back. I knew I had heard a chuckle and I have never been so pleased to see the sunrise and to know it was getting light and I would soon be on my way home.

We all had to take a turn at this job and it was one none of us wanted, but at one time or another we were all lumbered with the Winchester Bug. We would see those two words written against our names on the duty roster and know we faced another creepy nightshift. But lighting the fire at night, with no one around in the shed, and there was never anyone in sight on the station, was a daunting prospect, because it was just you, that graveyard and the chuckling ghost.

Waterlooville Ghosts

Hopfield House in Waterlooville is the subject of much discussion on the online forum of the Hampshire Ghost Club. This former Victorian house has now been converted into a block of flats and stories of ghostly happenings have been replaced by reports of 'bad feelings' about the building. However, it has a long and unhappy history of tragedy.

Built by a parvenu, a Mr Ferriby, in the middle of Queen Victoria's long reign, it was meant to be his family's house forever and Mr Ferriby stated this in his last will and testament. After Mr Ferriby died, all was well until the family, knowing that they must not sell the property, decided to let it, as it was too big for their needs. This is when the problems started.

The first tenants received a visit from an angry Mr Ferriby, his irate ghost telling them to go. He threatened violence if they did not leave. They took the hint and left.

The next tenants were a mother and daughter and they soon fell foul of Mr Ferriby. The mother was found dead soon after they moved in. The daughter, distraught at the unexpected death of her mother, departed abruptly.

After that the family decided to sell the house. They must have done so with their fingers firmly crossed behind their backs. The unsuspecting buyer was soon found stabbed to death in his home. His widow departed in haste.

A rich family man bought Hopfield in the 1920s. He lavished time and money on doing the property up and could not understand the various reports of the bad atmosphere felt in the house by visitors and friends. He was soon to find out what they meant. His son, a student at Oxford and well liked by all who knew him, blew his brains out in the basement for no apparent reason. His wife, unable to get over the shock of her son's death, died a short time later and the man himself died inexplicably soon after her. The daughter of the house lived. Grief stricken, she boarded up the house and, unsurprisingly, left.

Now the property has been converted into apartments, perhaps Mr Ferriby's rage has died down and he has come to terms with the reality that his house is no longer his family's home? Or perhaps the 'bad atmosphere' in the building is Mr Ferriby biding his time?

Ghosts do not just haunt houses in the town. There are several reports of a haunting in Hulbert Road in Waterlooville. A young girl is supposed to have appeared suddenly in front of a woman's car on a foggy night in 1976. As the occupants braced for impact, none came; the girl had disappeared. Considerably shaken, the driver and her husband told friends about the incident and learned that theirs was one of several sightings in the same spot. Apparently a girl had been run over while hitching back from Waterlooville to her home in Leigh Park. A further report was from a man who had actually given a lift to a girl in the pouring rain from the same spot to Leigh Park. When he drew up the girl, who had been sitting in the front seat, was gone and only the wet stain on the seat showed she had been there.

Nursing Ghosts

Formed in 1949, the Queen Alexandra's Royal Army Nursing Corps, QARANC, has continued the long service started by its predecessors, the Army Nursing Service and the Queen Alexandra's Imperial Military Nursing Service. Since 1854 these nurses have looked after the British Army and their allies, prisoners of war and civilians. Nowadays QARANC staff serve in both NHS hospitals and in Ministry of Defence hospitals in the UK and in the field.

The Cambridge Military Hospital, Aldershot, admitted its first patients in July 1879. It was named after His Royal Highness the Duke of Cambridge, who was then the Army's Commander-in-Chief. It was the first United Kingdom hospital to receive First World War frontline casualties and the first British Military Hospital to have a plastic surgery unit. It grew to accommodate not just soldiers but also civilians living locally. In 1898 a new wing, the Louise Margaret Hospital, opened to provide care for the servicemen's wives and children. It was named after Princess Louise Margaret, the Duchess of Connaught. This closed down in 1995 and the Cambridge Military Hospital itself also succumbed to the demands of modern thinking soon after. The structure of the building was then in need of much maintenance and it was felt that this would be too costly for the Ministry of Defence to bear. After much ceremony, the hospital closed it doors for good in 1996.

The hospital's claim to fame was its mile-long corridor. This was a perfect spot for the hospital's ghosts to lurk. There are reports of many Grey Lady hauntings up and down the country. The Cambridge Military Hospital's Grey Lady was thought to be a Queen Alexandra's Royal Army Nursing Corps nursing sister who had given an accidental overdose to a patient. Overcome with remorse when the patient died, she had thrown herself off the upper floor walkway. She was then seen fleetingly as she hurried along the upstairs corridor between wards ten and fourteen, leaving a faint trace of lavender scent in her path. Staff would take care to avoid that section of the corridor at night, which would chill when she appeared.

This caring ghost would also be seen standing beside very ill patients who would usually die soon after she visited them. Was she offering them comfort? It seems as if she was trying to make amends for her mistake long after the sad event.

The Royal Victoria Military Hospital in Netley opened in 1866 at a cost of £350,000, a huge amount in Victorian England. The main building, on the banks of Southampton Water, was huge and it was reportedly built using 3 million bricks and 3 million cubic ft of stone. It was thought at the time to be the largest military hospital in the world as it was a quarter of a mile long and postmen used bicycles to travel around its many interior corridors delivering the mail.

Netley had several ghosts. In his book *The Ghosts of Netley*, Philip Hoare notes that the Grey Lady haunting the hospital was a Victorian nurse who was 'a grey shadow in a crinoline dress'. She was supposed to have given her young man a fatal overdose and subsequently committed suicide by throwing herself off the hospital's chapel tower. This story is remarkably similar to the Grey Lady story at the Cambridge Military Hospital, Aldershot, except a crinoline was not mentioned there. The QARANC website mentions that this Grey Lady also appeared shortly before a patient died, again echoing the Aldershot ghost.

Another ghost said to have haunted Netley was the Blue Nurse. Nursing uniform dresses were blue and this nurse was said to have fallen in love with a patient. She later found out that he was dallying with another woman and so killed him and then committed suicide. She was regularly reported as having been sighted until the hospital's demolition in 1966.

Both these ghosts have seemingly been laid to rest by the destruction of the hospital. Nowadays only the chapel and cemetery survive. The site has become a country park and resounds to the laughter of children playing, the little steam train which operates when children are not at school, and the odd car driving to the car park. It is a far cry from the hustle and bustle of its time as a military hospital.

The Brushmakers Arms, Upham

As long ago as 1236, the Parish of Upham was mentioned as a tithing of the Hundred of Bishops Waltham, according to Hampshire County Council's excellent Hantsweb site. Oliver Cromwell and his men used the village as a campaign stop in 1644, the church being utilised as a stable as Cromwell was no friend to religion. It therefore seems fitting that a village with such a long heritage should have an inn with its own ghost.

The Brushmakers Arms, situated in the delightfully titled Shoe Lane, takes its name from the once-vibrant brush-making trade in the area. The ghost, who is still seen today, is reportedly that of one Mr Chickett, a travelling brush maker. He was one of several who frequented the area during tours of the countryside selling their handmade brushes and brooms. These brushes were fashioned from hazel, which grew abundantly in the surrounding countryside. Mr Chickett was known to be very careful with his money and this was his downfall as, while sleeping at the Brushmakers Arms, he was set upon and murdered in his bed. His grisly remains were found the next morning but his purse, which was with him at all times and which he put under his pillow at night, was nowhere to be seen. Despite extensive searches, his murderer was never caught and his money was not recovered.

Mr Chickett now haunts the room in which he was murdered, looking for his money, or his murderer, for all eternity. Animals who are taken to the pub frequently show fear near the room, with flattened ears and whining. Can they sense something we cannot see?

The Hyde Inn, Winchester

Reports differ as to how the female spirit reputedly haunting the Hyde Inn, the oldest Inn in Winchester, actually became a ghost. The inn was formerly part of Hyde Abbey, hence its name. It offered shelter to travellers in need. All records agree that the lady was a pilgrim who asked for food and shelter at the inn. Some reports say that the request was denied and the lady was later found dead, all skin and bone; other reports state that she was given food and shelter but was found dead the next morning.

All agree that no one has actually seen the lady ghost of Hyde Inn. Instead, they feel her presence as no matter how tightly tucked in the bedclothes are, they are often found in a heap on the floor some way from the shivering guests! Is she trying to keep warm in death, or is she getting her revenge by making sure that no one sleeps warmly while she is around?

'A strange greate light…'

In her 1953 book in celebration of the city, *Southampton Cavalcade*, Elsie Sandell recounts the tale of one of the prisoners at the Bargate in 1636. The hapless man saw 'a strange greate light' and swore a deposition on oath to the Mayor the next morning, stating that he had seen 'a bull, a white bear and three little puppie dogs without heads' in his cell. Furthermore, he asserted, just in case there was doubt in anyone's mind, that when he made the deposition he was 'waked and in his perfect senses and remembrance'.

Itchell Manor

Major Edward Moor, in the appendix of his 1841 book *Bealing Bells*, cited in John Ingram's *The Haunted Homes and Family Traditions of Great Britain*, tells the tale of the haunting of Itchell Manor. Both of these volumes are available to peruse at the British Library and they make interesting reading. Major Moor was at pains to give a brief history of the house:

> Ewshott House, or Itchell as it was formerly called, is in the parish of Crondall in Hampshire. It is a respectable old Manor House, and in very early times was the principal residence of the Giffords, one of the most ancient and eminent families in Hampshire. It was afterwards a seat of the Bathursts and was in their possession for several generations. About the year 1680 the chief part of the ancient mansion seems to have been pulled down, and the present house erected in its place. The remaining portion of the old house was allowed to stand, separated only by a party wall, and was let as a farmhouse to the tenant of the adjoining property.
>
> The estate came into the possession of Mr. Lefroy in the year 1818; by which time Ewshott had already acquired the reputation of being 'haunted'.

Major Moor published a letter from his nephew, Captain A.H. Frazer, RA, as a testimony to the veracity of some of the ghostly happenings at Itchell. Dated 19 July 1841 and written in Carlisle, Captain Frazer gives a frank account of his time visiting the house twenty years earlier, when Lefroy had invited him to stay.

It would seem that the Lefroys were happy to reside in the house with its ghostly occupants. The ghosts were not mentioned to new servants and, as a consequence, the family had a high turnover of staff, particularly of maidservants. When the let part of the building, which Major Moor had mentioned, was being vacated, the Lefroy family asked the outgoing family what they had been doing night after night, for it was from that part of the old house that much banging and knocking had emanated for years. The family hotly assured the Lefroys that they had not caused the disturbance and it was then that the owners took more notice of the nocturnal noises they heard nightly.

Investigation showed that a former owner, called Squire, had been somewhat eccentric and was generally felt in the area to be a dubious character. He had travelled the Continent when he was younger and had arrived home with a manservant, an Italian valet, described as also being 'a character'. The pair lived in seclusion and rumours abounded as to their doings at the house. All in the neighbourhood agreed though that Squire was a miser. One day the noises started. This coincided with Squire's disappearance. Locals were convinced that he had been bricked up alive within two walls of the house by the avaricious valet and the knocking sounds were made as Squire banged with his hunting whip to be let out.

Captain Frazer described the noises he heard most nights from 11 p.m. or midnight as being 'as if someone was striking the walls with a hammer, or mallet, muffled in flannel'. He also heard footsteps in the house and cited other members of the family and visitors to the house as hearing footsteps or wheeled carts outside in the drive. Each time these were investigated there was nothing to see.

The ghostly goings-on at Itchell Manor continued into the twentieth century. Eric Walter Geden-Tysoe was a new Scout Leader with 1st Basingstoke Scouts in 1951. He was part of a group of a dozen leaders and assistant leaders, with four instructors, who were invited to Itchell Manor by the Assistant District Commissioner of the county, Mr Lefroy, the owner of the house, to camp in the grounds and study for their Wood Badge, which involved a week-long course.

'We were doing our first testing on becoming leaders,' said Eric, speaking in July 2009. 'We were learning to train. We had never been there before'.

The Scouts hiked seven miles to the house and arrived late in the evening. The group pitched their tents in the rose garden, an elevated garden to one side of the house, by a brick wall, which separated the garden from the stony main path to the front of the house. There was an iron gate in the wall by which entry to the garden could be made from the path. By the time their camp was pitched it was very late. Most of the group went to bed but Eric and three friends stayed up, sorting the camp out. Eric and one other decided to go in search of the woodpile, which had been made ready for them.

> It was early morning, one o'clock or thereabouts. We went out to look for some wood because it was left out for us, for a bonfire for the next three or four days. We were round the corner, following the wall where they had the wood, and all of a sudden we heard what we thought were horses and a cart or something like that. We could hear them rattling slowly up the stony road, trit-trot. We thought it was some of the instructors coming up to tinker, because one or two things that we left out had gone, we should have put them away. We were this side of the wall and they were coming up the stony path to the front of the house. We thought that it was three of the trainers, playing a joke, but we looked through the gate and there was nothing there.

Their two friends joined the pair and they started back to their camp with the firewood.

> It went quiet and next thing was we looked round and the glass door of the house opened up. There were four of us and we just stood there and said, 'Good god, how's that?'

She came out of the house; we thought it was bits of wind, cloud, will-o'-the-wisp, whatever you call it. We were scared, wondering what the hell it was. As it came nearer to us we saw it was shaped like a woman. She was dark haired, was dressed in white, and as she went through the gate she turned round and looked at us. She was a young lady, thirty to thirty-five years old, and small. She had a nice figure. She was 15ft away from us, so near we could actually see her facial features. She was wearing long clothes, a long flowing white robe and her hair was black. It came down a little, to ear length, short, not hanging down her back. She came up into the garden and turned around and smiled at us. Then she went through the gate. We saw her for two or three minutes.

Considerably startled, the quartet went back to the camp where their friends were still soundly sleeping:

Next morning one of the chaps went into Fleet and there was a book about ghosts there and it was in there. He came back and showed it to us. 'There it is,' he said, someone had written about Itchell Manor's ghosts.

The others thought we were pulling their legs, they didn't believe in ghosts. Us four did, absolutely. I can see it now.

Hannah, Eric's wife, found the tale hard to believe too. 'I thought it was a tall tale. He'd been at the strong tea! I don't believe because I have not seen a ghost'.

Nevertheless, this disbelief in the story did not deter Eric, who later spoke about the ghostly experience on David Frost's 1950s television programme. The story was also recounted in *Hampshire, The County Magazine* in 1975 in an article by Ian Hayes. This same edition gave a potted history of the old house, which was demolished in 1955 to make way for a new, more modern building.

Eric went on to become the Basingstoke Scouts District Commissioner in 1966. Sadly, Eric Geden-Tysoe has passed away since this interview. The author sends her condolences to his family and friends.

Bramshill House

It is said that Bramshill House at Eversley, near Hartley Witney, is the most haunted place in the country. The list of ghostly forms seen flitting about the house and grounds is legendary.

The original house was mentioned in the Domesday Book, but the present mellow red-brick building at the end of a one-mile long drive was built between 1605 and 1612, although it incorporates an earlier, fourteenth-century premises. The builders of Holland House in London designed it for Lord Zouche of Harrington, Ben Johnson's patron. In the grounds, the lake covers five acres. Zouche lived in Bramshill House until his death in 1625. The Cope family owned Bramshill House from the seventeenth century until 1936, when it was sold to Lord Brocket as his family's second home. He lived there until 1953, when the house was sold to the Home Office. It is now the Police Staff College.

The story of one of the alleged ghosts haunting Bramshill House is of the White Lady, whose story is told in Thomas Haynes Bayley's (1797-1839) 1828 poem, 'The Mistletoe Bough', reproduced below. Several country houses have laid claim to the story, including Marwell Hall in Owslebury, Hampshire.

The Mistletoe Bough

The mistletoe hung in the castle hall
The holly branch shone on the old oak wall.
The Baron's retainers were blithe and gay,
Keeping the Christmas holiday.

The Baron beheld with a father's pride
His beautiful child, Lord Lovell's bride.
And she, with her bright eyes seemed to be
The star of that goodly company.
Oh, the mistletoe bough.
Oh, the mistletoe bough.

'I'm weary of dancing, now,' she cried;
'Here, tarry a moment, I'll hide, I'll hide,
And, Lovell, be sure you're the first to trace
The clue to my secret hiding place.'

Away she ran, and her friends began
Each tower to search and each nook to scan.
And young Lovell cried, 'Oh, where do you hide?
I'm lonesome without you, my own fair bride.'
Oh, the mistletoe bough.
Oh, the mistletoe bough.

They sought her that night, they sought her next day,
They sought her in vain when a week passed away.
In the highest, the lowest, the loneliest spot,
Young Lovell sought wildly, but found her not.

The years passed by and their brief at last
Was told as a sorrowful tale long past.
When Lovell appeared, all the children cried,
'See the old man weeps for his fairy bride.'
Oh, the mistletoe bough.
Oh, the mistletoe bough.

At length, an old chest that had long laid hid
Was found in the castle; they raised the lid.
A skeleton form lay mouldering there
In the bridal wreath of that lady fair.

How sad the day when in sportive jest
She hid from her lord in the old oak chest,
It closed with a spring and a dreadful doom,
And the bride lay clasped in a living tomb.
Oh, the mistletoe bough.
Oh, the mistletoe bough.

There is a carved chest at Bramshill which is marked 'The Brides Chest' and is at the centre of the story. There are several variations but the most common runs along the lines of Bayley's poem. On Christmas Eve, the family was celebrating the wedding of the daughter of the house. The place was decorated with holly and the bride held a sprig of mistletoe. By all accounts a beautiful young lady, the bride proposed a game of hide and seek to her husband. He happily agreed. She ran away to hide and was not seen alive again. The whole household hunted for her with increasing anxiety. Finally, the family was forced to concede that she could not be found. Time passed. Reports say that the unfortunate bride's family left the house and set up home in France. Years later they decided to return and Bramshill was being made ready for them. A servant opened a long forgotten trunk, the kind that could only be opened from the outside and, instead of the expected spare sheets, found the mouldering body of a young bride in her white wedding gown, still holding the dried remains of the mistletoe. The bride is said to have haunted the Fleur de Lys room ever since.

Looking at the history of the house there is much to support the claim that this story has its basis in fact. Peter Underwood, former President of the Ghost Club of Great Britain, in his excellent book *Ghosts of Hampshire and the Isle of Wight*, reports the investigation undertaken by Lieutenant-Colonel the Honorable E. Gerald French, DSO, which was published in *Hampshire, The County Magazine* in 1964. French looked at the history of the house and found that the lady in question could well have been Anne Cope, the 6th Baronet Sir John Cope's eldest daughter. She had married Hugh Bethal in February 1727 and is recorded as being buried, in the words of Sir William Cope in a book written by him which investigated the story, 'in January 1728 or 1729'. If it were 1729 that would be two years after the wedding. Underwood speculates about the probability of the story being true and points out that the wing of Bramshill in which the bride was allegedly found was said to have been demolished in an orgy of grief by the family. That the house has been altered, and these alterations are recorded about this time, lends credence to the story.

That the Mistletoe Bride is still in residence is also given credence by Underwood's citing of the Romanian royal family who stayed at Bramshill House after the Second World War (*Nights in Haunted Houses*). King Michael is alleged to have asked for another room for his children so that the 'young lady in white' who walked through their bedroom every night would not disturb them.

Other ghosts haunting Bramshill are many and various. One is an old man with a grey beard. He is thought to have been the White Lady's father or her mourning husband. He is seen either peering through windows or into the chest.

The house would not be complete without its Grey Lady and this ghost is seen in the library, the Roman Catholic chapel or on the terrace. Whenever she appears the atmosphere chills and there is a strong smell of lilies of the valley. This lady is described variously as 'beautiful', 'sad looking' and 'golden haired'. She often has tears on her cheeks and has been seen walking through wooden and brick walls.

The Grey Lady's husband is thought to have been executed in the seventeenth century at Bramshill. One senior police officer got a nasty shock at a classical music evening in the chapel drawing room when he realised that he was sharing the settee with the decaying ghost of this gentleman. The shock and the stench made him abruptly leave the room to be violently ill over the terrace balustrade. No one else had seen the apparition. The unfortunate ghost supposedly met his death at the stable block, where he is also seen.

The Fleur de Lys room also contains the ghost of a small child who fleetingly attempts to hold a visitor's hand. The child is also heard crying in the library. It is thought that the Grey Lady could have been the child's mother.

The Green Man, a member of the Cope family who threw himself from the cliffs not far from Brighton in 1806, is sometimes seen near the lake in the garden. He loved the colour green and everything he wore, apart from his boots, and all he ate, was green. He is seen as an apparition who is transparent from the knees down.

A young man in 1920s tennis apparel is frequently seen passing through the reception. He is thought to be a member of the Cope family who loved tennis. He was killed, so the story says, when he fell from a train.

The little boy on the terrace usually appears when there are children in the vicinity. He is thought to have fallen off the roof in the eighteenth century.

The gardener drowned in the lake and the area near where he died has an aura such that both people and dogs hesitate to go past the spot.

A knight in armour and a woman dressed in the style of Queen Anne have been seen in the chapel drawing room, whilst a nun and a lady dressed in the style fashionable in Charles I's time manifest themselves in the Roman Catholic chapel.

The Police College accounts department frequently has the heavy scent of lilacs filling the air, which has been experienced by college staff and students alike.

The stories go on and on. There are tales of the chapel drawing room being full of ghosts in period costume one minute and empty the next, while there is often a strong scent of flowers at the top of the Queen Anne staircase. Bramshill House is truly an amazing place, filled with a variety of manifestations which challenge belief.

The Eclipse Inn, Winchester

'Hanging Judge' George Jeffreys was born in Wrexham in 1648. As Lord Chief Justice, he was the leader of the judges at the 'Bloody Assizes', the trials that took place following the collapse of the Monmouth Rebellion at the Battle of Sedgemore in 1685.

The first trial took place in Winchester on 27 August. Dame Alicia (also known as Lady Alice) Lisle, a respected, gently born lady of over seventy years of age, was accused of treason. She had taken into her home at Moyles Court, Ellingham, near Ringwood, two fugitives: John Hickes, a person known to her as a minister, who had sent a message asking for sanctuary, and a man he brought with him and whom she had never before met, Richard Nelthorpe, a wanted outlaw. Spies had immediately carried the news of the arrivals and Dame Alicia said at her arrest and at her subsequent trial that she had supposed that Hickes was wanted for poaching or for something connected to his ministry.

Dame Alicia was the widow of John Lisle, who had been a member of Cromwell's House of Lords. He had been assassinated in Switzerland for his role in the execution of Charles I. According to Alice Lisle's entry in the *British Dictionary of National Biography* (Oxford University Press, 1997) John Lisle had sentenced Royalist John Penruddock to death. His son, Colonel Penruddock, was King James II's arresting officer in the subsequent treason case against Dame Alicia. As such, it could be argued that Colonel Penruddock was hardly in a position to be a fair judge of what he found at Moyles Court on 26 July 1685.

At the trial, no evidence of either Hickes' or Nelthorpe's offences were admitted and the one witness, the messenger, Dunne, stood fast, despite haranguing from Judge Jeffreys. By all accounts, Dame Alicia withstood a tirade of abuse from the notorious judge. Nothing connected Dame Alicia with Monmouth sympathies but the jury found her guilty under direction from Jeffreys. Dame Alicia was sentenced to be dragged through the streets on a hurdle and then burned at the stake that same afternoon. However, on hearing the news, the local townspeople's horrified reaction delayed the execution. When James II heard the news, he decided that the sentence was a little too drastic for the people of Hampshire to take quietly and so decreed that she should be beheaded. She spent her last night at the Eclipse Inn, just along from Winchester Cathedral.

The inn, dating from about 1540, has a varied history; as a private house, a rectory, an alehouse and an inn. The night before the execution, wooden scaffolding was erected outside the inn and Dame Alicia went to her grisly end the next morning. She was buried in Ellingham Churchyard, her cortege followed by many of the townsfolk in silent protest at the execution that was widely seen as unlawful.

Since that time, the figure of Dame Alicia has regularly been seen either in the upper bedroom she occupied at the Eclipse Inn or in the corridor just outside. Dressed in a long grey gown, she stands motionless in a corner recess.

She is also regularly seen at her home, Moyles Court, where her attire is more that of a rich lady. Reports persist of her silk dress rustling as she walks along corridors or in the courtyard, and of her driverless carriage being heard along Ellingham Lane in Winchester.

Fort Brockenhurst

Fort Brockenhurst, near Gosport, was one of five forts built to protect Portsmouth harbour and the naval properties around the town. They were built between 1858 and 1862, and were designed to protect against artillery shells.

Fort Brockenhurst today sits serenely in its moat, looking like a throwback to a past age as the water laps gently at the squat brick building. This appearance is reinforced by the fact that visitors enter the fort by drawbridge. The huge interior is full of atmosphere and cell three particularly so. It is here that Fort Brockenhurst's ghost likes to lurk.

It is thought that the ghost is that of a sergeant major who was stationed at the fort but details are sketchy. He is still making his rounds and his tuneless whistling and measured footsteps can be heard, although he has not been seen.

Portchester Castle

Portchester Castle, near Fareham, is the best-preserved Roman fort in Europe. It stands in a commanding position over the Solent, as it has done since it was built in the third century. In the twelfth century it became a Norman castle when a huge keep was added in one corner of the nine-acre site. Successive kings have stayed there, either for pleasure or while assembling an army, usually to fight the French. Following the marriage of Richard II to Isabella, the seven-year-old daughter of the King of France, a miniature royal palace was built for her within the castle walls. Gradually the castle declined in importance and by the eighteenth century it was just a prison, albeit a full one during the Napoleonic Wars.

Today Portchester Castle is a shadow of its former self but several of its old residents are still in evidence, although details of them are sketchy. There is the apparition described as 'a tall, whitish object' that appears regularly. This is thought to be the ghost of a long-dead prisoner who vowed to return. It could also be the manifestation of an uninvited actor, just popping in to give a performance and then disappearing once more. A monk is said to walk along the front of the castle, although he gradually fades as he walks by. There is also a sad woman seen crouching over a grave at the medieval church which stands in the castle grounds.

The Ghost of HMS Mercury

Dr Philip MacDougall, in his book *Phantoms of the High Seas*, tells the story of the ghost of Eagle Block at HMS *Mercury*, which was in East Meon, near Petersfield, for over fifty years.

HMS *Mercury* was the specialist shore training establishment for the Royal Navy's communications branch. It was opened in 1941 and its Latin motto,

Celer et Fidelis, or 'Swift and Faithful', summed up the ethos of the branch. Chris Rickard wrote an excellent history of the school, 'HMS *Mercury*: Swift and Faithful, 1941-1993' in 2006.

The original building, Leydene House, was the home of Lord and Lady Peel, who had the house built between 1914 and 1925, with a break during the First World War. Lord Peel was the grandson of the founder of the Metropolitan Police, Sir Robert Peel. The house was requisitioned from the widowed Lady Peel during the Second World War as a home for the communicators, following the decision to move them from the original Signal School within HM Dockyard, Portsmouth. The dockyard was coming under increasing aerial attack and it was felt that all the training, research and accommodation facilities should be moved to safer places away from Portsmouth.

HMS *Mercury*, as Leydene House was commissioned on 16 August 1941, grew to incorporate 100 Nissen huts and over fifty other buildings, including barrack buildings, a guardhouse complete with cells, and a cinema. The estate, the house and 120 acres of land was bought from Lady Peel by compulsory purchase for the sum of £60,000 in 1947.

A new classroom block was opened in 1962, having taken four years to build. This was Eagle Block and it catered to those learning Morse code as well as providing a range of formal classrooms. Philip MacDougall describes Eagle Block as having 'as much character as a cement barge on the River Thames'.

Eagle Block soon earned the reputation for being haunted. It is thought that the ghost who made strange noises, turned on lights in locked rooms or by pulling impossible-to-reach broken pull cords and who opened sky lights, was a young Women's Royal Naval Service (WRNS) rating who, in February 1961, had been struck by falling masonry while the building was under construction. She had died soon after. Her antics led to much excitement as routine patrols called in the emergency party to investigate. It was thought that intruders were causing the occurrences which, being a military site, were well documented and reported.

6 August 1993 was the day that training stopped at HMS *Mercury*. Most of the buildings were demolished and Leydene House was converted into luxury flats. What became of the Eagle Block ghost, nobody knows.

Odiham Castle

The delightfully named village of Odiham, which itself is the dwelling place of a ghostly little black dog that runs down the High Street, is home to the crumbling ruin called Odiham Castle. Known locally as 'King John's Castle', it was the place that King John set out from on his way to Runneymede and the Magna Carta in 1215, and it was the castle to which he returned.

Odiham Castle was built between 1207 and 1214 and cost more than £1,000 to build. It was said to be John's favourite castle and was strategically built half-way between Windsor and Winchester. In 1216 the castle survived a two-week siege by the French. It was owned by the powerful de Montfort family during the thirteenth century but had declined to the status of a hunting lodge by the fifteenth century. By 1605 it was described as a ruin.

The once-proud castle is now home to former prisoners, shadowy figures glimpsed now and again in costumes of yesteryear, and to a minstrel, fleetingly seen on rare occasions but more often heard. A chill in the air usually heralds his arrival and then the haunting strains of a pipe or a lute are heard together with muted singing.

The Dolphin Inn, High Street, Botley

The Dolphin Inn in Botley, just outside Southampton, was once called the Garrison Inn, reflecting its status as a garrison town in days gone by. It is sup-posed to be haunted by the spirit of a Civil War Cavalier, who is seen now and again in its rooms.

Footsteps outside a bedroom and noises in the cellar have also been heard at the inn. The dining room has a cold spot and there is the feeling of a presence there. There is also a story that the landlady in 1980 saw something, an 'outline', rushing past her that she described as 'tall and slim'.

The Theatre Royal, Winchester

The ghosts that haunt the Theatre Royal have not been around long in haunting terms. There seems to be no record of supernatural happenings on the site before John and James Simpkins purchased the building that had been the Market Hotel. They converted the old hotel into a variety theatre which opened in 1914.

Phil Yately, whose book *Behind the Curtains, Scenes from the History of the Theatre Royal, Winchester* (written in conjunction with Madelaine Smith) tells the story of the theatre, its history and inhabitants, notes several spirits in the theatre:

There may be more but the main ghost is that of John Simpkins. John and James Simpkins bought the hotel in 1912. They were the first owners. They worked in partnership, but John was the sleeping partner. James was the general factotum, the working man behind the project. Over the proscenium arch there's a crest, a cartouche, and on it are the initials JS. John said to his brother that he thought that it ought to be J&JS for James and John Simpkins. James promised his brother that it would be done and it never was.

John died [in 1923] and it is said that his ghost haunts the theatre to find out if the initials were ever altered. He is supposed to come out of what used to be his office on the far side and walk around. We call it the 'Ghost Walk'. He walks into one of the boxes. He looks at the cartouche and then disappears through the wall. A former crewmember swears blind that she saw an apparition dressed in a black cloak disappear through that wall.

Another ghost is that of one of the dancing girls, who has been seen to dance once more up on the stage. Phil Yately says:

There used to be dancing girls in the early review years, like the Tiller girls, but they were known as Dainty Maidens. One of the dancing girls was keeping company with a spot light operator, a 'Blinder' as they used to call it when they operated the spot lights from the prompt corner. He was called up in the Great War and was sent to France. She fainted one night and Jimmy Simpkins went on stage and said, 'What's the trouble?' She said, 'I've just seen the operator in the corner'. He said, 'You couldn't have done, he's serving King and Country abroad'. At that particular time the following day, the boy's mother received a telegram from the War Office to say he had been killed in action in France. We think that apparition was something she saw of her boyfriend who had been killed.

The third ghost is a Victorian lady. Michael Bentine, one of the Goons, used to do One Man Shows. He came here and we had nice chats in the bar. He said to me that he had had a lovely lady on stage with him that night and I said, 'Well, that's strange, it's a one man show. Who was it?' He said, 'I don't know, I'm asking you. She was dressed in a Victorian costume and she was a very friendly spirit. Do you know who she was?' The only thing I could think of was there used to be a big place at the top of Tower Street, known as Tower House, and the theatre site would be the garden of the whole house. I said, 'Well, maybe she was the owner?' He said, 'Perhaps she came down to look at the garden?'

Mr Yately has been involved with the Theatre Royal for thirty-five years, during which time he has been on the Operating Board, was the House Manager and an usher. He visited the theatre as a boy with his parents, when it was a cinema:

I have never seen a ghost but I think I felt an apparition one day when I was working here, when the theatre was completely dark. I went in to switch the lights on and there was a terrific sort of gush of wind. I know I locked all the doors. The fire bucket though was just below me and I would have fallen over it if I hadn't stopped. I would have gone right down and kicked the bucket!

We have had ghost hunters here. The last pack was here in 2008. The Chief Executive and the House Manager stayed all night and all sorts of things happened, things really did go bump in the night! I stayed with one group of ghost hunters from London and there were very high readings in certain parts of the theatre and that is where they think there was some sort of spirit lurking about, so…

These are things that have happened since our Chairman, James, turned the hotel into a theatre. Perhaps the hotel didn't like to be part of the theatre life?

The Angel Inn, Lymington

Lymington was once a shipbuilding port exceeding the might of Portsmouth. Now nothing is left of this legacy apart from the yachts bobbing in the harbour. It is obvious though that the town has known prosperity. The Georgian houses that line the picturesque streets tell of better times. One of these buildings is the Angel Inn, a sixteenth-century coaching inn which was formerly known as the George.

The Angel has several ghosts, recorded by Roger Long, which pop up to meet the unwary at odd moments. One story tells of a sailor, who may possibly be a shipbuilder, who made the inn's relief manager jump in the 1970s. Appearing late at night, the tall, bearded man was dressed in an old mariner's coat complete with shiny brass buttons.

Also seen several times is the coachman waiting for his free supper, who appears with his nose against the kitchen window.

The landlord's brother and sister-in-law stayed in the bedroom next door to the old ballroom. On their first night they heard the tinkling of ivory piano keys being played energetically. Despite a search, no piano or pianist was found. The inn's piano had been removed the day before the couple had come to stay as it was in disrepair…

Hinton Ampner

Ghosts at the old Manor House in Hinton Ampner, near Alresford, are well documented by Peter Underwood. The house was demolished in 1793, as no one would live in it for fear of the disturbances within.

The village, which gets its name, a corruption of 'Almoner', from its connection with the Priory of St Swithun at Winchester, is dominated by the Manor House. The present building was built about 50yds from the site of the earlier Manor House, which occupied the site of a large medieval house that burnt down in Tudor times. The building today encompasses the Georgian structure, built in 1793, and was extensively altered in the 1930s and badly damaged by fire in 1960. Today it is a pleasant and quiet place to live.

The Manor House it replaced was neither pleasant nor quiet and for many years all who lived there had their lives punctuated by unexplained and supernatural phenomena which drove out every tenant.

In 1719 Mary Stewkeley, ancestor of Sir Thomas Stewkeley who had lived at the house at the end of the sixteenth century, married Edward, later Lord, Stawell. They lived at the house with her sister, Honoria. Twenty-one years later, Mary died and her husband and sister continued to reside in the same house. Rumours soon began to circulate about the pair, as inevitably they will in a small community. It was said that a baby was born to the couple and that it had been murdered there.

Honoria died in 1754 and her brother-in-law a year later. Soon afterwards reports of sightings of Lord Stawell began to be whispered. A groom at the manor said he had seen his late master 'in drab coloured clothing'.

In 1765, after years of the house being used infrequently during the hunting season, it was let to the well-to-do Ricketts family. Mrs Mary Ricketts, home alone with her children for long periods while her husband was in Jamaica, gave accounts of her experiences with the Manor House ghost in letters to her husband, William Henry Ricketts, and in a description of the events which took place while the family resided at the house, written for her children. These included doors slamming for no discernible reason, even after the locks were changed. The family's nurse swore she saw a man 'in a drab-coloured suit of clothes' walk in to her mistress' apartment and the Ricketts' groom also said he saw a man wearing similar clothing. All the servants at the house had been replaced when the Ricketts' moved in and so they did not know of the previous sightings of a ghostly apparition.

Following these sightings, over the next years there were similar glimpses of a woman in a dark, rustling silk dress and footsteps, groans and more rustling noises were heard by several of the residents. These sounds intensified. A maid was heard groaning in her room, while music and heavy knocks were heard elsewhere.

Mrs Ricketts heard a tale, told by one of the villagers in West Meon, that the floorboards had been taken up in the dining room to conceal something. The storyteller did not know what was hidden.

Thereafter the haunting events followed one on top of another. Sixteen years after Lord Stawell's death, heavy knocking, indistinct conversations between a woman and two men, crashing and shrill cries were all heard. A family friend, Captain Luttrell, sat up with a servant and Mrs Ricketts' brother, later to become Lord St Vincent, to hear for themselves the sounds emanating from all areas of the house. They also heard the sounds of a gun being fired and more footsteps as they sat up night after night.

In August 1771 Mrs Ricketts and her children moved out of the Manor House, unable to bear living in the building any longer. The Lawrence family then occupied it for two years and little was heard of the happenings inside, although the female apparition was said to have appeared.

After the Lawrences left, the house was empty for twenty years before it was pulled down and the new house built nearby. At this point a child's skull was found under the floorboards in one room.

THREE

SAINTS, ROYALTY AND CELEBRATED CITIZENS

'God bless us every one!' said Tiny Tim, the last of all.

Charles Dickens, born in Portsmouth

A Christmas Carol

Hampshire abounds with saints, royal visitors and citizens who did amazing things. This chapter celebrates just a few of those folk who, for one reason or another are, or should be, remembered in Hampshire with pride.

St Ethelflaeda

Present-day tabloid newspapers fixate on the fact that the patron saint of Romsey's Abbey Church is best remembered for the fact that one of her saintly habits was to go to the nearby River Test at night, disrobe and stand naked in the freezing water while chanting psalms. Whilst certainly startling, this was just one of several events which led to her sainthood.

Romsey Abbey, the Abbey Church of St Mary and Ethelflaeda, owes its existence to the nuns settled by King Edward the Elder, the son of King Alfred the Great, the celebrated Saxon king, on the site in AD 907. He put his own daughter, Elflaeda, in charge of the group.

The saintly Ethelflaeda was the nunnery's second abbess. One of the stories told of her miraculous acts says that she used the glow from her fingertips to light up the Bible she was reading in the pulpit when the candles blew out in the abbey. Another tells of the time when, after accidentally giving away money a bailiff had placed for safe keeping in the abbey's strongbox, she prayed and then found the coffers full again.

The nunnery was highly regarded by both Saxon and Norman kings and provided education for the daughters of kings and noblemen. In about AD 960 King Edgar re-founded it as a Benedictine nunnery. At its height over 100 nuns lived there, but later the Black Death reduced that number to just nineteen.

In 1120 the church was begun and it was completed over a century later, in Henry III's reign. St Ethelflaeda appears on a wax seal used by the clergy at the abbey and her likeness, taken from the seal, is enshrined in Romsey's Charter Stone, unveiled by Queen Elizabeth II in 2007.

In October 2009 the first Ethelflaeda Festival was held in the town. On the opening day of the three-day festival, Canon Lucy Winkett, from St Paul's Cathedral, gave a free lecture on the influence women have had on the Church throughout history. This was followed the next day by the premiere of a musical drama based on the life of the saint. Dr June Boyce Tillman MBE, Professor of Applied Music at the University of Winchester, specially wrote this piece for the festival. It was performed by seventy of the town's children and a small orchestra. On the final day of the festival, a psalm which the abbey's Director of Music, Robert Fielding, wrote for the event was presented. After this the worshippers proceeded to St Ethelflaeda's Chapel.

St Ethelflaeda would undoubtedly have approved of the festival. Long may it last.

St Clement

St Clement, the patron saint of blacksmiths whose day is on 23 November, was celebrated in Twyford for many years until 1880. An effigy of the saint was paraded through the village and set down for general inspection outside the Bugle Inn, where it was usual to collect money for the blacksmiths for a celebratory meal, the Clem Feast or Supper.

Blacksmiths were important people in a time when the science behind the world was not understood. The craftsman who could make the tools needed to till the earth held a special place in society, hence the importance of celebrating the blacksmiths' patron saint.

At the Clem Feast the toast, 'The Blacksmiths', was followed by the reciting of the tale of how King Solomon was convinced of the importance of the blacksmiths after failing to invite them to a dinner for artificers, to which all the other craftsmen who had helped to build a temple were invited. The smiths protested at being ignored and eloquently gave evidence of their importance. King Solomon realised his mistake and gave them pride of place at the meal, ahead of the other craftsmen.

After the recitation, the blacksmiths 'fired the anvil', exploding gunpowder in their anvils, a practice whose origins seem to have been lost in time. To do this, a small hole was drilled in the anvil and was filled with gunpowder. A plug covered this and a hole was drilled through it. Gunpowder was then trailed from the plug and set alight. The result was spectacular as anvils weigh about 300lbs and the blast would force them into the air.

In *The Folklore of Hampshire and the Isle of Wight*, Wendy Boase tells us of another variation of the story of how the blacksmiths are the most important of the craftsmen. She says that King Alfred chose the tailor as the most important craftsman. When the blacksmiths heard this they were so annoyed that they said they would not work until the king changed his mind. Over time the other craftsmen's tools broke or rusted and things got so bad that, when the king's horse needed a replacement shoe for one he had lost, a group broke into a smithy and tried to make a new one themselves. The result was complete disaster and the anvil is said to have fallen on the ground and exploded. The blacksmith is said to have appeared, with St Clement, and King Alfred apologised. He then announced that the blacksmith was the most important of the craftsmen. It is said that this story was acted out at the Clem Feast.

St Clement, the third Bishop of Rome from AD 92 to AD 96 was, according to later fourth century sources, martyred by being thrown into the Black Sea while tied to an anchor. Whether this is true or not is debatable, as older sources do not mention this. He is depicted as either wearing an anchor about his neck or carrying an anchor, and is the patron saint of anchor forgers and blacksmiths in general.

St Swithun

Most of us will have heard of the rain on St Swithun's Day. If it rains on St Swithun's Day, so the saying goes, it will rain for forty days and forty nights. If it is fine on St Swithun's day, it will be fine for forty days and forty nights. Who was St Swithun and how did it come about that he had so much influence over the weather?

Swithun was born around AD 800 and was the Prior of Winchester Cathedral monastery before becoming Bishop of the cathedral in AD 852. He had taught both King Ethelwulf and his son, Alfred the Great, and was renowned for his learning. Indeed, it is said that Ethelwulf set great store by Swithun's advice, not just in religion, but also in matters relating to finances and war. He built many churches and liked to oversee the building work himself, sitting nearby and watching, to give his workers the impetus to work harder. He was said to be a humble man and went to the dedication of these churches quietly, on foot and often at night so as not to draw attention to himself.

He was known for his kindness and this led to the one miracle during his lifetime for which he is remembered. Seeing that many of the poor had to wade across the Itchen River on foot to come into the city to sell their wares, he ordered that a substantial bridge, made of stone, be built at Winchester's eastern gate. One day, as he was crossing the bridge, a passing monk bumped into an old peasant lady who was taking her eggs to market. The eggs landed on the cobbles and were all smashed. The old woman was loud in her grief, for the eggs were a major source of income and had been lost. Swithun picked up the eggs and the woman found that they were whole once again. This miracle was commemorated in the 1962 shrine dedicated to St Swithun at the cathedral, which has a broken eggshell on each of its four candlesticks.

Swithun died on 2 July AD 862 and was buried, according to his dying wishes, outside the north wall of the Old Minster. In this lowly place the rain would fall off the eaves and hit the grave and those worshipping at the church would walk over him. Despite the Winchester Cathedral canons' perception that this was too humble a place of rest for one so highly thought of, Swithun stayed there for a century. During this time tales of the miracles performed by Swithun from beyond the grave began to circulate and pilgrims came from ever-greater distances to visit his final resting place. Reports of specific miraculous events, such as a hunchback lying on the grave and rising to find himself straight, lent credence to the legend that was growing about him.

On 15 July AD 871 Swithun's body was scheduled to move from its grave into a new resting place inside the minster. However, it started to rain forcefully and continued to do so for the next forty days. The translation had to be halted. Not for nothing did the ancient Flemish know July as *wedermaend*, the month of storms. 15 July became St Swithun's Day, the date the saint is remembered.

Eventually King Edgar 'the Peaceful', grandson of Alfred the Great, succeeded in having Swithun's remains moved, and they were placed in a shrine in the New Minster. This was expedient for Aethelwold, later St Aethelwold, Bishop of Winchester at the time. In an age of reform, when Benedictine monks were replacing the secular canons, Aethelwold needed a character that could be used to appease those displaced by the reforms. Swithun was just what he wanted as he had not been a monk. His remains were placed in the new shrine, in a gold and silver reliquary, and this became very popular with pilgrims. It is said that in the ten days after his relocation there were 200 miracles as sick people were healed. As the resident monks had to give thanks every time there was a miracle performed, the tired monks soon started complaining. According to Wendy Boase, this discontent only stopped when St Swithun himself appeared to them and expressed his disapproval.

When the Normans rebuilt the cathedral, Swithun's skeleton was placed on the new altar. By now it was headless as the Bishop of Winchester, Aelheah, had taken the skull with him when he went to Canterbury in 1005. A century later and the skull was in Évreux in France. David Keys, writing in *The Church Times*, suggests that Swithun's skull might have been taken there after being given as a diplomatic gift, the Bishop of Évreux having been in England for the second coronation of Henry, the Young King, in Winchester in 1172. In the meantime the skeleton was further plundered as an arm bone was taken to Stavanger in Norway for the cathedral consecrated there in Swithun's name.

Over the following centuries, Swithun was credited with more miracles and he became a cult figure. A new shrine to him was built in 1476 but this was a victim of the Reformation less than 100 years later in 1538 when it was demolished and the materials reused elsewhere.

Winchester had no idea where St Swithun's skull was until it was traced to Évreux, where it still resides. St Swithun's first resting place has now been established and there is a marble slab which marks the spot on the cathedral green.

Today, Dr John Crook, FSA, Architectural Historian for Winchester Cathedral, is engaged in tracing pieces of the 1476 shrine in the hope that it may be possible to reconstruct it.

St Boniface

Boniface, originally named Winfrith and also known as Winfrid and Wynfrith, was born around AD 675 in the west of Wessex, possibly in Crediton. He came from a well-to-do family and showed promise as a scholar from a young age. Boniface decided to dedicate his life to the Church after hearing monks preach at the age of five. He pestered his father for permission, eventually given, to join the Benedictine monastery at Adescancastre, now the city we know as Exeter. He studied there for seven years before moving to the abbey in Nhutscelle (Nutshalling), present day Nursling, just outside Southampton. The abbey was a Benedictine monastery, renowned as a seat of learning. Here he studied under Abbot Winbert and taught in the abbey school. It was while he was at Nhutscelle that he wrote the first Latin grammar book in England. He became known for his preaching and the depth and breadth of his learning and was held in high esteem by the ecclesiastical and secular authorities. He was called to the priesthood at the age of thirty and it was after this that his thoughts turned to spreading the word of God beyond England's shores.

He obtained permission from his abbot to travel to Germany, which was largely heathen at that time, although some missionaries had had a little success in converting small pockets of the population to Christianity. Boniface wanted to build on this beginning. He set off for Friesland, modern-day Holland, in AD 716 but returned to Nhutscelle briefly because of political disturbances in Germany. When Abbot Winbert died in AD 717 he was asked to take his place. He refused as the call of the missionary work was too great and soon set off for Rome to see Pope Gregory II on his way back to Germany.

The Pope welcomed Boniface warmly and gave him full authority to preach the Gospel to the heathens in Germany. Boniface toured the country and found that in Thuringia, where St Killan had preached for some time, prominent converts had been murdered and the local people had largely turned their backs on Christianity. Boniface tried to inspire the local priests to go out into the community to bring back their wayward flock but had less success than he had hoped for. Boniface then spent three years studying and working with St Wilibord in Friesland, before moving on to establish a centre in Upper Hessia for training local clergy.

In AD 722 Boniface returned to Rome and Pope Gregory consecrated him as a Regional Bishop with the name Boniface, meaning 'the doer of good'.

When he returned to Upper Hessia it was to find that many had fallen back into paganism while he had been away. In a final bid to make his point the new bishop chopped a mighty oak tree down at Geimar, which the local population thought was sacred to the god Thor. He had a chapel built from the timber and the local villagers were so amazed that nothing had happened when the tree came down that there were large numbers of converts and word spread. This was his breakthrough in his quest to spread Christianity in Germany. Over the next years he succeeded in building chapels and founding monasteries and a steady stream of the pious came to help him in his missionary work. When Pope Gregory II died in AD 731, Pope Gregory III made Boniface an archbishop and bade him appoint bishops wherever he thought fit. Boniface set to with a will.

Boniface was under the protection of Charles Martel (AD 688-AD 741), the legendary Frankish general and grandfather of Charlemagne. He wrote many letters back to England and in one, to a friend in Winchester, he claimed that he could not have overcome the obstacles he had faced if it had not been for the friendship of Martel.

At an age when most would have put their feet up to rest, Boniface led a mission to Frisia once more, determined to try to finish the work he had failed to do there at the start of his missionary career. On 5 June AD 755 he and his companions were set upon by local heathens and all were killed. This day has become St Boniface's saint's day.

The date of Boniface's canonisation is unclear. Now St Boniface's relics lie scattered in several countries across the world and he is revered as the patron saint of Germany and the Netherlands. In England there are churches dedicated to St Boniface all over the country, most notably Crediton in Devon and in the county that he lived in at the beginning of his career, Hampshire. There is a St Boniface Church in both Chandlers Ford and in Shirley, Southampton.

It is claimed that St Boniface created the Christmas tree. Legend has it that when the oak fell at Geismar, a fir tree grew amongst its roots. St Boniface is reported to have said, 'This humble tree's wood is used to build your homes: let Christ be at the centre of your households. Its leaves remain evergreen in the darkest days, let Christ be your constant light. Its boughs reach out to embrace and its top points to Heaven, let Christ be your comfort and your guide'. The fir tree is said to have become the symbol of Christmas in Germany and has since spread through the world.

Alfred the Great

In Winchester, at the lower end of the Broadway, stands the towering statue of King Alfred the Great. Erected in 1899 and designed by Hamo Thorneycroft RA, it caused much interest when it was unveiled. Hundreds turned out to see the suitably heroic looking statue of Wessex's greatest leader and the Bishop of Winchester graced the event with a speech. Crowned and with his shield on his arm, he holds his sword upside down so that it resembles a cross held aloft. He looks what he was, a devout Christian who happened to be a warrior king.

The area that was Wessex has a long history. It was formed from the kingdom of the West Saxons. Cerdic (AD 467–AD 534) is generally held to be the first King of Wessex, although there had been a long line of chieftains before him. Wessex began in Berkshire and grew to encompass the whole of the south of England below the Thames.

Alfred was born in Wantage in Berkshire in AD 849. His father, King Ethelwulf, meaning 'noble wolf', (AD 806–AD 857) had succeeded his father,

King Egbert, that tenacious ruler who had opposed and been defeated by Beorhtric, the rightful heir to the throne who ruled between AD 786 and AD 802. Egbert had sought refuge after this defeat with Offa, the powerful King of Mercia whose daughter was then given in marriage to Beorhtric; this made life difficult for Egbert and gave Offa even more power. Egbert was forced into exile in Charlemagne's court in France, where he learnt much about politics and warfare. Charlemagne subsequently closed his ports to Offa's ships, which brought problems for traders in Hampshire and its main port of Southampton. Egbert returned to Wessex on Beorhtric's death and used his newfound knowledge to his advantage, taking the Wessex crown in AD 802.

On Egbert's death in AD 837, Ethelwulf took the crown and proved, despite his ecclesiastical leanings, to be a good ruler. Ethelwulf left a tenth of his lands to the Church and the deed for this was written in Winchester, which grew in importance during this period. Ethelwulf died in AD 856 and was succeeded by each of his sons, Ethelbald (AD 856-AD 860), Ethelbert, (AD 860-AD 865) and Ethelred (AD 865-AD 871). Their reigns were plagued by attacks from Danes, who had invaded England in the eighth century and were intent on conquering far and wide. The Norsemen had made peace with the East Angles and the Mercians and now they wanted Wessex. King Ethelred and his brother, Alfred, defeated them at a fierce battle at Ashdown, near Lambourn in Berkshire in AD 871, but before they could enjoy the victory they were defeated at Basing in Hampshire two weeks later. Ethelred died soon after this battle.

Alfred was crowned King of Wessex in AD 871. He made Winchester his capital, thus ensuring its place in history. Life was not quiet for the new king. The Danes had not gone away after winning at Basing. Over the next eight years, Alfred found himself battling to keep his kingdom. It was during this period that the most widely known story about him is set, although it was not in circulation until nearly four centuries later and is not mentioned by either of the leading primary sources for the period, the *Anglo-Saxon Chronicle* (AD 890), the book Alfred himself commissioned, or *The Life of Alfred the Great* (AD 893) by Asser, the Welsh monk.

In the winter of AD 877-878 the Danes controlled much of Wessex. Alfred withdrew to Athelney in Somerset. Here, so the story goes, he took refuge in a lowly cowherd's hut. Unrecognised by the local people, he was asked to keep an eye on the cakes baking in the housewife's hearth. Preoccupied with seeing to his equipment, he forgot the baking and the cakes burned. The housewife scolded him vigorously and the story has become a defining one for Alfred. Alfred later commanded the building of a monastery at Athelney.

After the Battle of Ethandun in AD 878, which Alfred won decisively, the Danes were starved into submission in Chippenham. It was the beginning of a period of peace for Wessex. The Danish leader, Guthrum, converted to Christianity and Alfred and Guthrum agreed to split their territories between them. Guthrum brought Danelaw to East Anglia, but Alfred retained the mints in London. All was quiet for several years but the Danes chafed at the bit and Alfred was obliged to retake London in about AD 886. It was at this time that he styled himself King of the Anglo-Saxons.

Alfred was under no illusions. He knew that there were more Vikings waiting to sail to England and he looked to shipbuilding to repel them. He established shipyards, building ships larger than the esks that the Vikings sailed in. These had sixty oars, twice the number of the enemy craft. These small beginnings could be said to be the basis for the Navy. The naval shipyard on the Itchen at Woolston was probably one that was started in Alfred's time.

In AD 897 these ships were put to the test when they were engaged in a battle in the Solent. Danish invaders, together with their wives and children, arrived in their hundreds. Both sides sustained heavy casualties but Alfred's fleet eventually emerged victorious.

Alfred himself was a very pious man and was devoted to education although, according to Hone, he did not learn to read until he was twelve. He surrounded himself with learned men, nicknamed 'Alfred's scholars', who were there to help him with his quest to spread learning in Wessex. Among them were Asser, the Welsh priest of St David's whose *Life of King Alfred the Great* is now so valuable to us in twenty-first century Britain; Plegmund, a Mercian cleric who became the Archbishop of Canterbury; Werferth, later the Bishop of Worcester; Grimbald of St Omer; and John, described as a continental Saxon.

When Alfred died he was buried in the Old Minster in Winchester. However, the monks there were extremely fearful that Alfred's ghost was haunting the building and so his body was moved to the New Minster and subsequently to Hyde Abbey. His final resting place was respected until the Reformation, when the buildings were pulled down on the orders of Thomas Wriothesley, the Earl of Southampton. However, he did not disturb Alfred's tomb. This happened in 1787-1788, when the building of a gaol on the old abbey site left Alfred's remains scattered to the winds.

Alfred split his kingdom up and left parts of it to each of his children in his will. The areas now known as Hurstbourn Tarrant, Bishop's Sutton and Alton were left to his eldest son, Edward, later King Edward; Aethelweard, Alfred's younger son, inherited Meon, Twyford and Southwick; his eldest daughter, Ethelfleda, received Wellow; his younger daughter, Ethelgiva, received Clere and Candover; and his nephew, Ethelm, was given Crondall.

Canute

Cnut, the Viking raider we know now as Canute, fought his way across the Anglo-Saxon counties to become King of England. The Witan, the Saxon council, is believed to have named him as king in 1016 in Southampton. Shortly thereafter Canute and Edmund, the son of the dead Saxon king, Athelred, who had been named as his father's successor by the Witan in London, led their forces to Andover and the first of a series of inconclusive battles for supremacy. Eventually the pair agreed to share the country between them and whoever survived the other would take the crown of England as a whole. His sons would then succeed. This plan was admirable but there is suspicion about the role the traitorous Hampshire nobleman, Edric, played in Edmund's early demise a few months later. What is certain is that Hampshire and the rest of England enjoyed peace and prosperity for the next twenty years due to Canute's strong rule. It was at this time that Winchester rose in prominence as a seat of administration, as Canute was not just the King of England but also of Denmark and later Norway too.

We have all heard the story of how Canute placed his throne on the beach and commanded the waves to stop advancing. According to Henry of Huntington (1080–1160), the Archdeacon of the Diocese of Lincoln in his *Historia Anglorum*, or *History of the English*, when the waves lapped at Alfred's feet he is said to have stated, 'Let all men know how empty and worthless is the power of kings, for there is none worthy of the name, but He whom heaven, earth, and sea obey by eternal laws'. He is said to have never worn his royal crown again after this time. Apocryphal the story may be, but Southampton is the place that tradition has it where this was supposed to have happened. There is a plaque today on the wall of the Canute Hotel in Canute Road in the town that bears the inscription: 'Near this spot Canute reproved his couriers'.

In his informative *History of Hampshire*, T. W. Shore, writing in 1892, mentions that Canute's palace was still visible in Porter's Lane, although he does say that in celebrated antiquarian and scientist Sir Henry Englefield's day (1752–1822), the property was in better repair.

Canute is recorded in the *Liber Vitae*, the Winchester confraternity book or memorial book for the New Minster, begun by King Alfred in AD 900, as being the monastery's benefactor, donating the Winchester Cross, large amounts of silver and gold coins and relics of several saints. Canute died in 1035 at Shaftesbury Abbey in Dorset, and while his heart is said to have been buried at the abbey, his body was buried in Winchester in the New Minster, now known as Winchester Cathedral. During the English Civil War Canute's bones, in addition to those of his wife, Emma of Normandy, the Red King, William Rufus, and other buried

English kings were scattered on the floor by marauding Roundheads looking for plunder. They now reside in chests which can still be seen in Winchester Cathedral.

William Rufus

Canterton Glen, in the middle of the area described by T. W. Shore as 'Malwood', is the picturesque site of the Rufus Stone. A great slab of iron, which John Wise in 1880 described as: 'Of a taste on a par with that of the designer of the post office pillar-boxes' (in Peter Tate's *The New Forest 900 Years After*, 1979), was erected in 1841 around the original stone monument by John, Lord Delaware, to mark the spot where a huge oak tree once stood. The arrow that killed William Rufus is said to have bounced off this oak and hit the king, mortally wounding him. Today the spot is a calm and serene place amidst the leafy fronds of oak and beech trees in the New Forest, with a convenient car park nearby.

The land that was to become the New Forest was a wild and furzy place back in 1079 when William the Conqueror (1028-1087) first cast eyes on it. Then it was known to the Saxons as 'Ytene', which Peter Tate helpfully tells us rhymes with 'Brittany', meaning the 'land of the Jutes and furzy waste'. The gorse, which is a feature of the landscape now, was just as much in evidence then. The local chroniclers at the time painted William as a brute, driving out the local population to make the land into his private hunting ground and executing any man who killed a deer there. There were harsh penalties for harming a deer too, with the offender often losing both his hands for the transgression. As Wendy Boase points out though, these rules were probably no more severe than the rule of the Danes whom the Normans had replaced. William had to be ruthlessly efficient in his dealings with the local population. He spent much of his first years as King of England quelling uprisings and he needed to stamp his mark on a rebellious land. Certainly it can be said that the chroniclers of the time exaggerated William's crimes and it seems certain that he did not displace whole populations or destroy legions of churches, as myths about him state. However, a forecast, allegedly made by an elderly local whose house was demolished to make way for the hunting ground, said that William's sons would die within the New Forest. This prophecy soon came true, as a stag killed Richard, William's second son, in the New Forest in 1081.

By the time his third son, William II (1060-1100), was hunting in the New Forest on that fateful day, the 200 square miles of forest land were there for the king's pleasure and resentment against the new regime, seen as foreign, strict and different, was high. William had taken over the English crown after his father's death and his reign was as tough as his predecessor's. He dealt with rebellious nobles with ruthless efficiency; subdued, for a while, King Malcolm of Scotland; and, after damping his elder brother, Robert Curthose's, pretensions to the throne, waged war in France on behalf of that same brother, who was also the Duke of Normandy, while he was away on the Crusades.

According to the monk William of Malmesbury (1080-1143), one of the main chroniclers of the day, in his *Gesta Regum Anglorum* (*c.* 1128), William was 'small and thick set and ill-shaped... His face was redder than this hair and his eyes were of two different colours'. It could possibly be that it is from this description that the nickname Rufus comes, referring to his ruddy complexion, although according to Barlow he was not generally known by this name until some time after his death.

Rumours abounded that the Devil was abroad and was seen by New Forest men. In addition to this, there was the story of the dream that Bishop Anselm, the exiled Archbishop of Canterbury, had had, which saw the king dragged before God and condemned to dwell in Hell for all eternity. The king himself had had a dream the night before the hunt, in which his doctor had let his blood. The red current washed up to Heaven and blotted out the daylight. The dream was so frightening that William insisted on having lights and company in the room for the rest of the night.

At daybreak a monk insisted on telling his ruler of another nightmare concerning him. This time the king had gone to a church and torn off the limbs from the crucifix, using his teeth. Flame had then shot from the crucifix's mouth, in a torrent similar to that of the blood William himself had dreamt of. He was shaken by the violence of the image. Later versions of this dream have the church richly hung and crammed with books, ivory and other luxuries. These vanish and William Rufus is left with the body of a man lying on the altar. He tears into his flesh with his teeth, whereupon the man rises up and admonishes him. With so many portents of disaster, it is not surprising that the hunt was postponed until the evening.

On 2 August 1100 the hunting party finally set out. The king had laughed at the last minute message from Serlo, the Norman Abbot of St Peter's in Gloucester. He sent to warn the king of impending doom. One of his monks had had a dream in which Christ, surrounded by a heavenly choir, was beseeched by a virgin at his feet to take pity on the English people who were subjected to William's cruel rule. William ignored the dream, which Serlo thought to be the foretelling of a change on the English throne.

The hunting party contained, in addition to William Rufus, the king's younger brother, Henry; William de Breuteuill, the Keeper of the Treasury; and

Walter Tirel (also Tyrell and Tyrrel, born 1065), who was known to be a crack shot with the bow. Orderic Vitalis (1075-1142), in his *Historia Ecclesiastica*, tells us that the king chose four arrows for himself and gave the remaining two to Tirel. The party set off and, in the ensuing chase, the king and Tirel were separated from the rest. What happened next comes to us not from those involved, the king and Tirel, but from second-hand sources written retrospectively. Malmesbury's account has the two of them by themselves, whilst Vitalis' report says there were others with them too. They both agree that these two were at the fateful spot on that day. Tirel fired an arrow at a leaping stag and instead of hitting the beast the arrow pierced the king's chest. Seeing that the king was dead, Tirel fled the scene, afraid that he would be thought guilty of murdering the monarch. He rode swiftly for the coast and the safety of his home in Poix-de-Picardie, France.

William Rufus' body was abandoned where it had fallen. Henry hastened to Winchester to ensure he inherited the crown. William de Breuteuill followed in pursuit to try, in vain, to claim the throne for Robert, William Rufus' elder brother who was on his way back from the Crusades. It was left to Purkis, a local charcoal burner, to transport the corpse to Winchester in his cart. It is said that the body dripped blood all the way through the forest and that Tirel stopped to wash his hands in the waters of Ocknell Pond, which is why it turns red every year on the anniversary of the king's death. Tirel was supposed to have crossed the Avon at Tyrrell's Ford and was also said to have bribed a blacksmith to shoe his horse backwards to fool pursuers. As late as the nineteenth century, the blacksmith in Avon Tyrrell had to pay a fine of £3 10s annually as penance for this trickery.

William Rufus was laid to rest in the Old Minster in Winchester with no ceremony; no bells were rung or divine service held. His soul was not prayed for and Henry instituted no enquiry into the circumstances of his death. It was only later that he attempted to reward Purkis for his trouble. Purkis was offered money and refused it, asking instead for the right to fell trees in the forest. This request was refused on the grounds that the forest was for deer hunting but Henry allowed him the concession of being able to cut any boughs within reach of his woodman's hook and crook. As Wendy Boase points out, this may be the origin of the saying 'by hook or by crook' which remains familiar to the present day.

Through the centuries that have followed William Rufus' death, there have been questions. Was it an unfortunate accident as suggested by the inscription on the Rufus Stone? Or was the death a political assassination, engineered by brother Henry, hungry for the crown? Perhaps we will never know.

Richard I

King Richard the Lionheart (1157-1199), was known as the 'Absent King' according to Elsie M. Sandell.

In 1194 Richard had just returned from captivity in Germany, following the successful Third Crusade against Saladin, the Egyptian leader of the Saracens. He had been crowned king in 1180 at Westminster and, apart from freeing his mother, Eleanor of Acquitaine, who had been imprisoned for fifteen years by his father, Henry II, for aiding an uprising against the Crown, he set about raising money to join the Crusades. A 'Saladin tithe' was imposed on the people of the land; honours, high offices, castles and mansions were auctioned off; and the imprisoned King of Scotland, William I, remitted 15,000 marks for his freedom and the commitments subjugating Scotland contained within the Treaty of Falaise, signed by Henry II in 1174. In 1191, Richard set forth from Southampton Water with an estimated 8,000-strong army, supplied with 800 hogs and 10,000 horseshoes by the Sheriff of Hampshire, to right wrongs in the Holy Land.

He defeated Saladin at Arsuf and then made peace-keeping arrangements with him so that he could return to England. Word had come to him of his brother John's activities in England and he realised it was time to re-assert his authority there. On his return journey, Leopold of Austria, no friend to Richard, captured him and he was imprisoned in Leopold's castle at Dürenstein, on the Danube. The German Emperor, Henry VI, another of Richard's enemies, then paid Leopold 75,000 marks for Richard and had him moved to Germany. Richard had to pay an enormous ransom for the time, 150,000 marks, for his release.

Richard returned to England from Antwerp in February 1194 on a ship commanded by Southampton captain Alan Trenchemere. His country was broke but that did not stop him from mounting a lavish ceremony in Winchester, which saw him being crowned for a second time. This was to end his brother John's interests in the crown once and for all and to reinforce his authority in England. Moving through Hampshire towards Winchester, he stayed at Kingsclere Manor in Freemantle and then Winchester Castle before taking up residence in St Swithun's Priory. On 17 April the Archbishop of Canterbury crowned him as King of England in Winchester Cathedral. Amongst those in the considerable throng of distinguished guests and Hampshire folk was William, the King of Scotland.

Soon after this Richard left Winchester and went to Bishop's Waltham, where he held his last English council before leaving England for France from Portsmouth. He was never to return.

Lord Palmerston

On the site of the old Audit House, in the middle of the Market Place in Romsey, stands an impressive statue of Henry John Temple, Viscount Palmerston (1784-1865). He was born at Broadlands House, the Temple family home since 1736, the second son of five children born to the 2nd Viscount Palmerston, Henry Temple, and his wife, Mary Mee. His great-grandfather, Henry (1673-1757), had been created the 1st Viscount Palmerston in Ireland in 1723.

Palmerston was elected to Parliament when only twenty-six years of age. He was first Junior Lord of the Admiralty and then Secretary for War. He served five successive Prime Ministers, as both a Tory and a Whig, for over twenty years in that capacity. He was appointed Secretary of State for Foreign Affairs in 1832 by Earl Grey and excelled in the position. He became the MP for South Hampshire after the 1832 Reform Act saw the disappearance of his Bletchley seat. His style though was abrasive and this led to the nickname 'Lord Pumicestone' being bestowed on him.

Popular in Parliament, Queen Victoria was not amused by his stand on foreign affairs. Palmerston saw the main objective of Britain's foreign policy as being to increase the nation's power in the world, sometimes at the expense of foreign governments. His achievements during this time included delivering Hong Kong to Britain as a trading base in 1842. The Queen and Prince Albert were more worried by the trend in Europe to depose their sovereign rulers, most of whom were relatives. Victoria was not impressed with Palmerston's sexual exploits either. His other nickname was 'Lord Cupid', given to him by *The Times*, who noted his handsome visage. After an embarrassing attempted seduction of a lady-in-waiting while a guest at Windsor Castle, Victoria had wanted him removed from office. She got her way when he publicly congratulated Bonaparte on his 1851 coup, which saw him become dictator and then Emperor of the French. Soon after this, Palmerston lost his job.

At the age of seventy-one Palmerston became Prime Minister, a position he held for three years. He then helped to form the Liberal Party in 1859. When he was seventy-five, he held the post of Prime Minister once more, this time for five years. His eight years as Prime Minister were turbulent times. He led Britain during the end of the Crimean War, the Indian Mutiny, the American War of Independence, Napoleon III's war with Austria and the domestic parliamentary reform debate.

Palmerston was again elected to Parliament at the age of eighty-one in 1865, but before he could take up the position he became ill and died later the same year. He was given a state funeral.

In 1839 Palmerston had married his long-time mistress, Emily, Lady Cowper, and her son, William Cowper, inherited Broadlands.

William Cobbett

Botley, just outside Southampton, is famous for its celebrated citizen, political commentator William Cobbett (1763-1835), writer of the *Rural Rides*, *Grammar of the English Language* and his weekly two-penny pamphlet, *The Political Register*.

The son of a publican in Farnham and grandson of a farm labourer, he was taught to read and write by his father. At sixteen he went to work for Revd James Barclay and read the books in this gentleman's library. He wrote his first book at this time, a history of the kings and queens of England. After a year of working for a lawyer in Grays Inn, he joined the Army where, in a largely ill-educated force, it was noted that he was literate. He became Secretary to Colonel (later General) Hugh Debbieg and furthered his education by memorising a book of grammar, which stood him in good stead in later years. Promoted to corporal, he was posted to Nova Scotia where he joined the 54th Regiment as clerk. It was here that he met his future wife, Nancy Reid, the daughter of one of his contemporaries. He also uncovered evidence of widespread corruption surrounding the distribution of provisions, which were being pilfered by some of the officers and men. He gathered information and, on his return to the UK and after being discharged from the Army in 1791, he took his information to the authorities. In 1792 he married Nancy but the pair fled to France for their own safety following the collapse of the court martial convened on Cobbett's evidence. Cobbett had uncomfortably realised that several of his friends would suffer if the court martial went ahead and so he offered no evidence at the hearing.

After six happy months in France, the French Revolution overtook the couple and so they sailed to America and settled in Wilmington, Delaware. Cobbett taught English to French émigrés and wrote a book of English grammar. He also began to comment on the political situation in France and America. This led to a hasty departure back to England in 1800 after being sued for defamation of character.

In 1805 Cobbett moved his family to Botley, where he had bought a farm. He had made contacts in publishing in London and now owned his own publishing company. He soon began his pamphlet, the *Weekly Political Register*, so called to escape the government's high tax on newspapers and thus to allow the poor masses to read his views.

Cobbett was tried and found guilty of sedition in 1809 following his public attack on the use of German troops to put down a militia mutiny in Ely. He was sentenced to two years in Newgate Prison and fined £1,000. He was further bound over to keep the peace for seven years when he was released, under a surety of £3,000. While in gaol he continued to write and have his work published.

There is a story that the Botley village parson, Richard Baker, did not share Cobbett's views. When the news came that Cobbett had been released from Newgate, he refused to surrender the keys to the church bell tower to the over-joyed inhabitants of Botley and so the bells were not rung in celebration. It is said that the villagers got their revenge on their parson by sending a false letter to him summoning him to London on the quest of a non-existent legacy. The villagers enjoyed a three-day party while he was gone.

In 1816 the Spa Fields Riot in London had a profound effect on Cobbett. The meeting that preceded the 'riot' consisted of little more than a few speeches on reform, but they were followed by some minor break-ins of shop premises nearby. This led to legislators sending out spies to gather evidence of those involved and to the suspension of the Habeas Corpus Act. Those named, along with 'chief incendiary writers', were to be rounded up and taken into custody. Cobbett's name was on the list. He and his two eldest sons fled to America. In his absence, his Botley farm and all his possessions were seized and sold by his creditors. His wife and remaining five children were made homeless and eventually found lodgings in London.

Cobbett wrote two more books whilst in America, another volume on English grammar and *Journal of a Year's Residence in the United States of America*. He returned to Britain in 1819, by which time the Habeas Corpus Act had been reinstated and he was safe from persecution. Between then and his death in 1835, he published *Rural Rides* in 1830 and was acquitted of sedition in 1831. Cobbett was elected to Parliament at the second attempt in 1833. He died five days after writing his last article for his *Political Register*.

William Cobbett dedicated his life to combating corruption and championing free speech. In doing so, he faced a life of hardship and persecution. Without him, many of the political reforms that came into being in the nineteenth century would not have happened.

Frederick Lee Bridell

The name of this tragically short-lived Southampton artist has been largely forgotten for many years. Thanks to the considerable efforts of Catherine Aitchison Hull

in researching Bridell's life for her book, *Frederick Lee Bridell*, this situation is changing amidst the growing realisation that a possibly great home-grown talent has been
ignored for too long.

Bridell, the third child of John Bridle, a carpenter, and his wife Amelia,
was born in the poor suburb of Houndwell in 1830. He lived his early life in
Pope's Buildings, tenements built to house the overflow of the town's teeming
population.

At the age of eight he began to draw ships and seascapes but after leaving
school at the age of twelve and voyaging on a coasting vessel, he realised that a
life at sea was not what he wanted. He began to work for a firm of housepaint-
ers in Southampton and it was at the age of fifteen that he furthered his interest
in art by joining a small painting club run by Philip Carter. Carter was not a
painter himself but, like all good mentors, had the knack of bringing out the
best in the club's members. At seventeen Bridell began to paint portraits, the
only commercially viable option for him at the time.

At the age of eighteen he began an apprenticeship with Edwin Holder, an
art dealer and restorer who had seen a portrait Bridell had painted of his friend
Henry Rose and recognised the inherent talent he possessed. Although he
had had no formal training as an artist, Bridell found himself copying the Old
Masters for Holder and learning much from the experience.

In 1851 Bridell submitted his first work to the Royal Academy, a great achieve-
ment in one so young and with little training. Holder sent him abroad to study in
1853, where he spent time in Paris and Munich copying works from the Louvre
and from the Dutch School artists Cuyp, Van der Velde and Berchem.

Back in Southampton, he completed works from his drawings made while
travelling and was increasingly sought by the well-to-do of the town for private
commissions. It was during this time that he began to exhibit regularly at the
Royal Academy, the British Institution and the Liverpool Academy.

With the patronage of James Wolff, a wealthy shipping magnate living in
Bevois Mount, who hung Bridell's pictures in his home and invited the public
to view them, Bridell was able to open his own studio in Highfield Lodge and
begin work on a major canvas, *The Temple of Venus*.

In 1858 Bridell travelled to Italy and set up a studio in Rome. He took letters with him for Robert Browning and his wife, Elizabeth Barrett-Browning.
He had met the couple at the home of author and biographer Sir Theodore
Martin (1816-1909). In 1859 the Brownings hosted Bridell's wedding dinner
after his marriage to fellow painter Eliza Florence Fox (1824-1903). Eliza was
later granted the opportunity to paint Mrs Barrett-Browning following two
sittings for a portrait.

It was while he was in Italy that he was at his most prolific, but it was to exact a toll. Ignored ill health eventually forced him to stop painting and he returned to England in 1863. In August of that year he died. He was just thirty-two years old.

Catherine Aitchison Hull, commenting on Bridell's achievements, suggests:

He had a 'natural' capacity to grapple with any subject and succeed. For example, trees, mountains, the human form, animals. He looked intently at how light works in a landscape. Now Turner in his paintings, for example, allows the light to dissolve the detail, which would be evident in a sunlit view. Bridell did not do this. He saw how the light reflects on certain surfaces and highlights some details. He does not lose the sense of perspective or space when he depicts a scene.

Bridell looked at the landscape of the Old Masters, Claude, Poussin and Rosa, absorbing the lessons of their work which was rooted in the Classical past. But he adapted these themes to 'add' to the beauty of the landscape, whereas when the Masters painted, the landscape was a backdrop to the action of the Classical heroes or 'nymphs' depicting an idyllic setting. Thus landscape itself, and capturing the movement of light, was the essence of his work.

He painted some large works on a very grand scale. He had an innate vision, which the reviewers of his work could only describe by the word 'grandeur'.

He painted from a sense of compulsion... which was, in the end, to his own detriment. The last few years, 1859-1863, were the period of his finest works and they are still being discovered.

By sheer dedication to art, I believe he overcame the limitations of his birth and was on the brink of obtaining the recognition he deserved when he died.

Southampton's Millais Art Gallery displays *The Colliseum at Rome by Moonlight*, described by Aitchison Hull as 'magnificent'.

The building Bridell used as his studio in Southampton still stands. Perhaps English Heritage or Southampton City Council should be thinking about erecting a plaque at the site, in commemoration of this long forgotten talent?

Jane Austen

In memory of JANE AUSTEN
Youngest daughter of the late reverend GEORGE AUSTEN
formerly rector of Steventon in this county.

She departed this life on the 18th July 1817, aged 44, after a long illness supported with the patience and the hopes of a Christian.

The benevolence of her heart, the sweetness of her composure, the extraordinary endowments of her mind, obtained the regard of all who knew her, and the warmest love of her intimate connections.

Their grief is in proportion to their affection. They know their loss to be irreparable, but in their deepest affliction they are comforted by a firm though humble hope that her charity, devotion faith and purity have rendered her soul acceptable in the sight of her REDEEMER.

So reads the inscription on Jane Austen's grave in the north aisle of Winchester Cathedral. Written by her family, it does not mention her literary achievements.

There has been much written about Jane. In a book this size, with so many competing demands for the limited space, there is room for no more than a brief skim over her life in Hampshire. That she was a Hampshire lass should not be forgotten, for her writing revealed life during her era while her wit and insight delights each succeeding generation.

She was born in the village of Steventon where the soil, Gilbert White stated, 'produced the brightest hops'. Her father was the Revd George Austen (1731-1805), a classical scholar and tutor nicknamed 'the handsome proctor' at Oxford University who, as Jenkins states, 'had his strawberry beds, his elm walk, his home meadows, his position in a pleasant neighbourhood as a much-respected country gentleman' to keep him occupied in between his parish duties.

Jane's mother, Cassandra (1739-1827), was intellectual, well-connected, wrote light verse and witty letters and was decidedly domestic. She bore eight children between 1765 and 1779: James (1765); Edward (1767); George (1766); Henry (1771); followed by a daughter, also called Cassandra (1773); then there was another son, Francis (1774). By the time Jane came along in 1775, the rectory was almost full. Mr and Mrs Austen's last child, Charles (1779), completed the family. Mrs Austen was known for the amount of darning she did, and would sit working on it in the living room regardless of who was visiting.

George Austen educated all of the boys except George, who was reported to be mentally abnormal and had fits and did not live at home. Thomas Knight and his wife, George's patron, adopted Edward, a less promising scholar than his brothers. He went on to inherit two estates and much wealth from his adopted family but remained on close and loving terms with his parents and siblings.

Jane, known as Little Jenny in girlhood, grew up in a happy, financially secure home. The children were all well read and several wrote verse and skits; indeed, amateur dramatics was a great part of family life in the Austen home.

Cassandra and Jane were sent to Oxford in 1783 to be educated by Mrs Cawley, a relation of Mrs Austen's sister, Mrs Cooper. Mrs Cawley, disliked by both girls and by Mrs Cooper's daughter, Jane, who was also studying with her, moved to Southampton where both Austen girls caught typhus fever and were very ill. Jane Cooper told her mother and Mrs Cooper and Mrs Austen took the girls home. Jane and Cassandra survived but Mrs Cooper, also catching the illness, was not so lucky and died. After this the girls were sent to the Abbey School in Reading for a year but this was not academically challenging, as well as being expensive, and so the girls returned home, this time for good. Jane completed the rest of her education by reading the books in her father's library.

Her first works were written between the ages of eleven and eighteen and she later copied a selection into three volumes to amuse her family, showing the promise of the comic insight she was to bring to her later works. Next came an irreverent history, again with her particular brand of ironic wit, and the novella *Lady Susan*.

While she was writing she was also a young girl growing up. She had many friends and family, went to balls and loved to dance; she could play the piano and was an excellent seamstress; she was also a devout Christian and helped her mother with her household duties. In short, her life was much the same as most of her contemporaries, apart from her love of writing.

In 1795 Jane's brother, Edward, lost his wife, Anne, suddenly leaving two-year-old Anna motherless. She was sent to live at Steventon and grew up to love her aunts Cassandra and Jane, the latter who made up stories for her. Edward later remarried.

Jane began work on *Elinor and Marianne*, later to be titled *Sense and Sensibility*. In 1796, Jane started writing what was to become known as *Pride and Prejudice*. The next year Mrs Austen took Cassandra, who was trying to get over the death of her fiancé in the West Indies, and Jane to Bath, where she met a young man, Sydney Smith. He was a clergyman employed as tutor to acquaintances of the Austen family. He was amusing and witty and Cecil speculates that he may well have been the model for the young man, Henry Tilney, in the novel Jane began the following year, *Northanger Abbey*.

When her father retired in 1800 the family moved to Bath, much to Jane's dismay. She disliked the town and the rectory had been her only home all her life. In 1802 she received her only marriage proposal, from Harris Big-Wither, a friend of the family and the heir to large estates near to Steventon. Although Jane initially accepted the proposal, she soon changed her mind.

In January 1805 Mr Austen died suddenly and the financial security surrounding the female members of the family disintegrated. In 1806 Mrs Austen,

Cassandra and Jane moved to Southampton, to live with Frank Austen and his wife in their house near the Bargate in Castle Square.

In 1809 Edward offered them the cottage at Chawton, which has become so well known in relation to Jane today. It was from here that four of her novels were published, all anonymously. *Sense and Sensibility*, published in 1811, lessened her financial worries. *Pride and Prejudice* was published in 1813 and almost immediately went into a second edition. *Mansfield Park* (1814) earned Jane more than either of the other two books. *Emma* (1815) was the last book published in Jane's lifetime.

Jane then became ill. At first she ignored it but soon had to acknowledge that she was weakening. She continued to write, but by 1817 was bed-ridden. Her brother, Henry, moved her and Cassandra to Winchester for treatment but it was too late. She died in the little house just along the road from Winchester College, at 8 College Street. Today it bears a forlorn little plaque telling of the building's sad claim to fame.

Persuasion and *Northanger Abbey* were published posthumously in 1817, with a note identifying the author for the first time.

Today Jane's house in Chawton, near Alton, is open to the public as a museum and the library at Chawton House is famous for its collection of early women's writings. The house also houses the collection of silver trophies owned by the Society of Women Writers and Journalists. Jane's work is now known all over the world and has been adapted for the large and small screen.

William Walker

The name of William Walker may not be one that immediately springs to mind, but to anyone with knowledge of Winchester Cathedral it should ring bells and bring a beaming smile.

The cathedral was consecrated on 15 July 1093. Nearly 1,000 years later, by the beginning of the twentieth century, it was sinking. The original construction had not given enough buttressing and the foundations were insufficient to hold the mighty load it had been asked to carry. Splits in the walls had been spreading for years and in 1905 things came to a head. Cracks in the south wall of the retrochoir, the area behind the choir, had been caused by subsidence in the east end of the cathedral and they had reached such a point as to be impossible to ignore. The cathedral needed major structural underpinning or it would not be long before disaster struck.

The cathedral's Dean, William Furneaux, put out a plea for £20,000 to pay for the work needed. A letter was published in *The Times*, repeated in the

Hampshire Chronicle, explaining the problem and the recommended solution. Money started to come in.

The main problem was water. Changes to the level of the water table had affected the bed of clay and peat, which the cathedral depended upon for support. Thomas Jackson, the Winchester Diocese architect, suggested bonding and grouting the walls and then underpinning them to the gravel bed 16ft below ground level. The consulting engineer, Francis Fox (1844-1927), who was knighted for his work in 1912, whose experience had already helped to build Marylebone Railway Station and the London Underground, was an expert on underwater foundations. He came up with the idea of sending a diver into the water to lay concrete directly on the gravel. Two divers were signed up to do the work; the lead diver William Walker (1869-1918) was the most experienced of the divers from Siebe Gorman Ltd, a company that had developed the closed diving helmet, which was watertight.

William Walker was trained as a diver in Portsmouth dockyard. In 1892, after five years of training, he passed out as a deep-water diver. He went on to work on the construction of the Blackwall Tunnel, the shipyard in Gibraltar and on rescue and emergency work in Wales.

In rescuing Winchester Cathedral, Walker worked in water 18ft deep as he systematically laid concrete into each of 235 4ft-wide pits, which were dug around the south and east subsiding walls. For six hours a day, five days a week, between 6 April 1906 and 8 September 1911 Walker toiled in a heavy diving suit. At weekends he would cycle the 150 mile round trip to his home in Croydon to see his family.

Walker worked in complete darkness as the water was so full of sediment that no light would penetrate. He removed the peat, levelled the gravel and laid bags of concrete. When the concrete had set, the water could be drained off and blocks of concrete and bricks were laid. In total 25,800 bags of concrete, 115,000 blocks of concrete and 900,000 bricks were needed to complete the work. The cost of the job escalated to £113,000 and meant that repeated appeals for funds had to be made. King Edward VII himself contributed £250.

A Service of Thanksgiving took place in the cathedral, which was presided over by the Archbishop of Canterbury, on 15 July 1912 at the end of the work, which King George V and Queen Mary also attended. They made it their business to stop and speak to those involved in the preservation work. For William Walker this was particularly poignant, as he had taught the king diving years before when he was a naval cadet.

William Walker was married twice and was a Member of the Royal Victorian Order (MVO). He died in the 'Spanish Flu' pandemic of 1918.

Lady Eleanor Peel

Many people in Britain today have much to thank Lady Eleanor Peel for. When she died on 9 November 1949, she left a legacy which went to provide for the Dowager Countess Eleanor Peel Trust, a charitable fund which, to 2008, had provided over £530,000 for medical charities and research, old people and those 'who have fallen on evil days through no fault of their own'. Some of this money has been used in Hampshire, most notably in East Meon.

Lady Eleanor was the granddaughter of James Williamson, the Lancashire textile king who made a huge fortune exporting fabrics and in inventing a floor covering by painting oil paints onto a cork backing. This became known as linoleum. He also gave the town of Lancaster a city park, which is known as Williamson Park to this day.

His son, also James, expanded the empire, in addition to being a Justice of the Peace, town councillor and Liberal MP. He was knighted in 1895 and took the title Baron Ashton. He had two daughters from the first of his three marriages; Eleanor, known as Ella, was born in 1871 and Maud was born in 1876. Maud died in 1906 at the age of thirty. When James died in 1930, he left nearly £5 million to his daughter.

Eleanor married William Robert Wellesley Peel in 1899. Peel was born in 1867, the grandson of Sir Robert Peel (1788-1859) the founder of the Conservative Party and the Metropolitan Police who served two terms as Britain's Prime Minister. William Peel's father, Sir Robert Peel's youngest son, William Wellesley (1829-1912), was also a politician and was Speaker of the House of Commons for ten years from 1884-1894. He was given a peerage for his work, which his son inherited on his death. Lord Peel was also a politician and held the offices of Secretary of State for India and Lord Privy Seal. In 1929 he was elevated to an earl. Lord Peel died in 1937 aged sixty. His son, Arthur William Ashton Peel (1901-1969), the Earl of Clanfied in the county of Southampton, succeeded him.

When Eleanor and Lord Peel married they were given a wedding gift by the bride's father that any young couple would be happy to receive: £800,000.

In 1913 the couple set about finding a suitable area to settle in. They found it in the rolling acres between Hambledon and Hyden Wood and decided to call the house they had built there Leydene, after Leydene Bottom, a hollow to the south of Hyden Hill.

Eleanor was renowned for saving her money. She would accept rides from coal lorries when walking home from one of the nearby villages, while a story from HMS Mercury, the Royal Naval training establishment which Leydene

House eventually became during the Second World War, tells of her suing the local council, Petersfield, for their delay in clearing snow from the roads; this meant that her guests had to stay an extra four days, at a cost of £7 17s for their food. This seemingly miserly attitude was to reap its reward for the charitable trust set up by the terms of her will after her death.

Eleanor seems to have been something of a character in other ways too. There is a story, told in the history of HMS *Mercury*, of her habit of exercising every morning in the nude on the balcony of her bedroom. Any of the estate staff seen peeping at her were summarily dismissed. On her way to breakfast she would minutely inspect the potted plants for dust and woe betide the butler and head gardener if she found any. Later she spent time in her bedroom with a telescope, making sure the estate workers were working properly and were not idle.

After Leydene House was requisitioned, Lady Peel moved to Scotland where she had a house built on the River Tweed. She died in 1949 and the trust made its first awards in 1951.

Sister Gerard

Romsey's best-kept secret is the fact that it is home to a miracle. The old convent, La Sagesse, contains a room in the middle of the building on the first floor, which is reputed to be the site of a 1927 event, which was hailed as miraculous.

Sister Gerard lay dying of tuberculosis and it seemed there was no hope. As her life lay ebbing away she had a vision of the Virgin Mary and of Louis-Marie de Montfort, who was formally recognised as a saint in 1947.

She was told that her work on earth was not yet over and that she had to get up. To the amazement of all around her, this is exactly what Sister Gerard did. Not only did she arise from her deathbed but she went on to work overseas as a missionary. It was this event that was the catalyst for St Louis-Marie's canonisation.

The Miracle Room was open to the public for many years but has now been closed as the site is deemed unsafe.

R.J. Mitchell

Sometimes the dividing line between what is folklore and what is history is distinctly blurred and the two often end up merging into one. One such example concerns Reginald Joseph Mitchell (1895-1937) and the Schneider Trophy.

Mitchell was born in Staffordshire and served an apprenticeship at the Kerr Stuart and Co. locomotive engineering works in Stoke-on-Trent before moving to Southampton in 1917. He initially worked in the drawing office of the fledgling company Supermarine Aviation in Woolston, but his talent was soon spotted and he climbed the promotion ladder rapidly. By the time he was twenty-four he was the company's Chief Designer and two years later he was their Chief Engineer.

Noel Pemberton-Billing formed what was to become the Supermarine Aviation Co. Ltd in 1913 in order to concentrate on marine aircraft. He located the company on the River Itchen and when he moved on just over two years later, his partner, Hubert Scott-Paine, took the company forward.

The Schneider Trophy was the prize for seaplanes announced in 1911 by the French Under-Secretary for Air, Jacques Schneider. It was worth the staggering sum of £1,000 and was meant to be a spur to aeroplane development. In the event, it did do its job and huge advances were made in aeroplane design and specification, but the competition became known for speed, with each country participating to show off the speed and dexterity of its greatest creations.

Britain had won the Schneider Trophy in 1914 and wanted to win it again. In fact, Britain desperately wanted to win it on three consecutive occasions. If she could do so, the trophy, and the glory attached to it, became hers permanently.

It was into this arena that Mitchell stepped. Supermarine's 1922 entry, the Sea Lion, stopped Italy's hopes in Naples that year by winning the race with a speed of 145mph. In 1925 the Supermarine S4 crashed before the race could start. In 1927 in Venice, the Supermarine S5s shot ahead of two other British companies' entries and finished the race first and second, recording a top speed of 281mph. Members of the government's 'high speed flight' piloted the aeroplanes and Flight Lieutenant S.N. Webster piloted S5 N220, the winning aircraft. At the next race in 1929, the Supermarine S6, powered by new Rolls-Royce engines, thundered home with a speed of 328mph. When the government stopped it's funding, Dame Fanny Lucy Houston donated £100,000 to sponsor Britain's entry into the 1931 contest, held in Calshot. The Supermarine S6B was the only entry that year, piloted by Flight Lieutenant John Boothman, and clocked up a winning run at 340mph, later increasing that speed to 379mph, a new world record. On the same day, 13 September, the aeroplane hit another world record at Ryde on the Isle of Wight when it reached 407.02mph.

Britain had done it! The Schneider Trophy, a bronze statue of a sea nymph kissing a wave, was presented to the Royal Aero Club in London. It has since been displayed in the Science Museum in London and, during the sixtieth anniversary celebrations for the Spitfire, in Southampton.

Mitchell's secret was to design an aeroplane with a single wing, to reduce drag and thus to be able to fly at higher speed. After this Mitchell looked at designing a fast fighter aircraft for the military and came up with the Type 224, which he was not happy with and which did not impress the Royal Air Force. He redesigned it with a retractable undercarriage and an enclosed cockpit and the K5054 was born. With its straighter wings, this was the prototype of the Spitfire.

Mitchell had had surgery for rectal cancer in 1933 and when this flared up again in 1937 he flew to Vienna for treatment at the American Cancer Clinic there. It was hopeless and he returned home to Portswood a month later. He lived long enough to see the K5054 fly. He was just forty-two when he died on 11 June 1937.

Norman Barfield, in his book *Supermarine*, calls Reginald Joseph Mitchell CBE, FRAeS, AMICE, 'Britain's most versatile aircraft designer and one of the great British heroes of engineering and of the twentieth century'. As such, he has earned a place in Hampshire's folklore.

Doris Cole

Woman Police Sergeant 1 (WPS1) Doris Cole, of the Southampton Borough Force, was the first woman to be attested in the Southampton Borough Force, in July 1942. With so many men called up for active service abroad, the force needed women to boost its numbers.

In 1915 a Miss Tate had been appointed as a policewoman, but she was never attested and so did not have the official police powers that came to Doris with attestation nearly thirty years later.

On 17 December 1945, WPS1 Doris Cole received the Chief Constable's Commendation for bravery after she was called to a public house in the city. A prostitute had threatened to shoot another woman, but Doris calmly searched the lady and recovered a loaded handgun from her pocket.

WPS1 Cole retired from the Southampton Borough Force in January 1965. In 1966 there was a woman inspector, a female sergeant and sixteen women police constables in the Southampton Borough Force, out of a total establishment of 499.

FOUR

WITCHES

For the Colonel's Lady an' Judy O'Grady
Are sisters under their skins!

Rudyard Kipling, a Southsea resident for five years
The Ladies

In days gone by, 'witchcraft' was often a convenient term to apply when events were not comprehended. Science was misunderstood and those people, usually women but not exclusively so, who understood nature, who often lived alone with an animal for companionship and were thought to be 'different' to their peers, were often branded 'witch', while the good they did was regarded as 'magic'.

When Dominican priest and witchfinder Heinrich Kramer published his *Maleus Mallificarum* in 1486 it was a sensation and was only outsold by the Bible. Horrified readers were told that witches 'drive to distraction the minds of men, such as have lost their trust in God, and by the terrible power of their evil spells, without any actual draught or poison, kill human beings'. Little wonder than that during the Reformation over 100,000 men and women were condemned as witches and met grisly deaths.

This chapter looks at some of Hampshire's alleged witches through the ages, about many of whom we know little detail, and then it looks forward to witchcraft in the twenty-first century.

Gypsies

Gypsies, of which there were many in Hampshire, particularly in the New Forest, used to guard themselves from the evil spells cast by witches by hanging snake skins from the fronts of their caravans.

Mother Russell

Old Mother Russell lived in a cottage in East Woodhay. One day a bark stripper, by all accounts a strapping, healthy man, was working on trees near her home and offered her some of the fallen remnants, which were a perk of his job. He could use these strips for his own use. She wanted more than he was offering her and took what she wanted, ignoring his protests. When he remonstrated with her, she gave him a look which changed his life. Almost immediately he was transformed from a fit and strong man to an ailing one. Never really ill, he was nevertheless not fit and found working on the trees much harder than previously.

This miserable existence lasted for some six months or so until the pair happened to meet once more. Mother Russell asked the man how he was and he told her honestly how he fared. She told him to cheer up and he would be fine in a few days, whereupon he did perk up and regained his former fitness. She had removed the spell.

Mother Russell later committed suicide while residing in Up Somborne. This was, of course, a sin in the eyes of the Church and so she could not be buried in consecrated ground. She was laid to rest at a crossroads in the village, with a stake through her witch's heart. The area is still known today as 'Mother Russell's Post'.

Mary Dore, the Beaulieu Witch

Little is known of Mary Dore, except that she was generally considered to be a witch. She lived in the eighteenth century and is commemorated on the second panel of the huge New Forest embroidery, hanging in the New Forest Museum in Lyndhurst. She is depicted as a little old lady wearing a black cloak, walking through the forest with her cat beside her.

Ivey, in her report on New Forest traditions, says that Mary Dore is mentioned in the Beaulieu estate papers as being 'Widow Dore' who had a cottage beside the Beaulieu mill. After being released from Winchester Gaol for an unspecified crime, she found her cottage had been demolished and voiced her displeasure at having to move into another house near the mill.

William Hone, writing in 1832, citing the Revd Richard Warner's 1793 *TopographicalRemarks Relating to the South-Western Parts of Hampshire*, calls her the 'parochial witch of Beaulieu' and says she died 'half a century since'. She apparently used her magic largely to extricate herself from trouble. Warner quotes the son of one who had, he claimed, seen her transform herself into a hare or a cat 'when likely to be apprehended in wood stealing, to which she was somewhat addicted'.

Changing into a hare seemed to be a popular pastime for witches according to legend. Hone tells us that to annoy 'squires, justices and country-parsons fond of hunting', witches often changed into hares to 'elude the speed of the fleetest dogs'. Consequently the country gentry had to take pains not to be overtaken by witchcraft, and so '…that never hunters nor their dogs may be bewitched, they cleave an oaken branch, and both they and their dogs pass over it'.

Kate Hunt, the Curdridge Witch

The village of Curdridge, near Botley, on Southampton's doorstep, has a church which reminds those interested that witches were once prevalent in Hampshire. On the south-east corner of the church tower grins a gargoyle, said to represent one of the seventeenth-century's witches.

Kate Hunt was said to have lived on the village side of the hill leading to Botley, then known locally as 'Kate Hunt's Hill' according to a parishioner cited in *It Happened in Hampshire* (1935). Kate was popularly supposed to have unnatural powers and was consequently blamed for anything that was unusual in the area. Beddington and Christy, the authors of the book, give an example: after trees were cut down and fell across her garden she was so annoyed that by the next morning they were found to have been flipped around and laid across the main road. Obviously, this lady was not to be trifled with!

Kate was popularly believed to be able to change herself into an animal. This is a common attribute for witches, many of whom choose, as Kate reputedly did, to become a white hare. This ability greatly troubled the villagers and they decided that the best solution to the problem would be to kill her. Village life would then be uncomplicated once again. As silver is well known to be the only metal capable of killing a witch, silver coins were cut in half to use in place of shot and they loaded a gun with them. The villagers then lay in wait at Pink Mead Farm, one of the hare's known haunts. The hunters were lucky as the hare was soon spotted and shot, but it escaped. Old Kate Hunt was later found to be dead in her home after suffering gunshot wounds.

Another story about Kate Hunt has her travelling on a gate from a local field to and from Bishops Waltham. How she travelled by gate is not told!

Nowadays the gargoyle resembling Kate, one of several depicting local legends to be found on the 84ft-high tower, looks down on all and sundry from the church tower, so it could be said that by being immortalised in stone in this manner, the witch had the last laugh on the Curdridge community..

Winchester Witch

Richard Bovet (born 1641), in his anti-Catholic epic *Pandaemonium* (1684), mentions the case of the begging Winchester witch who cursed a local school mistress when she refused to give her money. The witch sent her familiar, a large toad, to the teacher's home, after which she had 'most Tormenting Fits' and described her insides as being pricked with sharp pins or thorns. Attacks of pain were preceded by the arrival of cats, who howled until a great light appeared. The school mistress then suffered 'the highest extreme of misery.' Her plight continued for seventeen years.

The Witch of Liphook

There was once an unnamed witch who lived in Liphook and had the habit of bewitching children when she was not running about the countryside in the form of a white hare.

The story told about this witch tells us that when she was a hare, a dog mauled her so savagely that when she transformed into her human shape once more, she had bitten and torn skin on her hip and thigh.

After this she put a spell on a local lad so that he was unable to walk or to stand up and could only shuffle about. Whether he owned the dog that had caught her is not clear. She took to coming to his house to ask after his health, which greatly agitated the boy and his family.

One day, so the story goes, his parents took advice in the village and when the witch turned up at the house next it was to find that the building was completely sealed up. She stood outside and wailed, banging on the door as she did so. Meanwhile, inside, the family clustered about the huge log fire they had lit. The boy's parents had been told of a charm which they hoped would counter the evil effects of the witch's spell on their son. They put the charm into the oven and waited. Almost immediately the spell was broken and the lad could stand and walk about as normal.

Liddy Shears, the Over Wallop Witch

Liddy Shears lived in Over Wallop, near Stockbridge. Antony Brode, in his highly informative *The Hampshire Village Book*, tells us that in Old English 'waella' means 'stream' and 'hop' means 'valley'. The little cluster of villages known collectively as 'The Wallops', mentioned in the Domesday Book, take their name then from the stream running along the valley in which they lie.

Liddy Shears was reputed to be a witch. Legend has it that she always carried a three-legged stool with her whenever she went anywhere and it was this that she used to ride home on, like a horse. Of course, no one could swear to having seen her do this but they had heard the clip-clop of the stool's feet as she went by. All the villagers knew that Liddy did not own a horse or a pony and they reached their own conclusion.

It was well known too that witches could change their shape and become an animal at will. Liddy was popularly supposed to be able to change into any animal she chose. One day she was seen in her window pulling lead shot from her shoulder. The farmer who saw her doing this was the same one who had shot a hare out in his fields. It was injured but managed to escape. This was much too much of a coincidence for the good people of Over Wallop and her reputation as a witch was cemented.

Helen Duncan, the Last Prosecuted Witch

Witchcraft, by its very nature, can come in all shapes and guises. The 1735 Witchcraft Act, which was repealed just less than sixty years ago in 1951, claimed its final victim in 1944. Helen Duncan (1897-1956) was a Scottish housewife who worked part time in a bleach factory. She was also a medium who helped support her disabled husband and large family by travelling to give séances in spiritualist churches and family homes. She was so successful that she shook the wartime establishment.

In Portsmouth in 1941, she held a séance during which a dead sailor from HMS *Barham* materialised. This ship had been sunk by enemy fire but that fact had not been made public. One of the sitters at the séance telephoned the Admiralty and the Home Office and asked if the sinking was true and why the news had not been made public. He was told that to do so would shake public confidence.

Previously in Edinburgh, a similar thing had happened when the announcement of HMS *Hood's* destruction had been announced at one of Helen's

séances several hours before it was known at the Admiralty. Thus, the name of
Helen Dunmore was one that the Intelligence Services were familiar with. On
19 January 1944, at a chemist shop on the Copnor Road in Portsmouth, Helen
Duncan was arrested and charged with witchcraft, the last such prosecution in
the 224 year history of the Witchcraft Act.

Despite many witnesses for her defence, Helen was convicted and sentenced
to nine months in Holloway Prison in London. She left gaol vowing never to
conduct a séance again.

Witchcraft in the Twenty-First Century

Far from quietly dying away, witchcraft is alive and well, and living in the New
Forest. In fact, at the time of writing there are over fifty witches in the area. Julie
Forest is a local New Forest witch who has agreed to talk about twenty-first
century witchcraft for this book of folklore. She says:

> A witch is the name given to a person, male or female, who practices the art
> of witchcraft. Male witches are not called wizards. The word witch appears to
> come from an old European word 'weik', which has an association with magic
> or religion.
>
> The early witches were the nomadic tribal shamans, the oldest form of
> priest or witch. The shaman meditates and communicates with the spirit
> world, animals, birds and trees. They see what most people are unable to see,
> usually under a trance-like state during a ritual, which would involve raising
> energies and power by dancing and drumming.
>
> It is well known that most religions were originally dedicated to goddess
> worship. It is interesting to note that we all start life as female, it is only after
> the first six weeks that our sex is determined. The goddess provided the nur-
> turing and nourishment man needed to survive. The priestess would act as her
> channel and the priest her consort, thereby reflecting the male/female balance
> of nature: the priestess representing the dark mysteries of the moon and the
> priest the masculine heat of the sun.
>
> In pre-Christian times the goddess and god magick was called upon to
> bless the fertility of the earth and the safety of crops and animals. Ritual danc-
> ing was created to harness this energy. Early man depended on hunting to
> survive: the meat for food; the skins for clothing, warmth and shelter; and the
> bones for tools and weapons. Religion and magick were closely connected
> as early man believed in many gods. There was a god of hunting and in order

to be sure of a successful hunt, man would perform rituals prior to the hunt, either dressing up in an animal skin and dancing, and simulating the hunt and kill, and/or making models of the animal they were about to hunt and ceremoniously 'killing' the model. This was known as 'sympathetic magick'.

The goddess represented fertility, Mother Nature, mother earth, and was called upon to watch over the fields and the fertility of the crops and the tribe.

Women worked in the fields. It was their job to grow and harvest plants and herbs whilst the men hunted and did manual labour. In this way the women learned the potency of plants and how to use them in 'potions' to heal common ailments and problems. Some women learned the magical properties of plants and were able to create powerful spells, but this began to change with the birth of the Christian Church.

The Church felt threatened by the 'wise' women [witches] and men became frightened of women's power. Women were not allowed to be educated or to have knowledge and powers over men. Witches were blamed for everything that went wrong, from poor crops to bad weather, and they were called 'Devil worshippers'. Between the 1400s and 1700s some 9 million witches worldwide were hunted and executed by drowning, burning or hanging.

This state of affairs Forest describes as 'appalling' and, indeed, these bald statistics are both startling and horrifying.

Looking at today's witches, Forest says:

The witch of today is dedicated to helping and healing the planet and people. We celebrate the Earth and the Lore's of Nature. We call upon the elements (earth, air, fire and water) to aid in our work, and use the magickal and healing properties of herbs, plants, oils, trees and crystals to enhance and empower spells. We celebrate the phases of the Moon (known as Esbats) and the Eight Festivals (known as Sabbats).

We appreciate and respect nature and try to live in harmony with nature. We are dedicated to helping people and giving assistance freely and gladly in any way we can.

So being a witch today isn't about waving a magick wand to make things happen all the time, it is definitely more a way of life, going back to the old ways. Learning about the old plants and herbs, which are now often called weeds, and learning about their properties and how you can use them for alternative remedies as well as making incense. It is about tuning in more to yourself and nature. Learning to take time just to be you by sitting quietly inside or out and meditating on a regular basis.

Many of the stories we have been handed down from yesteryear mention witches in pointed hats and black garb, riding broomsticks and keeping black cats. Are these the essentials of twenty-first century witches?

We usually wear robes which are often black but can be white or coloured. You should have a robe, or robes, which you only use for magickal purposes when performing magick ceremonies or rituals, in loose comfortable natural material such as cotton or silk. The colour is up to you, white or black is usual, or even a more colourful robe of purple but it is your choice. Of course you can wear nothing, which we call Skyclad. Some people feel this puts them more in touch with nature. If you are working outside, especially with our English climate, you might also need a cloak. Ideally this is made of 100 per cent cotton and black is more practical, but the lining can be in a different colour, such as green or purple.

I do not wear a pointed hat or believe that a witch ever would. It is not a very practical piece of clothing. Our robes usually have hoods.

The pointed hat I believe was an invention of the Christian Church. The shape represented the church steeple and they were called 'steeple' hats. The hat was placed on the head of a 'Witch' prior to her execution in the hope that the Church symbol would draw salvation to her soul.

The besom or broomstick is a masculine symbol. Traditionally it was made from ash, for protection, the handle representing the male principle. The brush was made from birch twigs, for protection and purification, and is the female principle. The twigs are bound with branches from the willow tree for protection, healing and love.

The besom's main use is for sweeping negativity and evil entities out of a magick circle prior to commencing rituals. Originally it was used as a riding/dancing pole during crop fertility rights, when witches would go out on a full moon and straddle their besoms, jumping as high as they could in the fields to encourage the crops to grow high and strong. It should stand handle down, twigs up when not in use.

The besom is also used in pagan wedding ceremonies, known as Handfasting, when the couple jumps over the besom declaring their love and commitment to each other, for as long as they both desire it. The handle of the besom can be carved with runic or planetary symbols of your choice.

I don't have a cat. It is not a prerequisite of being a witch. A witch will often have what is known as a 'familiar'. This is an animal she works with when doing magick. Traditionally a cat is the typical familiar but it can be a dog, a bird or any animal. It doesn't have to be a living animal. You can have a spirit guide or familiar in the spirit world who you can communicate with when necessary.

In the modern world, with its sophisticated lifestyles and fast pace, it may seem that there is little place for witchcraft. Julie Forest disagrees:

> I feel there is a great need for witchcraft in the twenty-first century. Christianity has lost a lot of its popularity and power and needs to be replaced by something else. There are such a vast amount of alternative religions and beliefs in England now as we become more and more multi-racial and I feel witchcraft is a good way of life, which can be practiced by anyone no matter what their religion is.
>
> I am always getting asked to do spells for people. The most requested types of spells are for love and relationships, money or for removing bad luck or hexes. A lot of the time I just talk to people and try to help where I can.
>
> There are many, many witches active today. I work mainly on my own, but on occasions I work with two other witches. I am the only member of my family who practices the craft. Family, friends and work colleagues accept me for who I am and my way of life is not a problem for people who know me.

Julie Forest did not make a conscious decision to become a witch:

> I didn't 'decide' to become a witch, it just is. When I was a small child I used to collect plants and mash them with a stick to make a 'healing' potion. I obviously had no idea what I was doing; it was just instinct. I believe inherent memory from previous lives has helped me on the path. I genuinely believe I have been a witch, wise woman, and healer in previous lives and I have just brought the knowledge through and developed it.

Julie Forest's words bring insight into the background of witchcraft. It is interesting that the thoughts of a witch of today answers questions about some of the witches mentioned in this book. Fear is a powerful force for some of the actions taken against so-called 'witches' in the distant and not so distant past. It is a shame that these women were not given the chance to articulate their views as the twenty-first-century witch may do today.

1 Susannah Morley receiving the Tichbourne Dole. (Photograph courtesy of Richard Gordon)

2 'Sir' David Priestley being 'knighted' by Knight in Charge, 'Sir' Fred Rolfe after winning the Knighthood of Southampton Old Bowling Green competition. (Penny Legg 2009)

3 Overton Mummers in Freefolk in the late 1920s. Photograph taken by George Long. Long lived in Whitchurch and was a keen photographer all his life. His interest in folkore seems to have started in the mid-1920s and he photographed the Overton, Longparish and North Waltham Mummers in the 1920s and 1930s. (Photograph and caption courtesy Paul Marsh)

4 Eastleigh Railway Works Centenary, May 2009. (Penny Legg 2009)

5 The late Eric Walter Geden-Tysoe, whose encounter with a ghost at Itchell House stayed with him. (Penny Legg 2009)

6 The Eclipse Inn, Winchester, haunted by the ghost of Dame Alicia Lyle. (Penny Legg 2009)

7 Winchester's Theatre Royal, which has several ghostly inhabitants. (Penny Legg 2009)

8 St Ethelflaeda in Romsey, the patron saint of Romsey Abbey. (Penny Legg 2009)

9 Alfred the Great in Winchester. (Penny Legg 2009)

HERE STOOD
THE OAK TREE,
ON WHICH AN ARROW
SHOT BY
SIR WALTER TYRRELL
AT A STAG,
GLANCED AND STRUCK
KING WILLIAM
THE SECOND,
SURNAMED RUFUS,
ON THE BREAST,
OF WHICH HE
INSTANTLY DIED,
ON THE SECOND
DAY OF AUGUST,
ANNO 1100.

10 The Rufus Stone in the New Forest, which marks the spot where King William 'Rufus' was killed in 1100. (Penny Legg 2009)

11 The statue of Lord Palmerston in Romsey. (Penny Legg 2009)

12 Frederick Lee Bridle, Southampton's forgotten painter. (Photograph courtesy of Catherine Aitchison Hull)

13 The house at 8 College Street where Jane Austen died. (Penny Legg 2009)

14 The sun sets behind the Spitfire, R.J. Mitchell's masterpiece. (Penny Legg 2009)

15 Woman Police Sergeant 1 Doris Cole, Southampton Borough Police's first female policewoman, who was commended for bravery in 1945. (Photograph courtesy of the Hampshire Constabulary History Society)

16 The witch looks out from the top of the tower of St Peter's Church, Curdridge. (Penny Legg 2009)

17 Warrior, the equine hero who gave long service to Hampshire. (Photograph courtesy of the Hampshire Constabulary History Society)

18 Selborne's St Marys Church, the peaceful final resting place of Gilbert White. (Penny Legg 2009)

19 Brusher Mills, the New Forest snake catcher. (Penny Legg 2009)

20 The Winchester Morris Men. (Photograph courtesy of Mike Slocombe – www.urban75.com)

21 Moses Mills, who sang twenty-four songs for Hampshire folksong collector George Gardiner. (Photograph courtesy of the Hampshire Records Office and the late Paul Marsh)

22 The Axford Five, left to right, Emily and Hazel Askew, Carolyn Robson, Moira Craig and the late Sarah Morgan, keeping Hampshire's songs, collected by folksong collector George Gardiner, alive. (Penny Legg 2009)

23 Romsey Abbey (Penny Legg 2009)

24 King John's House, Romsey (Penny Legg 2009)

25 St Peter's Old Church, Stockbridge, is well worth a visit. (Penny Legg 2009)

26 The royal cypher, dated 1588, inside St Peter's Old Church, Stockbridge (Penny Legg 2009)

27 Eling Tide Mill, the last working tide mill in England. (Penny Legg 2009)

28 The General Military Hospital at Netley, which Florence Nightingale said was 'hopelessly out of date' when she saw the plans. (Photograph courtesy of the Lingwood Netley Hospital Archive)

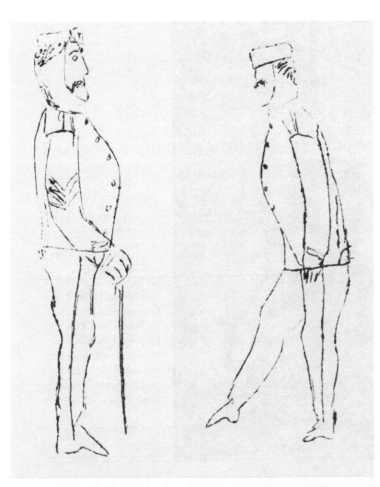

29 The etchings made by an inmate at the General Military Hospital at Netley. (Image courtesy of the Hampshire Constabulary History Society)

30 The Virgin's Crowns at Abbotts Ann. Once a widespread custom, now Abbotts Ann is one of the few areas in the country to award the Crowns and is the only one to award them to both male and female virgins. (Penny Legg 2009)

31 The legend of Sir Bevois is ingrained into Southampton. The lions guarded Josian, Sir Bevois' love. Now, proposed specialist treatment will mean they will guard the Bargate into the future. (Penny Legg 2009)

32 Otterbourne Mummers, 2009. (Penny Legg 2009)

FIVE

The Natural World

How often have I said to you that when you have eliminated the impossible, whatever remains, however improbable, must be the truth?

Sir Arthur Conan Doyle lived in Portsmouth and is buried in the New Forest
The Sign of Four

Hampshire has a rich legacy of mythical beasts and animal heroes. It has also been home to folk who have understood the natural world they lived in and who have left their mark on the county.

This chapter looks at Hampshire's natural world and offers a snapshot of heroes and customs, hard work and legends, which combined show Hampshire for the diverse county it is today.

The Grampus

Ralph Whitlock studies the phenomenon of the beast in folklore in his excellent book, *In Search of Lost Gods: A Guide to British Folklore*. He points out that many have common traits; they are unfriendly to their neighbours, and have to be vanquished either by exorcism or by the dashing exploits of an often self-sacrificing hero.

In Hampshire the Grampus is a well-documented, dolphin-like beast which forsook the water to live in the old yew tree near the church at Highclere. Tradition tells us that this was a somewhat timid creature which, nevertheless, sometimes liked to peek out from amongst the branches and harass the local population, in particular the young girls in the area. Some reports state that it 'blew like a whale', whilst others say it sounded as if it was snoring. Either way, the breathing of this beast caused much consternation amongst the neighbouring population and the local clergyman was called upon to help.

The intrepid vicar advanced upon the fearsome beast armed with his Bible and successfully managed to banish it to the Red Sea for a period of 1,000 years. Thus freed from the threat of the dreaded beast's breathing, the locals were able to breathe easier themselves. As there is no date to this tale, one wonders when the time will be up and the Grampus will return. Will the locals be as intimidated by his behaviour now as they were then?

The Bisterne Dragon

This fearsome beastie lived on Burley Beacon and terrorised the people of the little village of Bisterne, near Ringwood. Described as being covered in scales and breathing fire, this was a dragon, an old mythical monster.

Each day the village quailed in fear as the dragon descended from its lair and demanded a bucket of milk to drink. As it was also partial to both cattle and people, the villagers always complied.

However, after a while they tired of living in fear and hired themselves a champion to rid the area of the dragon forever. The champion was a well-known knight, Sir Maurice Berkeley, who, with his two faithful canine companions, agreed to do battle on behalf of the villagers.

The brave Sir Maurice covered himself in birdlime and powdered glass to make himself a less tasty mouthful and set off to meet the dragon in Dragon Fields. What ensued was a battle so fierce that when the victorious knight emerged from the fields, he was a changed man. Both of his English mastiff companions were killed and he himself died soon afterwards, a broken man who could not bring himself to speak of the ordeal he had faced.

The dogs and the dragon are commemorated in stone at Bisterne Park. The heroic canines now guard the terrace of the Manor House and the dragon is carved over the door. One of the local lanes is still called Dragon Lane.

The Wherwell Cockatrice

The Cockatrice, like its fearsome cousin the Basilisk, is a feared being which, according to the Parson in Chaucer's *The Canterbury Tales*, 'sleeth folk by the venym of his sighte'.

This strange creature is a cross between a reptile, a rooster and a dragon. It is usually portrayed as having a scaly body, the head of a cock and a dragon's tail. It normally had wings and some accounts state that it breathed fire like a dragon. All agree that, like a Gorgon from ancient Greek mythology, once it stares into your eyes, you are dead.

There are several versions of the tale of Hampshire's own Cockatrice. Marc Alexander, in his comprehensive *British Folklore: Myths and Legends* tells us that the Cockatrice at Wherwell was hatched in the cellar of Wherwell Priory, whereas Wendy Boase in *The Folklore of Hampshire and the Isle of Wight* tells us it was hatched in a dungeon beneath the priory. The Wherwell village website cites it as being hatched in the crypt of Wherwell Abbey. All agree that the egg, in medieval mythology usually laid by a cock but in Wherwell's case laid by a duck, was incubated by a toad and produced the awful Cockatrice. At first this creature was treated as the village pet and the villagers were happy to have it amongst them, but as it grew it became more than the villagers could handle, for its appetite could only be sated by human flesh. It would fly from its ecclesiastical lair and snatch tasty villagers to be eaten later.

Such was the terror in the village it was decided that this state of affairs could not continue. The good people of Wherwell were so desperate that eventually it was decided that the Cockatrice had to be killed. Anyone who could rid the village of the menace would receive a reward of four acres of land, a generous prize for the time. Many tried and died. A man called Green, described as an 'ingenious servant of the Priory' by the good ladies of the Hampshire Federation of Women's Institutes in *It Happened in Hampshire*, learning from the mistakes of his predecessors, wondered if the creature might be fooled into thinking that another Cockatrice was invading his territory and try to fight it off. He spent time polishing a sheet of metal to a mirror finish and then carefully lowered it into the Cockatrice's lair. The creature, thinking that it had a rival, repeatedly attacked the mirror image of itself, battering itself into exhaustion in the process. This was just what Green had hoped would happen. Taking up his spear, he plunged it into the recumbent Cockatrice, killing it instantly. The village of Wherwell was free, at last, from its tormentor.

It is whispered the villagers would not eat duck eggs for many years after the Wherwell Cockatrice was slain. To this day there are four acres of treeless land in nearby Harewood Forest, which are known as Green's Acres. Today the village, situated between Winchester and Andover, is a quiet place thanks to the ingenuity of Mr Green.

Warrior

Warrior was a magnificent white gelding, standing sixteen hands high. He had served with distinction in the First World War as an Army cavalry horse from 1914 to 1918. He served through the retreat from Mons, was at the Marne and Ypres and was unfortunate to be wounded by shrapnel in the advance to the Aisne. After this he went on to serve loyally with the Southampton Borough Police for sixteen years.

Time caught up with Warrior five years before the Second World War. After a day on duty, Southampton's most famous police horse died in his sleep. There is a memorial to him in Southampton Sports Centre, which remembers his earlier service, and his hooves were later mounted. One forms the gavel for Southampton's branch of the Old Contemptibles Association and two hooves, which were made into inkstands, were presented to the mayor. The Hampshire Constabulary History Society has retained one of Warrior's hooves in the force's museum. This equine hero is still regarded with affection and memories of him endure.

Fritz

During the Second World War the Royal Hampshire Regiment found itself with one of the enemy as a mascot. Fritz was a large and friendly St Bernard, described as 'handsome' by Major T.J. Edwards. He was originally a German police dog.

When the 1st Battalion attacked Arromanches on 7 June 1944, the fearless giant canine was seen in the battle zone in the thick of the fighting. He was picked up with German officers taken prisoner at the battle and taken with them to England. As there seemed to be no use for him and as he was in the way, he was given a death sentence. Luckily for Fritz there was one person who wanted him. She was Leading Wren V. Elgar, who volunteered to take responsibility for him and pay his quarantine bills.

When Fritz came out of quarantine Elgar made a present of him to the Royal Hampshire Regiment as she had heard that they were on the lookout for a regimental mascot.

The regiment was delighted to receive him and on ceremonial occasions he was dressed elegantly in a harness and coat emblazoned with regimental badges and the embroidered names of the countries the regiment had served in during the war. Fritz led the soldiers when the Royal Hampshire Regiment was granted the Freedom of Portsmouth in 1950.

The Hampshire Hog

Hampshire people are known affectionately as 'Hampshire Hogs'. The origins of this nickname seem to be shrouded in the mists of time, but Evans acknowledges, in his version of the *Brewer's Dictionary of Phrase and Fable*, that the name derived from the pigs Hampshire is famous for producing.

A hog is a male swine, castrated and bred solely for its meat. Hampshire folk have always been proud of the hogs they produce and, according to the Southern Life website, when military bands from Portsmouth passed by in days of old the excited country folk would be determined that their pigs would also enjoy the music. They would drive them out to line the streets as the bandsmen marched through, playing as they went.

Wendy Boase notes that it was thought that pigs had psychic powers and could predict windy weather by flinging about the straw in their sties.

The Hampshire government website notes that in 1790 the term had been included in the dictionary and was a 'jocular appellation for a Hampshire man', the definition linked to the fine pigs and bacon produced in the county.

Today, in Winchester, there is a lone Hampshire Hog on display outside the Hampshire County Council headquarters building.

The County Flower

A county flower is a flower chosen as an emblem of the county it represents. In 2002 the plant conservation charity, Plantlife, ran a competition to choose plants to represent the counties in the British Isles to celebrate the Golden Jubilee of Queen Elizabeth II. The flower chosen for Hampshire was the dog rose or *rosa canina*.

This common rose, often seen in hedgerows, is a deciduous shrub, often growing more than 3m in height. It has sharp thorns used for clinging as it climbs. The white or pink five-petal flowers bloom in June and July. The flowers ripen into rose hips in autumn and for many years these were collected to make rosehip syrup, as they are rich in Vitamin C.

The ladies of the Women's Institute noted that the rose has long been associated with Hampshire. It is used to ornament many of the county's buildings and is part of the Hampshire County Badge.

It is possible that Henry V, in 1415, first granted the rose to the bands of men from the county who were trained in Hampshire. Another theory is that it was granted after the Battle of Minden in 1759, when the victorious Hampshire Regiment gathered red roses from the heath land on which the battle had raged and wore them in their caps.

Gilbert White

One of the great names from Hampshire is that of the Revd Gilbert White (1720-1793), author of *The Natural History and Antiquities of Selborne*. White is remarkable for being the first naturalist to use observation to describe the natural world in which he lived rather than to dissect dead specimens. It has been claimed that he was the first ecologist in England. In an age when respect for nature was not high, he stands out amongst naturalists of his time. His book, one of the most published in the English language, has been continuously in print since it was first published in 1789.

Born in the rural village of Selborne, midway between the towns of Alton and Petersfield, where his grandfather was the local vicar, he went to Oriel College, Oxford, in 1740. He became his Uncle Charles', who was also a vicar, curate in 1746 and was ordained in 1749. He held appointments in various Hampshire and Wiltshire parishes, including Selborne and, in 1752, was appointed Dean of Oriel. In 1763 he inherited the family house in Selborne, The Wakes, from his uncle and lived there from 1784 to the end of his life.

In 1751 he began the detailed *Garden Kalender*, which was a record of activities in his garden and which he continued until 1767. A keen gardener, he was receptive to new crops and was the first potato grower in the area. All his experiments were keenly observed and he kept a record of them.

The Natural History and Antiquities of Selborne is a compilation of his letters to naturalist Thomas Pennant (1726-1798), whose replies have unfortunately been lost, and to the barrister and naturalist Daines Barrington (1727-1800). He was interested in all aspects of nature, but primarily in birds. He distinguished different species of similar looking birds through their varied calls by field study, a new concept in his time. He expanded his interests and wrote about such seemingly unimportant creatures as earthworms and their importance to the soil as the 'great promoters of vegetation' and, with William Markwick (1739-1813) who was working in Battle, Sussex, recorded details of periodic plant and animal life cycles over a period of twenty-five years.

In 1780 White's aunt, Rebecca Snooke, died and he inherited her pet tortoise, Timothy. He wrote extensively about this tortoise, with keen observations, which have inspired works by later authors on the subject, even into the twenty-first century.

Gilbert White died in Selborne in 1793 at the age of seventy-two. He left behind a legacy of groundbreaking work, which inspired other naturalists, including Charles Darwin, who based some of his work on White's keen observations and records.

Today the village of Selborne remembers its most celebrated son. The Wakes is open to the public and proudly on display is the original manuscript of *The Natural History and Antiquities of Selborne*. The Zigzag path is supposed to have been made by White and his brothers, who dragged a large stone up Hanger Hill, from neighbouring village Farringdon. The stone is now called the Wishing Stone and those who manage the walk up the winding path painstakingly cut by White will find it at the top, along with a seat in which to rest, admire the view, make a wish and catch their breath.

Brusher Mills

Harry 'Brusher' Mills was a unique character in the New Forest and a snake catcher par excellence. He was born on 19 March 1840 in Silver Street, Emery Down, near Lyndhurst and lived there until 1861. In 1881 he is listed on the census for that year as living in Clayhill with his widowed sister, Fanny Whithorn. Although he was listed as a 'labourer' he was already catching snakes in the mid-1870s. In an age when the National Health Service was decades away and snakes were common, Brusher's work catching them and producing homemade remedies for snakebites was invaluable. He was also trustworthy, which was more than could be said of the New Forest gypsies who were widely considered to be rogues and who offered snakebite remedies of their own. The gypsies called Brusher 'Sapengro', which means 'snake catcher' in Romany.

Looking at surviving images of him, he has a strange appearance to modern-day eyes, with his long forked beard, sturdy boots and gaiters. His multi-layered attire was completed with flamboyant neckerchief, metal-rimmed spectacles and battered fedora. The accoutrements of his trade, tins and sacks to hold the snakes in, hung from his waist. There is a lifelike image of Brusher reproduced on his gravestone at St Nicholas' Cemetery in Brockenhurst.

He is reputed to have had no fear of snakes, catching them in the woods at Sporelake Lawn with his bare hands. Those that were not used to produce ointment to cure bites were sent to London Zoo as food for the animals there.

Brusher got his nickname from his love of cricket. When a match was on at Bulmer Green, he would go along and brush down the crease between innings.

Brusher, who said he was 'born a gardener', lived outside in a funnel-shaped charcoal burner's hut, which was sparsely furnished and had a bracken bed. This hut was near Hollands Wood campsite and he lived there for almost the twenty years needed to claim squatter's rights over the land he lived on. It is said that with eight months to go until this milestone, he was given notice to quit by the local council and his home was set alight to prevent him returning. He never got over this eviction.

He was bitten on numerous occasions. When an adder bit him he would cut the wound open with a knife, allow the blood to flow and then rub his snake fat ointment over the wound.

On 1 July 1905 Brusher was enjoying his favourite tipple, rum, at the Railway Inn at Brockenhurst. This was his local hostelry and it had enjoyed his patronage for many years. After a meal of bread and pickles he left but he did not make it to his home in New Park. He was found dead nearby. A doctor certified death from heart disease. He was sixty-five.

The local police constable arranged the simple funeral, which was attended by his nephew and one sister, in addition to the constable and the landlord of the Railway Inn (now known as the Snake Catcher). Brusher's beautifully carved headstone stands just ahead of a smaller, much simpler memorial, which simply reads: H.M. 1905.

In his lifetime it is estimated that he caught over 29,000 snakes in the New Forest.

The Hampshire Avon

When Robert Southey (1774-1843) wrote his poem 'For the Banks of the Hampshire Avon' in 1799, he recommended travellers in the area to:

> … let thy leisure eye behold and feel
> The beauties of the place…

Southey undoubtedly knew what he liked.

The word 'avon' means 'river' in Celtic and so the name River Avon actually means 'River River'. It runs along the Avon Valley with waters flowing as cool and clear now as they were in Southey's time. Fossil records tell us that the valley was once underwater. The whole area was a vast sea which teemed with life.

Now it flows through the New Forest with the odd town and village along its snaking banks. Fordingbridge was known originally as 'Forde', and the second part of its name was not added until the Great Bridge, with its seven arches, was built around 1286. The Avon was first spanned here.

The village of Sopley, with its narrow lanes and picture-postcard thatched cottages, looks out over farmland, the flood plain and the New Forest. A stream bisects the village and joins the Avon south of the church.

The tiny village of Hale, in the north-west of Hampshire, has the Avon as one border and the county line with Wiltshire as another. It was listed in the Domesday Book as 'the hide of land in Charford held of the King by Alwi, son of Torber' (Fordingbridge Council website). Apart from records of its residents being caught poaching, the most notable thing about the 'vill of Hale' was the fact that in 1328 Adam de la Forde applied for permission to hold divine service in his Hale manor. Today there are 223 residences within the parish boundary.

Ringwood, or Rincevede as it was known in the eleventh century, stands on a crossing point of the Avon, 'vede' meaning 'wade' and 'rine' meaning 'a river or watercourse'. The town was first granted its market charter in 1226. The cattle market for which it was famous has ceased but there is a weekly Wednesday market and the town was happy to celebrate the 750th anniversary of its market charter in 1976.

The Avon Valley and its settlements are still as beautiful to behold as in Southey's day and efforts are being made to conserve the sense of old world charm contained within the area.

The Swing Riots

Life for a farm labourer in nineteenth-century Hampshire was hard at any time of the year, but during the harvest and the winter it was particularly so. Both John Barton in his book *Hampshire Headlines*, and the Southern Life website, highlight the unrest this caused in the 1830s.

Until 1795 the earning potential for a farm labourer meant that they could at least afford to eat reasonably well, with meat, bacon and dairy produce all being on the menu. However, following the adoption of the Speenhamland system, the brainchild of Berkshire authorities in that town near Newbury, the standard of living for the average farm labourer and his family plunged and there were many living on just bread and potatoes. The reason for this was that the new system changed the way the labourers were paid. Wages would be subsidised from local rates. This meant that farmers could pay as little as they could get away with; in other words, subsistence rates. Farm labourers, no matter how hard they worked, could not increase the amount they earned.

William Cobbett, in his *Rural Rides* (see page 76), did not endear himself to the government or Hampshire's gentry by bringing the plight of the farm workers to light in his scathing social commentaries. In an age when trade unionism was unheard of and those in authority held the agricultural workers in contempt, Cobbett's voice was the only one raised to champion the workers' rights.

The clergy took tithes from most farms' produce and farmers would only consider increasing wages if the local parson would reduce the amount of tithe he collected. Thus, a division between the clergy and those who worked the land opened up. Discontent was widespread and, by 1830, the farm labourers became increasingly desperate, turning to the highly illegal and dangerous occupations of poaching, smuggling and thievery to help supplement their meagre incomes. The punishments for these activities were severe, including the death penalty or transportation.

One of the farm labourers' chief jobs was to thresh the grain after the harvest. This process, removing the chaff, the husks and straw, was for centuries done by hand or by driving a horse through the grain and using its weight to separate the wheat from the chaff. In 1732 Scotsman Michael Menzies invented the first threshing machine. It was not a commercial success as it was prone to breaking down and it was stationery; the grain had to be brought to it for its hydraulically operating flailing wheel to work, but it was the beginning of mechanisation on the farm. This spelt disaster for the farm labourer. When Andrew Meikle invented a more sophisticated and reliable threshing machine in 1786, shortly before the Speenhamland changes, many farm labourers found themselves out of work. By the mid-nineteenth century steam power was harnessed to increase the thresher's potential and this added to the misery faced by the agricultural labourer and his family. In addition, a tendency to hire workers for only fifty-one weeks instead of the full year, which would have entitled them to claim assistance from the parish, brought both resentment and real hardship. This, poor wages and increased mechanisation led to threatening letters being sent anonymously to farmers and landowners. However, soon they were signed 'Captain Swing' and were being printed in the press, the first published in *The Times* in October 1830. The name stuck. The workers demanded a minimum wage, tithe and rent reductions and the end of rural unemployment.

Violence erupted in Kent when a barn and hayricks were set alight, and it spread to East Anglia and along the South Coast. In Hampshire and Wiltshire the unrest reached a peak for two weeks in November 1830. Workers crowded the streets of Overton, near Andover, on 18 November, demanding better wages and food, but were pacified by farmers promising higher rates of pay. Political and social reformer Henry 'Orator' Hunt (1773-1835), who lived locally in Whitchurch, met the mob the next day and agreed to arbitrate. His suggestion that the workers' wages were increased from 9s to 12s a week and that rent payments were to be made by the employers was accepted by both sides. The mob then disbanded peacefully and work was resumed.

In and around Micheldever a huge mob destroyed threshing machines despite the promise of higher wages. Members of this mob also converged on the farm owned by the Baring family, known later for its banking enterprise. Henry Cook, aged nineteen, threw a sledgehammer at the family's son, William Baring. Although it did no damage and Baring was unhurt, Cook was arrested and charged with attempted murder. Troops were brought in to restore order.

In Andover on 20 November, 300 workers marched on the town at 11 a.m. Their leaders, John Gilmore and William Shepherd, interrupted a meeting between magistrates and farmers, which was taking place at the Angel Inn. The magistrates suggested an increase in wages in an effort to keep the peace and the farmers agreed, provided the rents and tithes they paid the landowner were reduced. The mob then marched on the Tasker Waterloo Ironworks, forced their way in and destroyed as much of the machinery as they could. They caused damage which the owner, Robert Tasker, estimated at £1,000.

In Selbourne on 22 November, a mob destroyed much of the workhouse and frightened the vicar into halving his tithes, from £600 to £300 a year. They did the same in Headley. The leader, who brought the labourers to Selbourne by blowing on a horn, was John Newland. He became known as 'the Trumpeter'.

There was a pitched battle between rioters and special constables in Itchen Abbas. At Fordingbridge in the New Forest, the ringleader was ostler James Cooper, known as 'Captain Hunt', who led his mob in an orgy of destruction from astride a white horse and, as such, became known as a hero amongst his following.

The fire resulting from arson at the Charles Baker sawmills in Southampton could be seen in Farnham in Surrey and in Portsmouth. This caused £7,000 of damage and put many more people out of work as the sawmills were a major employer.

All over Hampshire there was unrest, fires and unlawful assemblies. On 25 November 1830 the Duke of Wellington, the Lord Lieutenant of Hampshire, issued a suppression order and eventually the county quietened down. Landowners and farmers agreed to increase wages and threshing machines were not used for some time.

Justice was not slow in coming. At a hearing in Winchester on 18 December, 285 people were committed for trial. The illiterate Henry Cook was sentenced to death for his attack at the Barings farm. So too was folk hero James Cooper. They were hanged in front of all 150 rioters who were also sentenced to death at Winchester Gaol on 15 January 1831. The others were later reprieved. The leaders of the Andover riots were transported and John Newland, caught after going on the run, was sentenced to six months hard labour. He died in 1868 and is buried in Selbourne Churchyard. His gravestone displays the legend, 'the Trumpeter'.

Ultimately the Swing Riots did not produce the results the rioters had hoped for. The riots did influence the 1834 Poor Law Amendment Act and the 1836 Tithe Commutation Act, but wages and conditions did not improve generally and agricultural labourers continued to be at the bottom of the heap.

The Court of Verderers

The Court of Verderers, or Swainmote, is the second most ancient court in England after the Coroner's Court.

The Verderers are the guardians of the New Forest and all its creatures. The New Forest encompasses heath, bog, woodland pasture, centuries-old coppice and timber plantations, and provides pastures for cattle, ponies, pigs and donkeys owned by the Commoners, local people who have authorisation to use the Open Forest for grazing.

According to the Verderers' own website, their role is to:

> … protect and administer the New Forest's unique agricultural commoning practices; conserve its traditional landscape, wildlife and aesthetic character, including its flora and fauna, peacefulness, natural beauty and cultural heritage; and safeguard a viable future for commoning upon which the foregoing depends.

The Verderers are certainly busy people.

The Court of Verderers was originally set up by the Crown to deal with minor offences within the sovereign's forest and had the power to impose fines on miscreants. In the seventeenth and eighteenth centuries these powers were extended and there has been a history of conflict between those concerned with the rights of the Commoners and those whose first considerations were for the owners of the land itself.

A series of acts sought to deal with these problems. Common Rights were first given statutory recognition in the act of 1698, renewed in 1808. The New Forest Act of 1851 removed many of the deer from the forest and allowed the Crown to enclose 10,000 acres for timber growing. It also allowed fences to be moved as and when required, known as 'rolling powers', which, if it had been enforced, would have eventually led to the enclosure of the forest and an end to the Commoners' ability to graze their animals. The 1877 act, known as the 'Commoners' Charter' abolished the Crown's 'rolling powers' and allowed the Commoners to graze their animals on the Open Forest for the payment of a small sum. This act also formally stated the number of Verderers at the Court of Verderers and stipulated that an elective Verderer should own 'not less than seventy-five acres to which were attached Right of Common of Pasture' (Vesey-Fitzgerald). The 1949 act further refined the previous acts and added to the number of Verderers at Court. It also made the ballot for the election of Verderers secret for the first time. Now the elective Verderer should be the occupier of 'not less than one acre carrying with it Right of Common of Pasture'. This effectively opened up the list of those eligible to stand for election as a Verderer.

As an aside to the 1851 act, Peter Tate noted that in 1670 the fallow deer population was 7,500; in 1830 the census put the figure at about 5,000 and after the Deer Removal Act at 4,000. By 1892 it was down to 250 but by the time Tate was writing the numbers had increased to about 900. Today fallow deer are numerous but numbers of all deer, without a natural predator, are monitored and annual culls are held.

Vesey-Fitzgerald gives a list of some of the rights which might be granted to a holding and they make interesting reading. 'The Right of Common Pasture of Sheep', he noted in 1966, had not been exercised for some time. Sheep are not mentioned on the New Forest National Park website. 'The Right of Common of Marl' was important in the production of fertilizer and there were several marl pits in the New Forest. 'The Right of Common of Turbary' was an ancient and important right when peat was the primary source of fuel. Cottages in the New Forest had specially made ovens to burn peat and the right to cut turves was valuable. 'The Right of Common of Estover' gave permission to gather firewood in the forest (estover was a Norman term for the collection of fuel wood). The Commoners maintained the right to gather 'by hook or by crook'. The 'hook' was a sharp billhook which could be used to cut down small branches. This damaged the tree and so was unpopular with the authorities. The Commoners also fashioned a long-handled stave, resembling a shepherd's crook, to knock dead wood from the trees. Today the Forestry Commission supplies firewood to those holdings that have this right. 'The Right of Common of Mast' gives the right to turn pigs into the forest to forage for acorns, an activity referred to as 'pannage', and it is still a common sight to see pigs roaming in the forest in the autumn months. The pigs clear the ground of the majority of the acorns, which can upset the ponies' digestive systems. The most widespread right is 'The Right of Common of Pasture of Commonable Animals' which covers ponies, horses, cattle and donkeys. These animals have to be branded with a brand approved by the Verderers and ponies have to be tail-marked by the district Agisters, the forest stock managers, employed by the Verderers.

Today the Official Verderer is the Court's Chairman and is appointed by the Queen. There are five elected Verderers, with another four each appointed by the Forestry Commission, Natural England, the Department for Environment, Food and Rural Affairs (DEFRA) and the National Park.

The Court of Verderers meets at the Verderers' Hall, Queens House, Lyndhurst, each month except August and all but one of the meetings, the Court Committee meeting, are open to the public. The walls of the Verderers Court are decorated with deer heads, their antlers a magnificent display and a reminder that this respected court stands in the deer's ancient home.

The New Forest Embroidery

To celebrate the 900th anniversary of the New Forest in 1979, the New Forest Association commissioned the embroidering of a tapestry, which was to show a pictorial history of the forest. The project was designed and organised by Belinda Montagu, who went on to become the association's President. Her book, *The New Forest Embroidery*, detailed the years of work that went into producing the artwork, which is 25ft long and 2½ft high.

The embroidery was originally designed to hang in the Verderers' Hall in Queens House, but problems with public access meant that the embroidery was first exhibited in the New Forest District Council Chamber and then, since 1988, at the New Forest Museum in Lyndhurst.

The bold, fun panels depict many of the scenes from history and folklore, who those in the New Forest know and love. The tapestry also shows the forest through all four seasons. Sixty volunteers embroidered the trees and animals, the heraldic devices and the birds. Belinda Montagu herself embroidered all the people and she is depicted in the distance on the third panel astride her grey hunter, Allah.

The tapestry originated from rough sketches, which became a full-sized cartoon on which the various elements were juggled. It was slowly built up from the backing canvas using silks, taffetas, velvets, leathers, felts and even wool which, as Belinda describes, was 'straight from the sheep's back!' The entirety was then appliquéd and machine and hand-stitched together.

On the first panel it is spring and King William I sits regally looking out over the forest he established, under the words 'Nova Foresta Ytene'. 'Ytene', as we learnt in Chapter Three, is Saxon for 'land of the Jutes and furzy waste'. The forest is shown unfenced, with a red admiral, dragonfly, common snipe and a nightingale representing the fauna, with the edible fungi, the chanterelle, amongst the trees. The death of William Rufus is depicted (see Chapter Three) and above this the Domesday Book is open showing four of the forest's manors: Linhest (Lyndhurst); Broceste (Brockenhurst); Bovre (Boldre); and Truham (Througham). King John (see Chapter Two) is shown giving a model of Beaulieu Abbey to a Cistercian monk in 1204. The panel ends with the Charter of the Forest, listing the Common Rights (see the Verderers Court earlier in this chapter), which was granted in 1217 by King Henry III.

The second panel is in summer and depicts the 'Stirrup of Rufus', through which dogs were thrust to see if they were small enough to remain harmless to the wildlife in the forest. Larger dogs had their front claws removed to render them incapable of harming the deer. A deer, pony, badger, magpie, pannaging pig, Dartford warblers, a carrion crow, chaffinches, a snake and a butterfly demonstrate just how diverse the wildlife is in the forest. The coat of arms of the 1st Earl of Southampton, Thomas Wriothesley, is depicted. Belinda Montagu tells us that he bought Beaulieu from the Crown in 1538 and paid £1,350 6s 8d. Lord Delaware's Rufus Stone marks the spot in Canterton Glen that is traditionally thought to be where William Rufus met his death. The witch, Mary Dore (see Chapter Four), is shown along with her cat. At the end of the panel the oak trees, their leaves starting to fall as autumn arrives, give way to conifers, signalling the start of the plantations managed by the Forestry Commission.

The third panel opens in winter and shows the 1848 pony-deer, the alleged cross between a New Forest pony and a red deer. The steam railway arrived in 1847 and it is depicted running along the rails as the tapestry heads back towards spring. Rhinefield House sits in the background. This was the home of the Walker family who owned the Eastwood Colliery, made famous in the books by D.H. Lawrence. The only daughter of the family married a naval officer, Lieutenant Munro, and the couple decided to adopt the name Walker-Munro.

They spent her father's wedding present, £250,000, on building the Rhinefield estate. Snake catcher Brusher Mills (discussed earlier in this chapter) also has a place on this panel. The once plentiful, but now sadly gone, Natterjack toad, a rare white buck, a fox and a swallow are all part of the forest scene on this part of the panel. New Forest resident Alice Hargreaves, immortalised by Lewis Carroll, is shown, together with her final resting place, Lyndhurst Parish Church. Two Girl Guide badges reflect the fact that Foxlease House, near Lyndhurst, is the British Girlguiding centre. It was presented to the Girl Guides in 1922 on the occasion of the marriage of Princess Mary, the then President of the Girl Guides. The Forest in wartime is reflected in the camouflaged tents and the Spitfire flying overhead, developed at Southampton (see Chapter Three). The Victoria Cross awarded to Flight Lieutenant James Nicholson, 249 Squadron, in August 1940 nestles in the trees below the Spitfire. Bringing the embroidery up to 1979 are the oil refinery and campsites, and the sight of the Queen planting a new commemorative tree on 12 April 1979.

In all, the New Forest embroidery provides a snapshot of the evolution of the New Forest and its folklore, and is a credit to its creators.

SIX

HAMPSHIRE'S MUSIC AND DANCE

Them that asks no questions isn't told a lie.
Watch the wall, my darling, while the Gentlemen go by!
Five and twenty ponies
Trotting through the dark-
Brandy for the Parson,
'Baccy for the Clerk;
Laces for a lady, letters for a spy,
Watch the wall, my darling, while the Gentlemen go by!

Rudyard Kipling
'A Smuggler's Song'

Let's face it, most of us feel better for a laugh sometimes and our forebears were no different. Music, dancing and drama offered a release from the everyday stresses and strains of life for the people of Hampshire. A travelling entertainer was something different, to be enjoyed and talked about for months afterwards. Joining in was fun and brought laughter to friends and family. It could also bring in the odd much-needed extra coin in lean times. Strange but true stories could lead to events being commemorated with a song and new traditions begun. This chapter looks at some of the songs from the county and the dances enjoyed here. It also offers an insight into the world of the players and looks forward to the music of Hampshire in the future.

Entertainment in the Middle Ages

In the pampered twenty-first century we have got used to our wall-mounted
flat screen televisions, with high definition pictures and surround sound. These
bring us all the latest films, news, comedy and drama programming directly into
our living rooms via our satellite dishes and cable connections. We enjoy our
Digital Audio Broadcasting, or DAB, radios, which broadcast clear sounds from
all over the globe and we think nothing of listening to any one of hundreds of
radio stations playing many different types of music whenever we want to listen.
On our home computers, or out and about with our laptops or mobile tel-
ephones, we can surf the Internet, enjoying the latest YouTube video whenever
and wherever we feel like it. How lucky we are! We have unlimited, twenty-
four hour entertainment at the touch of a button and we take it all for granted.

In 1969 C.E.C. Burch researched a fascinating book entitled the *Minstrels
and Players of Southampton, 1428-1635*, which makes it clear that the entertainment offered in yesteryear was of a vastly different nature to that which we
enjoy today.

The minstrels, so Burch contends, were born of a tradition older than the
Romans. Much political mileage could be obtained by paying for entertainments for the masses. The three different kinds of Mimus (entertainment) were
Mimic drama, sung Mimus and recited Mimus. Juvenal's *Satire X* (AD 200)
pointed out that all Roman people seemed to be interested in were 'bread and
circuses'. Burch cites Graves' 1962 translation of *The Twelve Caesars*, in which
Suetonius tells us of Augustus' understanding of keeping his people happy. He
listed the entertainments that the emperor provided 'in various City districts,
on several stages'. These entertainments included actors, gladiators, jugglers and
fools, as well as musicians and wild animal hunts.

The coming of Christianity led eventually to a decline in the government-
funded spectacles but the everyday folk on the streets continued to amuse
themselves and their peers. By the Middle Ages jousts, feasts, mystery plays
and animal baiting had taken over as entertainments, although some of these
pastimes were only open to the privileged few. Mummers, jugglers, fools, con-
jurors, minstrels and troubadours now relieved the monotony of the daily grind
needed to make a living.

Germanic invaders and Roman Christian missionaries each spread their own
versions of their country's epic tales to Britain and, as Burch points out, 'the
Anglo-Saxon gleeman was affected by the Mimus of the former empire'. Over
time the Church took a progressively dimmer view of those who were involved
in providing such entertainment but the minstrel, as he became, endured.

The word 'minstrel' originally meant 'little servant' and referred to those who were employed at a castle or court as a musician or poet. Minstrels made up their own songs and short stories, often topically, about those around them. Minstrels were also famous for their 'chansons de geste'. These were long poems recounting myths and legends. Troubadours, who eventually replaced minstrels, sang of courtly love and told of far-off lands. When troubadours began to travel they were known as 'wandering minstrels'.

Burch tells us that William the Conqueror brought his minstrel, named Taillefer, along with him when he invaded England and landed at Hastings in 1066. Over the following centuries the reputation of minstrels generally began to fall due to widespread abuse of the freedom a minstrel enjoyed. The idle would claim food and drink by stating they were minstrels, which harmed the true minstrel to the point that the only way forward was by noble patronage. When travelling, the minstrels would wear something to identify the noble house from whence they came, either livery or some kind of badge.

In the Southampton Steward records, it is noted that in 1461-1462 'the Menstrelys of my lord of Kentts 5 Trompetts' were paid 3s 4d. 'The Fool of Lord Rivers' received 1s in the same records in 1470-1471.

Burch notes that the minstrels from over thirty patrons visited Southampton and are recorded as receiving payment from the Borough officials between 1428-1429 and 1483-1484. The town was not unaware that the minstrels represented important people. In the Southampton Steward's accounts there is an entry dated 1428-1429 for a payment to the King and Duke of York's eleven minstrels, noted as *pro honore ville*, meaning 'for the honour of the town'.

Later 'players', dramatic actors who swelled the ranks of the travelling entertainers from Elizabeth I's day forward, joined the minstrels. Originally players acted out the Scriptures for the illiterate flock of the Church. Later the great mystery plays emerged, under the guidance of the guilds. Those in York, Chester and Coventry rose to prominence but there were local plays all over England and the players travelled the country to perform in them. Originally amateur actors, soon they were being paid for their performances.

The players' popularity soared and they soon rivalled and then overtook the minstrels. They sought similar noble patronage deals too. The Southampton Steward began to record payments to both minstrels and players in 1485-1486, when the Earl of Arundel's minstrels were paid 3s 4d on 20 January and his players were paid 3s 4d on 23 January.

The players usually performed for the town mayor first and it was to this free performance that anyone could come and watch. The mayor would usually pay the players for the performance.

The 'players of the King's interludes', as the players patronised by both Henry VII and Henry VIII were known, came to Southampton more often than any others. The plays had become secular over time and by 1570 Burch found that they were moral in tone, warning of the dire consequences for dishonourable lapses. In addition to the minstrels and players who had noble patronage, there were also specialist entertainers such as bear wards, those in charge of bears for bearbaiting, jesters or fools, and jugglers. Once again it is one of Henry VIII's entertainers, his bear ward, who is most often mentioned in the Southampton records.

Edward Alleyn (1566-1626), the most famous actor in Elizabethan England, came to Southampton twice. In 1593 he came as an actor and again in 1623 when he was part of the reception committee for the Infanta of Spain, who had come to marry Prince Charles. Alleyn was made a burgess of the town at the time.

That a player could rise so high shows just how far entertainers had come. The records of so many of the payments to the minstrels and players who came to Southampton allows us, in the pampered twenty-first century, a glimpse of the entertainment available to our ancestors.

Winchester Morris

One day in 1972 Albert Wilkins was asked if he fancied going along to a Morris dancing group. The friend asking him didn't want to go alone. Albert recalls, 'We went along on a Wednesday night. He couldn't get on with it somehow and left. I stayed. That first evening I walked in, it sort of grabbed me'.

So began the start of an interest in Morris dancing which has lasted to the present day. Albert is now the Winchester Side Bagman, or General Secretary. 'I look after the money,' he says. In times past the Bagman went around the audience with a collection bag for donations. 'The Squire is the boss. He decides what we are going to dance and the Bagman does everything else really; organises places, gets the Side out, organises the police, is the General Secretary and keeps the books'.

Between April and July each year the Winchester Morris Men are busy dancers. 'We dance every Wednesday and then at odd fêtes. We could be out every weekend if I did not say "No". We did three weddings this year! Two on the same day!'

The Winchester Morris Side owes its existence to Cecil Sharp (1859-1924), as do many of the Morris Sides in England. Sharp was born in Denmark Hill,

London, and was the son of a slate merchant with an interest in archaeology, architecture and music. He read mathematics at Cambridge but music was his passion. He spent ten years in Australia, working his way upwards; first washing hansom cabs, then in a bank and afterwards in a law firm. At the same time he taught the violin and became known for his musical ability. He finally gave up the law firm to follow his music and taught at Adelaide College of Music, in addition to conducting and playing the organ and piano. In 1892 he returned to England and became the music master at Ludgrove Preparatory School, which prepares boys for Eton. A year later Sharp married Constance Dorothea Birch.

The origins of Morris dancing are shrouded in the mists of time. 'No one knows when it started,' says Albert. Morris dancing was popular in Tudor times in Court and has always been popular with the masses in towns and villages. Roy Christian, in *The Country Life Book of Old English Customs*, speculates that the origins of Morris dancing are a 'survival from the primitive past connected with food supply and the fertility of the soil, which gradually lost its original point in Christian times to become just another form of communal entertainment'.

Russell Wortley speculates that the decline of Morris dancing in the 1850s was probably due to the cessation of annual events such as gatherings at Whitsuntide. These were often rowdy and could lead to a brawl, which was too much for staid Victorian England.

By the end of the nineteenth century Morris was all but dead. However, folk dance collectors Percy Manning and Thomas Carter persuaded the last dancers in Oxford to get together again and dance. This they did in March 1899. This rekindled enthusiasm for Morris and, as the dancers could earn a little from participating, it continued.

'The Great Revival happened in 1899,' says Albert. 'Cecil Sharp was staying with his mother-in-law at her home, Sandfield Cottage, just outside Headington, near Oxford, and saw the Headington Quarry Men, who came up on Boxing Day because it was snowing and it was cold and wet and they were all out of work. He recorded the tunes'. The dancers rightly thought they would receive a penny or two for their entertainment.

The Morris Ring website gives a description of the Headington Quarry Men whom Sharp saw that Boxing Day morning. They are described as being men dressed in white with ribbons decorating their costume, small latten bells were strapped to their shins and they were carrying colourful handkerchiefs and sticks. One man had a concertina and one was dressed as a fool. Six men formed a set of two lines of three outside Sandfield Cottage and began an agile, leaping dance to the lively music supplied by the concertina player. Sharp had seen nothing like it before. The dancers danced five dances and the concertina player, twenty-seven-year-old William Kimber Junior, later answered Sharp's many eager questions. Sharp recorded, in his ever-present notebook, the tunes Kimber played.

Sharp then began a keen study of the folk songs being collected at the time by Lucy Broadwood in Surrey and Sussex, and George Gardiner in Hampshire, amongst others, and realised that there was a difference between these songs and the printed versions he used to teach at school. He decided to go out and collect them himself to see what music he could find. Albert says:

> He was merely interested in the music rather than the dance. He then got interested in the villages in the Cotswolds, where the dances were still extant. They were recorded from the elderly men who were still there. The dancers were old but the musicians could still play, so he recorded all the tunes and then got some sketchy notes.

Before the First World War, Sharp travelled all over the country collecting music and dances, noting them as he went. He discovered Morris, Sword and Country dances and began publishing books of the Morris dances and their music from 1907. In the meantime, the dances were being taught from his notes at the Esperance Girls' Club in London from 1905. The book *Sword Dances of Northern England* did much to revive the obscure and almost extinct Rapper dances in Northumbria. 'They dance with long flexible swords and the dancers are very agile and very fast, especially doing the somersault!' says Albert. The books of Morris dances triggered the beginning of Morris and Country groups around the country. Albert continues:

> The Morris Ring is the umbrella association to which all men's clubs belong. The association keeps Morris Sides up to standard. It was formed in 1934. There are two other Morris associations, the Federation, which is just ladies, and the Open, which is mixed, men and women.
>
> The Morris Ring was very small and remained small for a long time up until the Great Revival in the 1960s. There was a great folk revival then. A resurgence of traditional jazz, folk programmes on the television on a Friday night and there were folk clubs springing up everywhere. There were two in Winchester at one time. The Winchester Side was formed in 1953. It's strange, I was born in the town and I had never seen them dance until I joined them. The man that started it, old Lionel Bacon, was a doctor, the Medical Officer of Health in Winchester, and when I joined he was very welcoming.

The dances that the Winchester Morris Men entertain their audiences with on warm summer evenings come from the original Cotswolds villages Sharp visited. These are places with pleasant sounding names like Evington, Bampton, Ledington, Sherbourne and Hinton-in-the-Hedges. Albert comments:

> It was an artisan thing to do. The dancers were mostly farm labourers, stonemasons and brick layers. Kimber was a bricklayer and a stonemason in the colleges of Oxford. Most of them were of that sort. At the Revival Sharp formed his own demonstration team and Morris was taught, all identically. There were no individual styles and everybody danced exactly the same before the First World War. It was choreographed and there was no deviation from it. It wasn't until the later revival that people started doing it their own way. The dances we do are attributed to the villages from where they came. There is, for example, a dance from Bampton. Bampton are still dancing it. They have had an unbroken tradition for 500 years. So we dance it. It probably does not look like what Bampton does. They change it most years, so we in Winchester think we've got it and then we watch them and think, 'Oh, that is not how they did it last year!'

Albert smiles wistfully when he recalls the reaction to the Morris Men turning up to dance locally:

> The response used to be really great. Now it is not so good. It is not anti, it is just that nobody goes to pubs anymore. Fêtes are always fine because people are there anyway. This season [2009] was not so good but last season was great because it was the first year of the smoking ban. So everybody was outside and it was brilliant! So people had a choice, put it out and go indoors or sit and watch us! This year they have either all given up smoking or, to get through the recession, people just don't go out. We used to have some wonderful times back in the late 1970s and early 1980s. Pubs that were packed and never shut!

The Winchester Morris Men are few in numbers nowadays, with only about ten active dancers and there are few other groups in the county, most notably in Southampton, Portsmouth and Yateley. Albert is the only Winchester Morris dancer who is actually a Winchester resident. It would seem too that long gone are the days, noted by George E. Frampton in *Hampshire, The County Magazine*, when it was worthy to record the amount paid, 3s 4d to 'singers, players and Morris Dancers on Maye Daye' in Southampton in 1562-1563. As the twenty-first century advances, we should be thankful that Morris in any form is still with us in Hampshire.

Beware Chalk Pit

It is not everyday that a person builds a mausoleum for his horse, but that is precisely what Sir Paulet St John did for his trusty steed in 1740. While out on a fox-hunt in the rolling chalk downs in September 1733, the pair apparently crashed some 25ft down into a chalk pit hidden amongst the brambles. Both were mercifully unharmed, but Sir Paulet was not unmindful of their lucky escape. He renamed his horse 'Beware Chalk Pit' to remind himself to take more care in future. In 1734 the horse was entered into the race for the Hunters Plate on Worthy Downs. He and Sir Paulet were the winners.

When Beware Chalk Pit died, Sir Paulet buried his friend under the 30ft-high triangular obelisk, which now stands in Farley Mount Country Park, west of Winchester. Inside is a plaque which tells the tale of Sir Paulet and his favourite horse.

Beware Chalk Pit is commemorated in a song written by folksinger Graham Penny and published in *Folk Songs of Old Hampshire*, edited by John Paddy Browne. It is reproduced here by permission of the publisher, Milestone Publications:

Beware Chalk Pit

There's a tale I'll tell to you,
It's remarkable but true,
Of Sir Paulet St John and his noble steed:
An event which you shall see
Back in 1733.
Of which Hampshire gentlemen should all take heed.

Chorus
Beware Chalk Pit, beware Chalk Pit,
As you go galloping over the downs
Beware Chalk Pit. [*Repeat all three lines*]

As Sir Paulet rode to hounds
'Cross the rolling Hampshire Downs,
He was riding hard as he was wont to do,
When he jumped a bramble hedge
And went headlong o'er the edge
Of a chalk pit that was hidden from his view.

Chorus
Beware Chalk Pit, beware Chalk Pit,
As you go galloping over the downs
Beware Chalk Pit. [*Repeat all three lines*]

Now the chalk pit's sides were steep,
It was twenty-five feet deep,
How they came upon it I cannot account,
But the strangest thing of all
– They both survived the fall
Without injury to rider or to mount.

Chorus
Beware Chalk Pit, beware Chalk Pit,
As you go galloping over the downs
Beware Chalk Pit. [*Repeat all three lines*]

Now Sir Paulet knew, of course,
That the fault was not his horse,
And for riding blindly he should take the blame;
By all rights he should be dead,
Of his horse he proudly said
He shall henceforth be remembered by this name–

Chorus
Beware Chalk Pit, Beware Chalk Pit,
The finest horse in Hampshire,
Beware Chalk Pit.

Now when Chalk he passed away,
Well his master then straightaway
Did on Farley Mount a monument erect,
And if you should pass that way
You can still observe today
This enduring final mark of his respect.

Chorus
Beware Chalk Pit, Beware Chalk Pit,
As you go galloping over the downs

Beware Chalk Pit.
Beware Chalk Pit, Beware Chalk Pit,
The finest horse in Hampshire,
Beware Chalk Pit.

It would seem that into the modern era Hampshire's singers are gaining inspiration and writing songs that continue the proud heritage of folk music in the county.

Making Music in Hampshire

There is a rich legacy of folk music in Hampshire. That many of the songs from the county have survived is due in no small part to the efforts of a Scotsman, Dr George Barnet Gardiner (1852-1910), in collecting them from singers all over the county. He collected over 1,000 songs from ordinary people in their villages and in workhouses in towns across Hampshire. Eighty of these songs were from five women in Axford, near Andover.

Gardiner collected from 1905 until 1909, when he published sixteen songs (*Folk Songs from Hampshire*). He published a further fifty songs in the *Folk Song Society Journal* in the same year. Gardiner usually noted the words and left a musician to note the tune. Henry Hammond (1866-1910) travelled with him in 1906 and went to Winchester, Micheldever, Twyford and Old Alresford, collecting from eight singers. Hammond himself also collected songs in Dorset with his younger brother, Robert Francis Frederick. The entire Gardiner collection is now housed in the Cecil Sharp Memorial Library in London.

Sarah Morgan, a long-established folk singer in her own right who runs the Winchester Community Choir as well as the Andover Afternoon Choir, teamed up with Moira Craig and Carolyn Robson, who runs the Alton Choir, in 2003 to form Craig; Morgan; Robson. As such they have toured England and America performing songs from their respective areas – Scotland, Hampshire and Northumberland – at folk festivals and gigs in towns and villages. In 2006 they were instrumental in celebrating the centenary of Gardiner's collection with a large concert by Winchester and Alton Community Choirs and the Andover Museum Loft Choir. Sarah says:

Gardiner came to the Preston Candover area in 1907. He made several visits and to begin with it was quite difficult because he came at harvest time. Everybody was too busy. But then he also turned his attention to people living in workhouses and so on, who were more of a captive audience. Trying to talk to working, labouring people in the summer months was disastrous because they were working all the time. It was very difficult but he did say that he found the Preston Candover area particularly rich, especially the women's songs in that area. He wrote to Lucy Broadwood, another collector based in Sussex, mentioning in particular that there were women's songs from Axford.

Moses Mills (1826-1916) was one of the male Preston Candover singers, who sang twenty-four songs for Gardiner. These included 'The Furze Field', which is described on the Forest Tracks website as a 'widely-known bit of amourous symbology'. Sarah continues:

Gardiner had been researching Folk Music before he developed an interest in English Folk Songs. He'd been to many European countries, looking at folk music. He was quite an erudite man and when he turned his attention to a folk song there was a huge revival of interest at the time. People like Cecil Sharp and other collectors tended to be generally middle class or upper middle class people who saw folk music and song as an element of Englishness, which was going to die out forever as part of our heritage.

The choice of song to record was very subjective. Sarah continues:

There were certain songs that collectors did not bother about because they did not think they were proper folk songs. You very rarely get the breadth of singers' repertoires, so you get quite a false idea sometimes from the collection. Collectors were working all along the South Coast at about the same time as Gardiner. It was suggested that Gardiner might turn his attention to Hampshire because little collecting had been done in the area. He collected hundreds and hundreds of songs, something between 1,200 and 1,400 songs.

There were some areas that do not feature in the lists of songs collected, and this could be because of his methods of collecting. Sarah explains:

There were certain places where he just did not meet the right person. He tells funny stories in the *Hampshire Chronicle*. For example, on one occasion he went to the house where he had arranged to see a lady about some songs and then when he got there someone completely different answered the door. He said he'd come about old songs, and they said 'We've no money to give for old songs!' Going along to the village pub or the blacksmith and saying 'Do you know anyone who sings any old songs?' was not always productive. If they didn't happen to know the person, then Gardiner wouldn't hear of it. If it was some elderly person who just happened to have been brought up knowing a lot of songs and she was just singing away to herself while at work, who would know?

Frank Purslow (1926-2007) was originally from Birmingham. His interest in folk songs was piqued at a young age as he was encouraged to sing by his family. Later he heard traditional folk singers in London, Suffolk and Norfolk and his enthusiasm grew. He volunteered at the Cecil Sharp Library and it was here that he came across the work of the Hammond brothers and George Gardiner. His offer to index the manuscripts led to much time-consuming work but his articles in the *Folk Music Journal* on both the Gardiner and the Hammond collections did much to publicise these collectors' work, and cement his own reputation as an authority on Gardiner and Hammond and their folk songs.

In the mid-1950s Purslow ran two folk clubs and this led to a collaboration with guitarist John Pearse. Together they recorded *Rap-a-Tat-Tat* in 1959, a selection of the songs collected by George Gardiner, Henry Hammond and Cecil Sharp.

Such was the interest in *Rap-a-Tat-Tat* that Frank was asked to produce a book of songs that people could actually sing from. Thus, in 1965, *Marrowbones* was published. This hugely successful book built on the sometimes fragmentary texts collected by Gardiner and Hammond, as Frank researched other versions of the same songs collected. *Marrowbones* resulted in three further books: *The Wanton Seed*, *The Constant Lovers* and *The Foggy Dew*.

Frank became interested in Morris and danced with several Sides in Abindon and Bampton. He then formed his own band, Morris Eight, which later became the Bampton Barn Dance Band.

Sadly Frank did not live to see the revised version of *Marrowbones*, published a matter of days after his death in 2007. Derek Schofield, the editor of *English Dance and Song* said of *Marrowbones* in Frank's obituary, 'This publication… serves as a reminder of Frank's important contribution to our knowledge and understanding of two invaluable song manuscripts and to their popularisation'. Frank had been about to receive a gold medal for his work from the English Folkdance and Song Society when he died.

In folk circles the name of Bob Askew is increasingly known. He is instrumental in celebrating George Gardiner's Hampshire work and knew Frank Purslow well. He and Paul Marsh, mentioned in Chapter One in connection with the Mummers plays, are behind the Gardiner Appreciation Group (GAG), which seeks to publicise Gardiner's work. Askew was also the catalyst for the work done recently in Hampshire by Craig; Morgan; Robson, who, together with Askew's daughters Hazel and Emily, formed the Axford Five to sing and record some of the eighty songs Gardiner collected from the five ladies in Axford. Sarah says:

Hazel and Emily Askew were already recording and singing a lot of Hampshire folk songs. We suggested to them that they might like to collaborate with us on the project and that neatly added up to five women, which happened to be the right number, so it was all meant to be! We were lucky enough to have the support of Doug Bailey, who runs a recording studio in Wherwell.

The CD, *Axford Five,* was released in 2009.

Gardiner's collections are now being taken into Hampshire's schools so that a new generation will learn about them and the heritage attached. This is an initiative through the English Folkdance and Song Society, called 'Take Six'. This is a searchable database of six of the most prominent of the folk song collectors in the country. Sarah remarks:

I think Gardiner's legacy, like that of other collectors, is that he has given us an absolutely wonderful resource. Martin McCarthy once said, and I may be misquoting him, 'The only thing you can do to damage these songs is not to sing them'. They have so much vitality, you can arrange them, you can sing unaccompanied, you can put them with instruments, and you could probably sing them to a reggae beat! Gardiner has given us a snapshot in time, of what people were singing, which I think is wonderful. Probably fifty or 100 years ago it wouldn't have been like that. He has put down a line in the sand if you like and so whatever we do to change or modify those songs if people want to go back and see what a song was like when it was collected, we can find out what the original was like. It is a marvellous resource. Gardiner's collection is like having a huge book of dressmaking patterns. You can make them up in different fabrics and alter them in different styles and then you can go back to the start and say, 'How did that start off?' Check, and then you can walk in a different direction. It's a treasure house.

Sadly, since this interview Sarah Morgan has passed away. The author sends her condolences to Sarah's family and friends.

The Southampton Philharmonic Society, a Fashionable Choir

Sometimes history creeps up, little by little, success after success, until, all of a sudden, 150 years have gone by and an organisation has a heritage, folklore of its own and a big anniversary to celebrate.

This is the case with the Southampton Philharmonic Society, which celebrates its 150th anniversary in 2010. This is a double celebration as the Choir's celebrated Musical Director, David Gibson, also celebrates twenty years with the Society in the same year.

In 1961 the archives at the Southampton Central Library were searched for all mention of the Choir and the results help to sketch a picture of a lively organisation, growing slowly into the dynamic force it is today.

The Southampton Philharmonic Choir began in an age when ladies were formally requested, in concert programmes, to 'conduce to the convenience and comfort of those sitting immediately behind them by removing their hats during the performance'.

Originally known as the Southampton Sacred Harmonic Society, it was founded in 1860 and was conducted by Mr Alexander Rowland, RSM. *The Southampton Times* gave notice of the first recorded concert, on 5 May 1860 at the Carlton Assembly Rooms. Handel's *Judas Maccabaeus* was performed and Mr Rowland was said to have wielded 'his baton as a magician would his wand' in the 12 May edition. This same concert was repeated in November 1860, when the same newspaper noted that 'there was a decided improvement in solos and chorus.' *The Southampton Times* reported, on 2 February 1861, that the *Messiah* was performed 'before a large and highly respectable audience'.

In 1874 the name was changed to the Southampton Philharmonic Society and by then it had become a fashionable pastime to attend its concerts. In December 1880, for a performance of the *Messiah* at the Hartley Hall, it was reported, in the 18 December edition of *The Southampton Times and Hampshire Express*, that crowds were so great that 'Southampton does not possess a hall large enough for an audience of this magnitude.' Many people were turned away and so missed 'A fine performance.'

Despite this apparent success, in 1883 the Philharmonic Society collapsed owing £57 because, 'Members had not supported the Society as they should have done,' (*The Southampton Times and Hampshire Express*, 24 November 1883). Alexander Rowland immediately set about forming a new Society and this began performing early the following year as the nucleus of what became known as the Test Valley Musical Society. Alexander Rowland retired in 1889, his baton being taken up by the Revd E.M. Moberly.

By 1891 the Southampton Philharmonic Society had its name back and was flourishing. *The Southampton Times and Hampshire Express* hoped, 'its life may be a long and successful one,' in its 11 April edition. However, performing at the ice skating rink at the Victoria Rooms was not always popular, 'Not a few of the audience left before the end, but the coldness of the hall was in a large measure accountable for this,' said the same newspaper on 28 November 1891.

Official patronage by the Mayor and the Southampton City Corporation at a performance of *Elijah* in 1892 was noted as it 'should have the effect of enlisting for it increased support, etc., etc.,' (*The Southampton Times and Hampshire Express,* 14 May 1892). However, by 1893, losses were mounting up and it was decided to perform at the Philharmonic Hall, instead of the chilly skating rink. The first fund raising event after this, a 'Conversazione and Sale of Work', brought in a profit of £21. Happily, by 1895 however, *The Southampton Times and Hampshire Express* reported that 'The Society has fallen on better times' (28 September). It was back in profit. The Society had taken advice from Sir Joseph Barnby (1838-1896), the conductor at the Royal Albert Hall Choral Society.

Over the next years the Society continued to provide Southampton with high quality concerts and these were so popular that the Society was soon calling for a first class concert hall, to hold 2,000 people. This call was made at regular intervals until the Southampton Guildhall was built in 1937.

In 1901, as a mark of respect to the late Queen Victoria, the concert programmes for the performance of *Elijah* were edged in black; the ladies took off their coloured sashes and sang in 'sombre attire.' *The Southampton Times and Hampshire Express* reported (9 Febuary), 'so persistent was the effort to impart a gloomy air to everything, that it almost seemed as if it must have been a pre-arrangement that all the electric bulbs in the hall went out suddenly in the second part of the oratorio – and were not seen again that night.'

The Society's history at the beginning of the twentieth century was a mixture of tried and tested works, performed to large audiences, and new music, such as Parry's *Judith,* which were often poorly supported. Consequently the Society's finances swung between profit and loss each year.

The Society joyfully celebrated the opening of the Southampton Guildhall with a performance of *Elijah,* conducted by D. Cecil Williams, a Southampton musician. Sir Adrian Boult conducted a joint event, the Festival of Britain, with the Choral Union, later to become the Choral Society, in 1951. In 1960 the Society celebrated its centenary with a programme of English music under the direction of Alwyn Surplice, the organist of Winchester Cathedral.

Professor Peter Evans conducted the Southampton Philharmonic Society for twenty-eight years, from 1962 until his retirement in 1990. During this time the repertoire expanded to include all major choral works, particularly by Benjamin Britten, and alliances with the University Choral Society (now known as the SU Phil) and professional orchestras were formed.

The BBC has broadcast the Society on several occasions, the first being a new work by Jonathan Harvey, in 1972, *Cantata VII On Vision*.

David Gibson took over the baton from Professor Evans in 1990. He is a veteran of the Philharmonia, Bournemouth Symphony Orchestra, City of London Sinfonia, London Mozart Players, The Hanover Band and the New London Sinfonia, which he founded in 1987. Having worked with the D'Oyly Carte opera company as Assistant Director of Music, Chorus Master and Guest Conductor, in addition to the Southampton Philharmonic Society, he is currently Musical Director of Basingstoke Choral Society, the Occam Singers, and the Croydon Philharmonic Choir.

The Society celebrated its 150th birthday with an Anniversary Concert in April 2010, at the Southampton Guildhall, performing Mozart's *Requiem* and Muldowney's *The Fall of Jerusalem*.

SEVEN

COUNTRYSIDE AND BUILDINGS

Of all the trees that grow so fair,
  Old England to adorn,
Greater are none beneath the Sun,
  Than Oak, and Ash, and Thorn.

Rudyard Kipling
A Tree Song

Hampshire is a large county and so has a rich mixture of countryside, coastline, hills and towns. It can truly be said that you do not have to go far to find whatever you desire, whether it be peace and quiet in a leafy setting or bustle in an urban one.

This chapter looks at some of the many places of interest in the county and attempts to show what a diverse area Hampshire is.

The Abbey at Netley

Near bustling Southampton is the tiny village of Netley. Here you will find the picturesque ruins of the Abbey of St Mary of Edwardstowe, otherwise known as Netley Abbey. The last Hampshire monastery to be established, it was founded in 1238 as a Cistercian abbey by Peter des Roches (d. 9 June 1238), the Bishop of Winchester under King John and, later, Henry III. He had previously founded Titchfield Abbey in around 1222, which, like Netley, is now an English Heritage site. The Cistercian order was named after the parent house at Citeaux in Burgundy and the Cistercian monks followed a strict regime in the Benedictine tradition, with hard manual labour being at the core of its values. Indeed, as Turner (*A History of Hampshire*, 1963) points out, the monks at Netley derived their income largely from sheep farming and forestry, as they had at Beaulieu, from whose abbey the first monks at Netley had come.

Des Roches died before the abbey was little more than a grand design, but under the patronage of Henry III it grew and flourished. Never an establishment destined for greatness, it had a reputation for coming to the assistance of travellers, particularly those from the sea due to its location just yards from Southampton Water.

Upon Henry VIII's Dissolution of the Monasteries it became a private house in 1536, occupied by Sir William Paulet, his Lord Treasurer. The new owner destroyed much of the original abbey to make a grand palace for himself.

William Seymour, the 2nd Duke of Somerset and 2nd Earl of Hertford, continued this destruction in the seventeenth century by selling off much of the fabric of the abbey to Southampton builder Walter Taylor, who wanted to use the materials for other building projects, most notably a house in Newport on the Isle of Wight. This action has created a legend that has been passed down to us through the centuries.

Taylor was concerned about a vivid nightmare he had had, during which he dreamt that he was killed by a falling keystone from one of the abbey windows. So concerned was he about this dream that he confided it to a friend, Isaac Watts, the father of the celebrated hymn writer Dr Isaac Watts (1674-1748), and asked for advice. He was counselled to have no further business with the demolition, as the dream was thought to be a sign of God's displeasure at the desecration of the site. However, greed got the better of Mr Taylor and, after much deliberation, he decided to carry on with dismantling the abbey building. Disaster soon struck when the keystone of a window arch fell from its place and hit Taylor's head, fracturing his skull. He died soon after. As a consequence, no further demolition work was undertaken at the site, Taylor's dramatic death being deemed an act of God. The result of this decision is the dramatic ruin that is Netley today.

The abbey has been a popular place to visit over the centuries since this incident. Jane Austen visited with her niece, Fanny Knight, and other family members and it is possible that this visit was the inspiration for her gothic novel *Northanger Abbey*. The finding of female human remains at the abbey inspired the Revd Richard Barham (1788-1845) who, writing as Thomas Ingoldsby, was the author of *The Ingoldsby Legends*, a collection of grotesque tales which became very popular at the time. The remains he said, perhaps with tongue firmly in cheek, were those of a nun who had been walled up inside the abbey. The story stuck and added to the folklore surrounding the site. As indeed did Richard Warner's *Netley Abbey: A Gothic Story* from 1795, which asserted that the abbey contained 'a mystery of a horrible nature…' (Southern Life)

The story of 'Blind Peter' also adds richness to the abbey's store of legends. The monk is said to have been the keeper of the abbey's treasure during the Dissolution of the Monasteries and hid the treasure to avoid it being seized by Henry VIII's men. The treasure was never found. A treasure seeker, one Mr Slown, is said to have tried to find the secret stash. Soon after he began to dig in a likely spot, something frightened him so much that he ran away from the site screaming and collapsed soon after, suffering a heart attack. His last words, according to Southern Life, were 'For God's sake, block it up'. Blind Peter is said to prowl the abbey ruins on Halloween night, still doing his duty and guarding the treasure.

The abbey ruins, being picturesque, have inspired many an artist. Turner (1775-1851) painted 'The Ruins of Netley Abbey, with Several Figures', in 1795. Francis Towne (1740-1816) produced 'Netley Abbey' in about 1809 and John Constable (1776-1837), who visited the abbey while on his honeymoon, created his own atmospheric 'Netley Abbey' in 1833.

Today the abbey is still open to the public, and family picnics and open-air theatre are the order of the day, although church services are also held there from time to time.

King John's House, Romsey

Romsey once focused on woollen cloth finishing, fulling and dyeing, and became a thriving and prosperous town. It was ideally situated between the sheep-shearing areas around Salisbury and the wool port of Southampton. It also benefited from its watermills and the local alkaline water was ideal for the industry. Walking around the town today there is evidence of this history still to be seen, for example at Sadler's Mill, a Victorian building constructed on the site of the earlier mill.

Romsey also owed much to the high ranking nuns at the convent of Romsey Abbey, who were able to use their influence to gain privileges from Court, not just for their Benedictine abbey but for the town as well (see Chapter Three on

St Ethelflaeda). The nuns educated many of the nobility's daughters and those of well-to-do local families.

In 1927 the little house off Church Street became the object of much interest. Miss Mabel Moody owned it, and her family also owned the nearby Victorian brick house, which now houses the Moody Museum. Miss Moody was curious about the building's history and so she asked an antiquarian living locally to investigate the house. By looking at the property deeds and the space in the roof, he judged that the house was very old indeed. The architect to Winchester Cathedral, T.D. Atkinson, gave advice and this led to exciting discoveries within the house. It was revealed that medieval features had survived behind partitions and hundreds of years of alterations.

In the ensuing excitement, the house was immediately hailed as being King John's long sought-after hunting lodge. It was known that John (1166-1216) had built a hunting lodge in Romsey sometime around 1206. John's son, Henry III (1207-1272), granted it to the Abbess of Romsey Abbey and the record of this transaction survives today.

Later analysis found that this assumption was incorrect by about forty years, but by then Romsey had found King John's House and the legend lives on today. In 1995 the central tie beam in the roof was analysed and dated as having been felled in 1256. No one knows the origins of the house or its purpose. Now it is a Grade I listed building and the pride of the town, although run by an independent trust.

The house shows signs of its former glory. It is thought that it once played an eminent or official role in the town, given its proximity to the abbey. It must be remembered that Church Street, which now stands between it and the abbey, was a much later addition to Romsey. An imposing outer stone stairway led up to the upper floor from the front of the house. The site on which the building sits, which originally extended up Church Street for some distance, invites supposition about the other buildings there. It would have been typical to have kitchens and a great hall, and stables must have also been included. The whole leads to the impression of an impressive property. More so because it was made of stone, like the abbey, which was a rare commodity in the town in the thirteenth century. Most people would have lived in small wooden-framed houses.

Inside the building today, fourteenth-century graffiti can be seen scratched into the stone. It is supposed that members of Edward I's (1239-1307) retinue made the images when he came to the town in 1306.

Over time the site was sold to successive owners. Some of the site was sold off and sub-let. There is evidence of a brazier having worked in the house, which archaeological research has confirmed on the ground floor. There is also part of an animal bone floor dating from before the eighteenth century, each bone laid carefully end-to-end, and it is thought that this would have offered a non-slip surface in an industrial area. In the seventeenth century craftspeople were drawn to the area, which has an abundant water supply.

A later cottage, known as Tudor Cottage, abuts King John's House. Its picturesque, distorted timber framing, bulging walls held in by braces, gives a chocolate box quality to the house which now stands in a period garden, growing flowers that would have been known to gardeners prior to 1714. This date relates to the now demolished row of 'Queen Anne Cottages' which once also stood on the site.

The Old Church, Stockbridge

Old St Peter's Church in Stockbridge is one that could easily be overlooked. A fraction of its original size, it stands on a prominent site just along from the roundabout at the east end of the High Street. From the outside it resembles a small village hall set amongst a pretty churchyard. It is the oldest surviving building in the town.

Parts of the church date back to an early West Saxon chapel on the site and the church was mentioned in the Domesday Book. The majority of what is left now dates back to the twelfth century.

Originally the building could seat 250 people and was a large, imposing structure. It was originally attached to the Parish of King's Somborne as a field chapel, but Stockbridge became a parish in its own right in 1842. It was partially demolished in 1870 because parishioners considered the building unfit for worship due to the damp and cold inside. Thus the new St Peter's Parish Church was built in the High Street. All that was left standing of the Old Church was the chancel, which was used as the town's mortuary for a while.

The Old Church was subject to rising damp and in the early 1990s steps had to be taken to restore the church if it was to be kept in use. An earlier renovation in 1963 had helped keep the building going, but thirty years later it needed major work. At the time the churchyard had also been allowed to fall into disrepair and was overgrown to boot. Local volunteers did much of the work. They removed the major cause of the damp, the cement liner in the inner wall, and cleared 130 tonnes of earth from the outer walls. £10,000 was spent on professional restoration of the Old Church's walls and a new pathway, named the Avenue Path, was built through the churchyard. On 2 June 1991 the Bishop of Southampton rededicated the chancel. It has been in regular use since.

Inside the Old Church there is a surprising amount of interest for such a small building, seating no more than twenty-five worshippers. On the south wall a medieval door is on display. It is made of oak and is studded, with strap hinges and a ring-shaped handle. It has been carbon dated to 1354 and it took nine years, and over 600 hours, to renovate. It is thought to be an original door to the building.

The murals on the east and north walls are of particular note. They were drawn in red and ochre paint and are royal cyphers. The date, 1588, tells us that the 'ER' referred to on them is Queen Elizabeth I.

The altar is a seventeenth-century communion table and behind this are two rare fourteenth-century windows. They are made of white glass and are decorated using the grisaille technique, which gives an illusion of light and shade; each tiny leaded diamond contains an image of foliage.

One of the gravestones out in the churchyard is worthy of mention. It is that of John Buckett, the landlord of the Kings Head Inn. He was the bailiff and the election manager for the town, a rotten borough, which returned two Members of Parliament for just 500 local residents. Queen Elizabeth I had granted this right, which remained in force until the passing of the Reform Bill in 1832, which disenfranchised the town and expanded the electorate. The Stockbridge Town Hall was given as an election bribe in 1790. John Buckett's epitaph reads:

In
Memory of
John Buckett
many years Landlord of the Kings Head Inn
in this Borough
who departed this life November 25th, 1802
Aged 67 years.

And is alas! poor BUCKET gone?
Farewell convivial honest JOHN.
Oft at the well by fatal stroke
Buckets like Pitchers must be broke
In this same motley shifting scene
How various have thy fortunes been!
Now lifted high, now sinking low.
Today thy brim would overflow.
Thy bounty then would All supply
To fill & drink & leave thee dry.

Tomorrow sunk as in a well
Content unseen with Truth do dwell:
But high, or low, or wet, or dry.
No rotten stave could malice spy
Then rise immortal Bucket rise
And claim thy station in the skies.
Twixt Amphora & Pisces Shine
Still guarding Stockbridge with thy Sign

Stockbridge today is a bustling little town and is proud of its Old Church.

Eling Tide Mill

Most people drive past the brown tourist sign for the Eling Tide Mill without stopping. If they paused in tiny Eling instead of charging off to enjoy the undoubted delights of the nearby New Forest, they could explore the last working tide mill in Britain and marvel at a quieter age.

The moss-dotted mill building blends intimately with its surroundings, the old boat-building village of Eling with its picturesque water and wildlife. John Hurst, the cheery former mill assistant/curator, has a way with fascinating facts. A chat with him unleashes a torrent of highly interesting mill information:

> Eling Tide Mill has been on this site for at least 900 years. It was here 'prior to the Roman Conquest' and those words were used in the Domesday Book. However, we don't know how much prior. It could have been a week; it could have been 100 years. There was a double mill from 1066 onwards, but most of the main mill building was completely rebuilt in the eighteenth century, so it is over two centuries old now. All the machinery would have been wooden prior to the nineteenth century because cast iron didn't exist.
>
> A double mill means two mills and two sets of machinery. It did fox the local historical society because they knew there were two mills at Eling. They assumed that it was two separate mills. Later they found documents, which repeatedly referred to this as the 'double mill'. It makes sense that they were both here, rather than one here and one somewhere else. That does imply that there has been a mill here for some time prior to that, because you tend to start off with these things fairly small and build up over time. The fact that by 1066 you had two watermills, two sets of machinery and four sets of stones running means it had been here for a while.

Outside the Tide Mill is a picturesque causeway between the huge millpond
and Bartley Water, filled with small bobbing boats. The millpond is a bird-
watcher's delight, as it is alive with scenic greenery and waterfowl. The guardian
of the causeway is the keeper of the Eling Toll Bridge. This is reputed to be
the last medieval toll bridge in Hampshire. Unless you are going to visit the
nearby St Mary's Church or cemetery, all motor vehicles have to pay a toll to
cross Bartley Water at this point. This has been the tradition for nearly 600 years
according to the earliest lease in existence, dated 1418. In 1800 the toll was 6d
for a four-wheeled carriage. In 2009 it was £1, which is now collected by the
New Forest District Council rather than the mill itself. John explains:

> The toll bridge is also our dam. We use it to trap water on that side of the mill and
> initially that was built as a causeway by the Romans in the fourth century AD.
> The causeway has been there in one form or another for the last 1,600 years. At
> one point it was the only route that joined the town of Totton to Eling.
>
> There is evidence to suggest that a number of tide mills were built in
> Western Europe. The oldest tide mill on record is actually in Northern Ireland.

Indeed, the earliest excavated mill found so far is Nendrum Monastery Mill in
Strangford Lough, which dates from AD 787. John continues:

> From 1382 to 1975 the mill was owned by Winchester College. William of
> Wickham, the Bishop of Winchester, left it to them as part of their endow-
> ment. He was born into relative poverty and was educated by the parish. By
> the time of his death he was incredibly wealthy. He knew he owed everything
> to his education. He left his holding in the manor of Eling to Winchester
> College to generate income.
>
> All mills were run as businesses. They belonged to the lord of the manor
> in medieval Britain. The lord of the manor wanted as much money and as
> much work out of the mill as possible. The miller would lease the mill but a
> lord who was an astute businessman would not just say, 'Thanks and anything
> you make is all yours'. He would say, 'Anything up to this point is yours, but
> anything you make after that comes back to me'. You had to keep the lord of
> the manor happy. He really was the absolute power.

The Eling Tide Mill's fortunes waned over time:

> All proper flour milling started to dry up by the 1900s. By 1920 the flour
> had ceased and the mill was concentrating on animal feed. This continued

until 1946 when all milling at Eling stopped completely. The last miller, Tom Mackerel, continued collecting the tolls from anyone crossing the bridge until he retired in 1970.

The mill fell into disrepair. New Forest District Council bought the site in 1975 and started restoring it. By 1978 the Eling Tide Mill Trust had been formed. Its purpose was to preserve it as a working tide mill, for the education and benefit of future generations. Lack of money meant the second water mill was never restored.

'It took five years of restoration just to get it to the state it is at present,' says John. 'Fundraising went on and a folk group called "The Flower of the Forest" sold their LP to raise funds. Mill enthusiasts and local volunteers did a lot of the work'.

Tide mills work by storing tidal water in the millpond and then releasing it through sluice gates to push the waterwheel around. This rotates the grinding stones to grind the wheat into flour.

'The working stones are made of French Burr,' says John. 'They were quarried about thirty miles south-east of Paris. They are the hardest you can get anywhere'.

The Tide Mill, with atmospheric low beams, displays its workings, history and heritage over three floors. A pleasant woody, salty tang to the air permeates the building. The indoor water wheel can be viewed rotating on milling days. Milling is dependent on the tide times but over six tonnes of flour is produced each year, which is on sale to regular customers and through the mill shop.

The Eling Tide Mill is undoubtedly part of the rich heritage of Hampshire.

The Dolphin Hotel, Southampton

The Dolphin Hotel in Southampton has had a long and prestigious history. Parts of the building date from 1250 and there is evidence of Elizabethan modifications. The exterior is gorgeously Georgian, with massive bow windows, which are said to be the biggest in England.

The hotel was formerly a post house. A daily postal coach ran between the hotel and the Swan with Two Necks in Lad Lane, London. The British Postal Museum has a beautifully printed turn of the nineteenth-century notice, which lists all the post coaches, their leaving times and destinations from the Swan with Two Necks. The coach to Southampton left this very busy postal coach hub every morning at 10 a.m. sharp.

Over the years the Dolphin Hotel has attracted many distinguished visitors. Queen Victoria stabled her horses here when she visited Osborne House, her home on the Isle of Wight. Jane Austen danced in the bow-fronted ballroom on her eighteenth birthday on 16 December 1793. William Thackery, Edward Gibbons and Orson Welles, amongst many others, all stayed at the hotel.

The Dolphin prided itself on its wine list, as that for 1936 shows, when Trust Houses Ltd owned the hotel. The helpful list offers advice and insight into the various wines on offer. It tells us, for example, that Sauternes are 'rich, luscious and sweet wines of unsurpassed excellence, much appreciated by Ladies'. A bottle of Château d'Arche-Lafaurie, 1928, could be had for 7s 6d.

The hotel is said to be haunted by several ghosts. Apart from that of a cat, Molly the cleaner is the apparition seen most often. She walks below floor level and so her legs do not appear. Whenever she is in evidence there is a marked drop in temperature. In 2003 the BBC set up webcams in the hotel and the one in the cellar recorded three strange lights, or 'orbs', which are supposedly balls of ghostly activity.

In November 2008 the Grade II listed hotel fell victim to the worst global recession in living memory and called in the administrators. A deal to build apartments in the hotel car park had fallen through and left the hotel in trouble, owing £4.7 million and in need of a buyer. In August 2009, after being boarded up since May, it was reported that the hotel had been bought for an undisclosed sum. It became part of the Duke of Buccleuch's huge portfolio and has been restored to its former glory. It is now named The Mercure Southampton Centre, Dolphin Hotel.

The Red Lion, Southampton

Just down the road from the historic Dolphin Hotel is the Red Lion public house. This majestic Tudor building has a cellar dating to 1148; the exterior has Tudor beams and the back of the building dates from the 1950s.

It is best known for the 1415 trial of three noblemen: Richard, Earl of Cambridge; Lord Scrope of Masham; and Sir Thomas Grey of Heton who plotted to kill Henry V (1386-1422) in what is known as the Southampton Plot. They were accused of plotting to assassinate the king at the Dolphin Hotel and replace him with Edmund Mortimer, 5th Earl of March. They were discovered when March was informed of the plot and told the king. The three ringleaders were tried in the half-timbered 'trial room' in the Red Lion. They were found guilty and executed at the city's Bargate. The two nobles were beheaded and Sir Thomas, a commoner, was hanged, drawn and quartered.

The Red Lion has its share of ghosts, including a procession of mournful people leading from the pub to the Bargate, just a few hundred yards down the road. The pub's landlord has been quoted as saying that there are about twenty-one ghosts, but there seems little to support this figure. Various paranormal investigators have visited the pub over time and have found evidence of ghostly activity. The most common is the sight of a lady aged about sixty who drifts through the bar area. It is thought that she is a former barmaid.

Follies

Follies are to be found dotted all over the country, a monument to the eccentricity of the British. What is it about these little, and not so little, buildings, which are normally found at the tops of hills, that draws us to them?

Hampshire's follies number in double figures and range from towers to pyramids and all shapes in between. The rich built them; they had the money to spare for such extravagance, as the buildings usually had no purpose but to be admired. As such they were a status symbol, similar to the sports car of the twenty-first century.

Heaven's Gate, the 60ft-high triple-arched folly built in 1731 as an eye-catcher, sits on the top of Sidown Hill, near Andover, in north Hampshire. An eye-catcher it certainly is, as its size and location are certain to get the building noticed. Made of gently mouldering bricks, it has a pediment over the large central arch, and is adorned with three ornamental urns, one on each side and one atop the pediment. A giant curiosity indeed, it is not open to the public and permission to visit it has to be granted by the owner of the Highclere estate, the Earl of Carnarvon.

Just north of Havant is Leigh Park. Now an overflow town for Portsmouth and Havant, the residential properties stand on part of the site of the Leigh Park estate, once owned by Orientalist and traveller Sir George Thomas Stanton (26 May 1781-10 August 1859). Portsmouth City Council bought the land in 1944 to house bombed-out residents, but 1,000 acres were kept as a public park. Here you can find the delightful, if slightly tatty, Beacon folly, built by Stanton on a hill in the park. It is a circular stone building resembling a Greek temple, with Doric columns supporting a domed roof. Steps lead up to its raised floor and the whole is reminiscent of a mini seafront bandstand.

Peterson's Tower at Sway in the New Forest is believed to be oldest building made of concrete in Britain. With walls 2ft thick and nearly 400 steps, the tower was designed and built by Andrew Thomas Turton Peterson (1813-1906), a judge who was allegedly inspired to create the design by Sir Christopher Wren during a séance – at that time, Wren had been dead for more than 150 years. It was completed in 1885 after five years of construction by local, unskilled labourers.

At 60m, or 218ft, it was the tallest un-reinforced concrete building in the world, with thirteen floors. Peterson built the tower as a philanthropic gesture, to bring work to the area at a time of hardship, and also to demonstrate the properties of Portland cement. It was reputed to have cost £30,000 to build. The stone used to build the structure is reported to have come from Milford-on-Sea's beach. Peterson originally planned to have a light on the top and clock faces on the sides, but the light was rejected as it could be mistaken for a lighthouse and the clocks were similarly resisted.

When Peterson died at the age of ninety-three, his ashes were buried at the base of the tower but were later interred in St Luke's Church in the mid-1950s. Now the property is a Grade II listed monument and is in private ownership.

Hursley

The village of Hursley, near Winchester, has a long and distinguished history, much of it bound to nearby Hursley Park.

Merdon Castle, originally known as Gains Castle, was one of six castles built by Henry de Blois, the Bishop of Winchester (1100-1171). Three of these, Merdon, Wolvesey and Waltham, were in Hampshire. Merdon, built around 1138, consisted of a motte, an artificially constructed mound, with a keep, the actual castle building, which sat atop it. The bailey, the outer defensive court-yard, surrounded the motte. The castle's church was built in the outer bailey.

It was erected on the site of an earlier Iron Age hill fort on a south-facing chalk point. When this was built its earthwork defences consisted merely of a ditch and a bank. The site had been a Saxon encampment and was later taken over by the Danes. What made Henry de Blois interested in this site particularly is not known.

Once built, the fortified Merdon – half castle, half palace – was useful to the Bishop, who was King Stephen's brother. He supported Stephen when besieg-ing their cousin, Empress Matilda (1101-1169), during the bitter struggle for the Crown following the death of Henry Longshanks, Henry I (1069-1135). Empress Matilda had been named as the rightful successor, an arrangement that all of Henry's nobles had agreed to, but she was in France when her father died, making it difficult to claim her inheritance immediately. In her absence, Stephen stepped in and usurped her, sparking the long civil war that ensued and which Stephen ultimately won.

Henry II (1154-1189) came to the throne in 1154. He was Matilda's son and no friend of one who had supported a usurper instead of the rightful heir. He seized all of the castles Henry de Blois had built. Merdon was supposed to be destroyed, but in fact it remained in use for the Bishops of Winchester until the middle of the fifteenth century. Lay brothers still utilised the decaying remains into the seventeenth century. The tower gatehouse is now a romantic ruin but the upper floor joists are visible. The castle is overgrown but the earthworks can still be seen.

It is said that the old well in the castle grounds was once used by Cromwell to hide a box of treasure in its waters. The treasure can only be raised in complete silence and, as such quiet is difficult to come by, it may still be there. The well water is said to be so deep as to be bottomless. Another story says that if a duck is dropped into the well it will emerge via an underground stream, minus its feathers, in the Pole Hole, a small pond in the village of Otterbourne nearby. There are rumours that this hypothesis was tested during the Second World War by bored workers at Hursley House, but whether this is true or not is open to conjecture.

The castle ruins sit in one corner of the Hursley estate, owned since 1958 by the computing giant IBM. This estate, which is now no longer open to the public, has a long history.

A hunting lodge was built on the site followed by the Great Lodge, which was the home of Oliver Cromwell's son, Richard, after his marriage to Dorothy Major, the owner's daughter. Richard, unfortunately nicknamed 'Tumbledown Dick', was rejected as his father's successor as Lord Protector of the Commonwealth by both the Army, because he was not a general like his father, and by Parliament, which refused to finance him. He lived at Hursley until the Restoration of the Monarchy made life too uncomfortable and he fled abroad. He returned to Hursley for the final eight years of his life and when he died in 1712, aged eighty-six, he was buried at the local church. When the Great Lodge was torn down the Great Seal of the Commonwealth was found hidden inside. This was mentioned in the 'Acts and Ordinances of the Interregnum 1642-60' in Article XI, and the seal was used in an age when few people could write as a visible and easily understood method to authenticate official documents. The present-day queen uses the Great Seal of the Realm today.

William Heathcote later built a mansion on the site and this forms part of the present house. His son, Thomas, rebuilt the church in 1752. John Keble (1792-1866), the founder of the High Anglican Movement, took over as rector in 1836. Keble had a distinguished career as a priest, an Oxford University tutor, where he was Professor of Poetry for ten years from 1831 to 1841, and published author. He is credited with being the 'Renewer of the Church' on the justus. anglican website. His book of poems, *The Christian Year*, spread his theological views and part of the proceeds helped to rebuild the church. Some of his poems are still in use as hymns today.

In the early part of the twentieth century the entertainment annex built by George Cooper at the now enlarged house kept the village amused with cinema, stage and dressing room. Functions were held there too and it operated, as Anthony Brode points out, very much as a village hall.

This was not to last though. During the First World War the house was used as a military hospital, whilst in the Second World War the Minister of Aircraft Production, Lord Beaverbrook, requisitioned it for Vickers-Armstrong to test Spitfire engines and improvements.

Archaeologists who have investigated the site have found evidence of the British and American soldiers who were stationed at Hursley Park in both wars.

Broadlands House

Broadlands House, the home of Lord Romsey, the grandson of Earl Mountbatten of Burma, and his family is an elegant mansion standing on the River Test at Romsey.

The land originally belonged to the Benedictine nunnery in the town and had been used as farmland since before the Norman Conquest. Following the Dissolution of the Monasteries it was sold to Sir Francis Fleming in 1547, who built a large house on the site. The house descended through the female line and the St Barbe family lived there for over a century. In 1607, the year that Romsey was made a borough, King James I stayed at Broadlands.

Broadlands passed to Humphrey Sydenham in 1723. He had lost his fortune in the collapse of the South Sea Bubble of 1720, when people all over the land who had invested in the South Sea Co., which was supposed to be underwriting the British National Debt, lost their savings overnight. Sydenham sold Broadlands to Henry Temple, the Irish 1st Viscount Palmerston, in 1736. It was Temple who began the process that was to have such a profound effect on Broadlands. He asked William Kent to 'deformalise' the grounds and open up the area from the house to the river.

The 2nd Viscount later continued this by booking the services of that most famous architect and landscape gardener Lancelot 'Capability' Brown. Brown soon saw the 'capabilities' of the Tudor and Jacobean house and set about transforming it. He continued Kent's work and then expanded upon it until the property had been landscaped out of all recognition. Between 1767 and 1780 he wove a spell that culminated with the production of the masterpiece we are familiar with today. The house was squared off in a Palladian style far removed from the old St Barbe Manor House, and Brown's son-in-law, the celebrated Henry Holland, designed the east front portico and the domed hall. The foremost plasterer of the day, Joseph Rose, designed and laid the decorative plasterwork in the main rooms.

The 3rd Viscount Palmerston, the great statesman, left the estate to his stepson, William Cowper. Eventually it passed to Edwina Ashley. She married Lord Louis Mountbatten, Earl Mountbatten of Burma, the last Viceroy of India and the house passed into the hands of the Mountbatten family. On Mountbatten's death in an IRA bomb attack in 1979, the estate passed to his grandson, Lord Romsey, who inherited the title Lord Brabourne on his father's death in 2005. The stables now house an exhibition on the life of Lord Louis Mountbatten.

Without doubt, Broadlands holds a place in the hearts of the local people of Romsey.

St Catherine's Hill

Less than a mile outside Winchester is the majestic St Catherine's Hill, once used as a point of navigation by Solent shipping. It rises on land owned by Winchester College and to reach the summit it is necessary to follow the path, which contours around the hill, and then to tread each of the 111 steps up the steep incline to the top, which is covered by beech trees.

On the way the walker sees firsthand evidence of thousands of years of history that the hill represents. The ramparts of an Iron Age fort, built in 150 BC, are still visible on the hillside and the path goes along the deep, hand-built Iron Age defensive ditch which is still impressive in the third millennium after it was constructed. On the edge of the beech trees are the remains of a Norman church, just visible, buried in the ground.

From the top of the hill the views are spectacular and it is possible to pick out major Winchester landmarks, such as the cathedral, St John's Hospital, Winchester College and St Giles Hill, the site of the huge medieval fair which outshone even Weyhill (see Chapter One). In the fields between the hill and the city, looking down on the terrain, it is possible to see the Dongas, the tracks through the land worn over centuries of use by wagons and carts.

On the top of St Catherine's Hill is the 90ft by 86ft Mizmaze. This is a series of nine rounded-edge squares, described by Wendy Boase as 'being cut by someone who did not understand the design'. The squares are cut into the chalk with raised grass banks, inches high, either side of the chalk path.

It has been conjectured that the Mizmaze has been on St Catherine's Hill since medieval times and was re-cut at intervals. However, the information board at the site states that it is unlikely to have been cut prior to the seventeenth century. One story as to its origin states that a pupil at Winchester College, who was under punishment for a misdeed and was detained at the school over a holiday, cut it to keep himself busy and pass the time. While he was doing this, he supposedly composed the school song, 'Dulce Domun'. It is also said that the Church adopted the Mizmaze at one point and monks had to crawl along it on their knees as a form of penitence. The various false paths and dead ends were regarded as metaphors for the sins that had to be overcome on life's journey.

There is one other mizmaze in Hampshire, in Breamore, which is a scheduled ancient monument and as such can be visited and marvelled at, but not followed. The St Catherine's Hill Mizmaze is open to the public and, because it has been designed for followers to walk on the chalk rather than the grass banks, as at Breamore, it is more deeply cut into the landscape as people walk upon it.

St Catherine's Hill has earned its place in Hampshire's folklore and is a joy to visit.

The Wallops

The villages of the Wallops, on the Romsey to Tidworth road, may sound strangely named to twenty-first-century ears but they have a long heritage. 'Waella' in Old English means 'stream' and 'hop' means 'valley'. The villages are therefore named after the stream in the valley, in this case the Wallop Brook, which winds its way towards the River Test.

Over Wallop was the property of Countess Gytha (Githa), who became the second wife of Earl Godwin (Goodwin) of Wessex (1001-1053) in about 1019. She was the mother of King Harold, who died at the Battle of Hastings, and she was also the sister-in-law of Canute. Her daughter inherited the Over Wallop estate. Her name was Godgifu, Old English for 'God's gift', but she is better known now as Godiva (1040-1080).

Godiva was married to Leofric of Mercia (d. 1057). It was his oppressive taxation that Godiva was trying to save the people of Coventry from when she agreed to ride naked through the city's streets. Her husband had challenged her to do so and, if she did, he agreed that he would ease the taxes. Of course, we all know the legend. She took her courage in her hands and only one person peeped at her, Peeping Tom, who was then struck blind.

Over Wallop was described in the Domesday Book as being the 'other Wallop', smaller than Nether Wallop.

Anthony Brode notes the vast, destructive fires which have been a feature of village life in Nether Wallop for centuries. One was in 1672, when he noted 'the Great Fire caused losses of £8,000 and upwards'. Two centuries later the Manor Farm was ablaze and a reward of a pint of beer was offered to all who would turn out to help fight the flames; this produced 210 volunteers. In 1928 the local cricket team and their opponents were called upon to help douse a blaze in thatched cottages in the village, which they stopped spreading to other buildings.

The village, which for many years was famous for its cricket bats made out of local willow and was beloved by the most famous cricketer of all, W.G. Grace, also boasts a curious pyramid-shaped memorial in the churchyard. This is to Dr Francis Douce, who left £1,000 to be used to educate local boys and girls. However, he counselled that they 'must not go too far lest it makes them saucy...' Any child found climbing on his memorial was to be deprived of their education, which was an effective way of keeping the pyramid in good condition.

Middle Wallop was the site of a Second World War airfield and is now the home of the School of Army Aviation.

The Southampton Docks

Historically, Southampton has long been a busy and important port, bigger than neighbouring Portsmouth. King John (1166-1216) received payment from the town's Burgesses for both the town of Southampton and the port of Portsmouth. In 1324 it was established that the port extended from Langstone in the east to Hurst in the west, and so included Southampton Water and part of the Solent.

Admiralty jurisdiction was granted to the Burgesses by Henry VI, which meant that they could hold an Admiralty Court, claim wrecks, regulate fishing and erect a prison. There was also an Admiralty gallows for the execution of criminals. The Mayor of Southampton was Admiral of the Port and had an oar carried ceremonially before him.

Southampton was a busy trading port until the middle of the fifteenth century. Links with Normandy tailed off eventually though and with it much of the cross-Channel trade. It was partially replaced by traders arriving from Bordeaux, Gascony and later from Venice, as traders came to buy the wool produced at the monasteries in Netley, Titchfield and Beaulieu. The port brought much prosperity to the Crown, and as Shore (*History of Hampshire*, 1892) notes, the port's customs fees were used as security for loans.

In the sixteenth and seventeenth centuries maritime trade dropped and dwindled to a point where it became almost non-existent. New and emerging trade routes to India were partially to blame for this decline. It was not until the nineteenth century that Southampton began to thrive as a port once again.

20,000 people turned out to witness the laying of the foundation stone of the new Southampton Docks on 12 October 1838. The Mayor and City Corporation led a procession through the town to the 216 acres of mudflats next to Town Quay, which had been acquired for £5,000 a short time earlier.

The Southampton Docks were the brainchild of businessmen who had the vision to form the Southampton Dock Co., overcome local opposition and get the massive project underway. The *Daily Echo*, in its pictorial souvenir on the history of the docks, published in 2005, reported that on the day the foundation stone was laid the shops closed, ships in the harbour were dressed with colourful pennants, which waved in the breeze and there was a general atmosphere of carnival. That this was also the date of the new Queen Victoria's coronation added to the general gaiety of the day.

The arrival of a rail link from London and the decision by the Royal Mail Steam Packet Co. to base themselves at Southampton Docks did much to boost the new venture. Ships now cruised to the Caribbean and the Americas from Southampton, their passengers able to travel from London to Southampton by train with ease.

During the Crimean War (1853-1856) the port was used for the deployment of troops, the beginning of a trend that stretched for over a century with many troopships leaving for different parts of the British Empire and various conflicts. In 1859 the port had to be enlarged to accommodate all the traffic flowing though it. Later, in the First World War, Southampton was the major military port when all the expeditionary forces and their stores embarked from the docks.

The Southampton Dock Co. was taken over by the London and South Western Railway in 1892. By 1893 the New York mail service had been transferred from Liverpool to Southampton. When the *New York* sailed into Southampton for the first time on 1 November 1893, it opened a significant chapter in Southampton's maritime history. The Empress Docks, whose facilities were more modern than those in Liverpool, were soon thronged with people and the port went from strength to strength.

In 1907 the White Star Line came to Southampton. It was this shipping company which owned the unfortunate *Titanic*, and many of the crew were from the town.

Vast quantities of imports came into Southampton as well as its cruise passengers. Mistletoe from France came in each festive season. In the 1930s fresh, dried and canned fruit arrived in enormous quantities. Nowadays the docks are an important receiver of the country's car shipments.

During the Second World War over 1,000 men were employed at the docks in building part of the Mulberry harbour used on D-Day. All records were smashed during the war years, with more men and equipment going through the port than at any time before.

In 1982 the ships leaving for the Falklands conflict were not just naval vessels from Portsmouth and Plymouth. They were also commercial ships, such as the liner *Canberra*, which had to be stripped and made ready for war service. Southampton Docks staff worked all hours to get the ships ready and soon residents were waving off the *Canberra* and the *Queen Elizabeth II*. Thousands lining every vantage point greeted their return and a flotilla of small boats escorted them into their berths at the docks.

Since then the *Queen Mary II* has arrived and the *Queen Elizabeth II* has left Southampton for the final time, amidst much fanfare and no little sadness. The Southampton Docks thrive, with cruise liners and cargo vessels filling the berths. Long may this success last.

Winchester Theatre Royal

Phil Yates, the Winchester Theatre Royal historian and a man who admits he has been fascinated by the theatre since he was a teenager, is a fountain of knowledge about the building.

The Simpkins brothers, John and James, bought the Market Hotel in 1912. This dated back to 1850, when it was a hotel built specifically to accommodate the large numbers of people who travelled on foot from surrounding villages to bring their animals to the cattle market nearby. Next door to the hotel site and the cattle market was the Corn Exchange, which opened in 1838. As Mr Yates points out, 'Farmers could not come in to Winchester and do all their business in one day and so they decided to build a hotel close by'. Nowadays the new Discovery Centre, formerly the city library, is on the site of the Corn Exchange, which closed in 1909. The cattle market closed its gates for the final time in 1937, bringing to a close a historic chapter in Winchester's farming history.

John and James Simpkins were the sons of a skilled carpenter who made furniture, coffins and similar items. Mr Yates says:

He had his own shop at 16 Jewry Street, which is a pizza restaurant today. I don't know why his sons decided to go into the entertainment business but they started off at St James House in 1910. That is where the first silent films were shown and, of course, there were variety acts between the films. They had that for about four years but they wanted a place of their own.

The brothers bought the hotel and sought planning permission in November 1913 to extend the ground floor out through the yard to build an auditorium and a stage. This was granted the following day.

The old Corn Exchange became the Regent Theatre in 1915, and the Regent Cinema in 1917 when the Simpkins brothers took it over. They thus dominated entertainment in the city at the time. The Regent closed in 1935 and was acquired by the City Council.

In the early days many future stars of stage and screen appeared at the Theatre Royal, including the future Gracie Fields, then known as Gracie Stansfield.

In the 1920s the popularity of variety theatre waned and the brothers converted the theatre to be used as a cinema. After John died in 1923, James sold the building to County Cinemas Ltd who were later taken over by Odeon Cinemas. Mr Yates continues:

It was an Odeon Cinema from about 1938 to 1950. Then Odeon leased the cinema to different lessees until about 1970. They wanted to get out of smaller towns as they wanted to concentrate on big multiplex cinemas so they decided to sell the Odeon Cinema, which was down the road, to Star Group who was buying up all these small cinemas. Their aim was to have part cinema and the other part bingo.

With the other cinema came the Theatre Royal. Star had no interest in the building or its history and wanted to demolish it and sell the land to the frozen food retailer Bejam, now part of Iceland. Mr Yates goes on:

That is when we formed the action group. It took us two years to negotiate with estate agents in London. They wanted £135,000 and we didn't have a dime. Eventually, after twos years we settled for £35,000, but we still didn't have the money. The City Council, bless their heart, came in with £20,000 and Lord Sainsbury of Preston Candover, who is still involved with the theatre as a patron, and Peter Cadbury who lived at Preston Candover, then stepped in. So the Cadbury Trust, the Sainsbury Trust and the City Council bought the Theatre Royal for us.

Dame Gracie Fields was the first patron of the theatre in 1978. Since that time hundreds of major stars have trodden the boards, including Dame Judi Dench, who has performed at the Theatre Royal on four occasions and is the President of the Winchester Festival, the annual celebration of performing and the arts, which takes place in the city.

Phil Yates is now the only founder member of the original action group left. The others have either died or moved on to other projects. He has been involved with the Theatre Royal for more than thirty-five years. During that time he has devoted himself in various capacities, from house manager to usher. Now the Theatre Royal historian, he is part of a community project funded by the Local Heritage Initiative, part of the National Lottery Fund, to bring the history of the site and its surrounding area to the public's attention.

The General Military Hospital, Netley

When Florence Nightingale (1820-1910), newly returned from the Crimean war, was sent the plans for the first General Military Hospital to be built in Britain, in Netley on the shores of Southampton Water, she was not impressed. As Elspeth Huxley says, she drew on 'researches going back to her youth both at home and in France, Germany, Italy and Switzerland' to tell the government, in the person of Lord Panmure (1801-1874), the Secretary of State for War, that the design of the hospital was 'hopelessly out of date' and completely unsuited for its purpose. She felt it would be too hard to keep clean and during wartime, when demand was high for the hospital's services, expansion to cater for these extra casualties would be difficult. She also criticised the fact that the magnificent windows that lined the building and gave outstanding views of the water were in corridors, which left the wards dark and gloomy.

It was too late. She was overruled. The hospital was at that point more than a plan on a page. Construction had started and £70,000 had already been spent. Despite speaking to the Prime Minister, Lord Palmerston, and his urging Panmure to 'stop all progress in the work till the matter be duly considered,' the hospital went ahead largely as planned.

Philip Hoare eloquently explains the problem in his book *Spike Island*. He says, 'Everything about the place was monumental. Its architecture aspired to eighteenth-century rationality, yet it spoke of nineteenth-century imperialism... designed by a team of architects whom no one had told to stop, its creators having suffered a fit of megalomania'.

Time though, proved Florence Nightingale correct. There are surviving photographs from the First World War which show corridors filled with patient's beds as there was not enough room in the wards for the extra casualties.

The hospital's red brick and Portland stone facade was impressive enough to become a landmark and something of a tourist attraction for shipping and the increasing number of passengers on cruise liners sailing past the hospital on Southampton Water.

In keeping with the monumental theme of the hospital, it seemed only right that the main entrance to the building opened into the hospital's natural history museum, complete with elephant skeleton and several glass-fronted cupboards full of skulls. It was a show of the mighty reach of the British Empire and an acknowledgement of the changing scientific ideas of the time, reflecting the interests of the hospital doctors. The impressive staircases rose on either side of the back of the museum, giving a grandstand view of the relics on display as they were ascended. The irony of having skulls on display at the hospital was not lost on the patients, who quickly dubbed the area 'Skull Alley'.

The hospital was divided into blocks and each functioned almost as a separate hospital in itself. The ranks were strictly segregated but, given that the hospital design was poor, ventilation was limited and so smells lingered, having no regard for the patient's rank or position.

Casualties arrived either by boat or by train, on a branch line from the Netley mainline station. The hospital took casualties from the Second Boer War and both World Wars. During the First World War a sea of Red Cross huts sprouted on the grounds at the back of the hospital and these became the overflow areas to allow Netley to accommodate 2,500 patients at a time, and treat 50,000 casualties between 1914 and 1918. The same happened during the Second World War when the hospital treated over 68,000 patients.

In the 1950s the costs of maintaining the hospital grew to be untenable and in 1958 much of the site closed. A fire in 1963 was the final nail in the coffin and everything except the chapel was demolished in 1966. The buildings to the rear of the main hospital, which housed the psychiatric facilities and which had escaped the original closure, were vacated in the mid-1970s and these buildings were taken over by the Hampshire Constabulary as their Police Training Establishment.

Today the chapel stands in acres of parkland, the Royal Victoria Country Park, and the sounds of children playing and dogs yapping have replaced the noisy arrival of trains bearing wounded men. The small museum area at the main entrance of the Hampshire Constabulary Training Establishment contains several etched glass windows, completed by one of the patients. They are a reminder of the human face of the hospital, showing life as a patient. The cemetery is another reminder, with its rows of white war graves, maintained by the Commonwealth War Graves Commission, surrounding a huge, white, war memorial.

Hampshire Place Names

Some of the village names in Hampshire have an interesting history and it is worthwhile to stop and contemplate the origins of a few of these in the county, as Beddington and Christy did for the Women's Institute in 1936.

A 'bunny' is 'a hollow, narrow rift or valley' and so the beautifully named Chewton Bunny in the New Forest is named after the local landscape.

The many areas ending with 'bury' or 'borough' are Anglo-Saxon and are named after fortified places. For example Danebury, a few miles north of Winchester, was the site of an Iron Age hill fort originally built in the sixth century. Today it is a Scheduled Ancient Monument and a Site of Special Scientific Interest.

'Chester' comes from the Latin 'castra', meaning 'fort', and the number of place names in Hampshire ending in this word reflects the abundance of Roman forts that dotted the county. Thus we know that there was a Roman fort at Winchester, Portchester and Silchester. The Romans ruled England from AD 40 to about AD 450.

A 'dur' is a 'spring', whilst a 'ley' is a 'wood or open space in a wood'. Thus the village of Durley is named after the spring in the open space in the local wood.

'Ford' is Anglo-Saxon and means 'a place to cross water on foot'. In other words, the water at a ford was shallow enough to wade through. There were a number of such places in Hampshire, such as Chandler's Ford, Fordingbridge, Twyford and Alresford, derived from 'Aldersford', which means 'the ford over the river where the alder trees grow'.

A 'ham' was a 'homestead' and so such villages as Crookham (listed as Crokeham in the Domesday Book), Damerham on the Hampshire/Dorset/Wiltshire borders, and Odiham in north Hampshire, all began as humble homesteads in the area.

A 'holt' is a 'copse' and so the village of Sparsholt gets its name from a copse nearby. Nowadays Sparsholt is famous for its agricultural college and for the 'potting shed', which is the home of the popular radio show, *Gardeners Question Time*.

Eling, near Totton, Basing, Nurseling and Hayling all use the Anglo-Saxon word 'ing' meaning 'a place that was settled by a group or a family'. Stubbington goes one step further, as in addition to the 'ing' in the village name there is also the use of 'ton' (also 'tun'), which means 'an enclosure'.

Marchwood is named after the wood at the village boundary, 'march' being another name for a boundary.

Mottisfont, near Romsey, famous for its abbey and glorious grounds by the River Test, owes its name to the Norman word 'font' which means 'a well or fountain'.

There are several villages with very obvious French sounding names, echoing the Norman invasion in 1066 and its subsequent impact on Hampshire. 'Beaulieu' is French for 'beautiful village' while Dibden Purlieu comes from the Anglo-Saxon word 'den' (or 'dean') meaning a 'deep wooded valley' and the French 'pour allez lieu' referring to the deforestation caused by repeated walking through the forest in the area.

The word 'strat' is found all over England but in Hampshire this Latin word for a 'street' is used for Stratfield Saye, the home of the Dukes of Wellington since 1817, and nearby Stratfield Turgis, both just north of Basingstoke. The use of the word 'field' (also Anglo-Saxon 'fold') denotes a forest clearing where trees were felled.

As can be seen from this snapshot of the names of some of the villages across Hampshire, many derive from the landscape and features around them. In a largely illiterate age, it made sense to name a village after the local features which were plain for all to see. We, in the twenty-first century, can learn much about the lives of our forebears from the origins our place names.

EIGHT

STORIES, LEGENDS AND CUSTOMS

Old Arthur's Board: on the capacious round
    Some British pen has sketch'd the names renown'd
In marks obscure of his immortal peers.

Thomas Warton (1728-1790)
'On King Arthur's Round Table in Winchester'

This book has looked at seasonal customs and spirits who cannot rest; the lives of the saints and of those who have contributed to the history of our celebrated county; the music and dancing which Hampshire residents have enjoyed over the years; and the buildings they have lived and worked in. Now it is time to look at the stories and legends, the ideas and beliefs, which have been handed down from generation to generation. Some of our quaint traditions and customs are alive and well, surviving into the twenty-first century, and some, sadly, have been forgotten. Enjoy!

Pie Poudre Courts

Ben Johnson's 1614 comedy *Bartholomew Fair* contains several references to Pie Poudre Courts. In Act II, Scene I, Justice Adam Overdo says: 'Many are the yearly enormities of this Fair, in whose Courts of Pye-poulders I have had the honour, during the three days, sometimes to sit as Judge'.

In Act III Scene IV, Leatherhead, a hobbyhorse seller cries: 'Is this well, goody Jone? to interrupt my Mar-ket in the midst? and call away my Customers? can you answer this at the Piepouldres?'

For centuries markets and fairs have been held all over Hampshire in the principal towns and villages. The Bishop of Winton granted the fair at St Giles Hill, not far from Winchester, its Pie Poudre Court by permission of Edward IV (1442–1483).

Historically, fairs were an important source of trade and entertainment to the local people, and attracted both those interested in the commerce of the day and those bent on not so honest pursuits. To deal with those who were caught in foul play, a Pie Poudre Court was set up at each fair.

The name derives from the French name for a vagabond, 'pied poudreaux', which literally means 'dusty foot' and is a reference to the tatty condition of the peddlers who were the court's chief litigants.

The Pie Poudre Court dealt with all civil disputes at the market, as well as collecting tolls from traders. It had a reputation for the speed in which it dealt out justice, which was just as well as those involved were often itinerant traders who moved on after the market was held. The Court of the Clerk of the Market, which Blackstone called 'the most inferior court of criminal jurisdiction in the country,' (*Commentaries on the Laws of England, 1765-1769*), dealt with criminal matters, including those dealing with weights and measures. After the 1878 Weights and Measures Act, this court's powers were taken over by Magistrates Courts and both it and the associated Pie Poudre Courts became obsolete. The 1971 Courts of Justice Act finally took the Pie Poudre Court off the statute books.

Chris Hayles, on his informative Southern Life website, tells us that privileged Southampton, which was listed as a borough in the Domesday Book, had an ancient Pie Poudre Court that was confirmed by charter in 1461. However, in the charter of incorporation of 1447, which gave the city the right to own a corporation seal, own lands as a corporation, have perpetual succession, to make its own by-laws and to sue in the Kings Courts, it was given exemption from the business of the Clerk of the Market, as well as from the Kings Constable, the Earls Marshall and the Lord High Admiral. This gave the city burgesses a free hand to control trade both in and out of Southampton.

Eventually the fairs and markets declined and ceased to be profitable. Many were turned into funfairs, became hiring fairs at which cheap labour could be hired, or disappeared into oblivion.

Hampshire's Smugglers

It seems to be human nature to look for a way to avoid paying a tax. Taxes, by their very nature, are unpopular and this has led to a tradition that in some parts of the world, not just in the United Kingdom, continues to this day. The smuggler may be more sophisticated nowadays than he was in days gone by, but the main point, that of cheating the taxman and outwitting his excise officers, has not changed.

Smuggling became a large-scale enterprise after the introduction of the 1671 Customs Act, which placed heavy duties on certain goods. In Hampshire many people turned to smuggling out of necessity. A fisherman can only survive for so long with poor catches and his knowledge of coves and the coastline was invaluable to the 'free traders', as smugglers were often called. A keg of spirits, a bolt of cloth, tobacco or another luxury tucked into his boat helped to keep his family fed. Once involved, it was hard to get out for trust was not the smuggler's middle name, and so smuggling whole cargoes soon became a dangerous way of life.

It is true that the Isle of Wight was the area's major smuggling haunt. The proximity of the Hampshire coastline to the Isle of Wight made the final stretch to the English mainland an easy hop for smugglers to bring their contraband in to distribute and sell on. Wendy Boase notes that 'almost every cave of Freshwater Bay, Dunnose Point and the Undercliff of the Isle of Wight harboured contraband'. Hampshire, though, had its fair share of 'gentlemen' as the free traders were known. Between the mid-eighteenth and nineteenth centuries, the trade's height, casks of brandy came across the Channel from France in false-bottomed boats, while tobacco was often woven into light rope and used in the boat's rigging. Hiding places all over Hampshire showed the imagination and ingenuity used to outwit the excise man. Contraband was hidden in cellars in cottages and inns, in lonely houses and in dense woodland. Table tombs in churchyards were handy places of concealment, as were the beds of nursing mothers. Soberton Churchyard was conveniently situated between Portsmouth and Medstead and so it came to possess a dummy vault near the chancel door. Wells were often the place of choice, particularly Chewton Bunny, near Milton, and Preston Candover, whose well entrance was said to be so big that a wagon and horses could drive into it. The hollow oak trees along the River Hamble at Warsash made excellent hiding places too.

Hiding places for contraband had to be big enough for the purpose. In East Boldre the Turf Cutter's Arms, which had a path down to the Solent along which the barrels of alcohol would be rolled, often had its oven utilised as a

convenient storage spot. The quarry at Wootton, near Bashley, also made a good
warehouse, the goods being covered with gorse and bracken. Heavy goods were
often taken up the Beaulieu River and sunk in deep New Forest ponds. They
were raked out on moonlit nights, hence the term 'Hampshire Moonrakers' for
smugglers in the county.

Fawley, near Southampton, now known more for its oil refinery than as a
smuggling haunt, was a busy free traders' lair. Ashlett Creek, now part of the
yachting marina, was used as a landing point and the caves to the south in the
woods at Spratt's Down were used for storage. The village of Spratt's Down
earned the nickname 'Lazy Town' because all the inhabitants worked at the
smuggling trade during the night and caught up on their sleep in the daytime.
Beddington and Cristy repeat the tale of the excise officer in this area who
always stayed for the evening at the home of certain elderly residents in Fawley.
That is, until one unfortunate evening when the hollow noise from beneath his
feet alerted him to their duplicity and his hosts ended up in Winchester Gaol.

There are many stories connecting Lymington to smuggling. One story,
found on the smuggling.co.uk website, is that of a well-rehearsed piece of
deception. A ship would come in and the sad faced crew and passengers would
announce that the captain had died and a doctor had to be called. This worthy
then confirmed the unfortunate man's death and the undertaker's hearse would
be loaded with the coffin. Then the solemn procession, which included the
town's customs officials, would proceed at a pace that the sombre occasion mer-
ited as far as the Angel public house, whereupon they stopped for refreshment
to drown their sorrows. The officials would be particularly well looked after and
it was a far less dignified group who would later leave the pub and proceed on
their way. At the first opportunity the hearse, complete with contraband hidden
in the coffin, would speed off and unload. The local vicar helpfully allowed the
tower at St Thomas' Church to be used for storage. There is also said to have
been a tunnel cut from the shore to the Angel which was wide enough for
smugglers to bring in their barrels unnoticed.

A quarter of a mile off the coast from Pitts Deep, South Baddesley, there was a
spot called Brandy Hole. This was so called because barrels of brandy would be
roped together, sunk and then the spot marked for later recognition and easy pick
up. A Pitts Deep cottage had a local reputation for the good quality of its brandy!

Cecilia Millson tells us of the Smugglers' Way, the route taken by contraband
into Hampshire. The table tombs in Boldre Churchyard in the New Forest were
handy places for brandy kegs to be hidden after arriving at Lymington. From
there they were transported to Sway, where they were secreted in both Sway
House and in the various cottages and inns in the village. From Sway House it

was said that there was a four-mile-long tunnel which ran underground from the cellar to the coast.

Burley was the next link in the chain. This village, four miles outside Ringwood, was the home of the delightfully named Lovey Warne and her brothers, John and Peter. Their house, Knaves Ash on Crow Hill Top, was the perfect place for stashing contraband. Lovey owned a bright red cloak, which came in very handy when the excise men were in the area. She would go to the top of nearby Vereley Hill and walk around making sure her red cape was visible to the entire local 'gentlemen' as a warning that they should stay away. Lovey, so it is said, also went to Christchurch harbour when a contraband packed boat came in. There she would visit the captain's cabin. Taking off her clothes she would wind smuggled silks around her body and then redress, hoping nobody noticed her sudden weight gain. Back at home she would reverse the process and the silks were spirited away to be sold on, tax-free. Apparently no one worried about her dumpy figure, one excise man finding it acceptable enough to invite her for a drink at the Eight Bells public house in Christchurch. The game was almost up when his hand went walking up her thigh and she had to protect her honour with a swift poke in his eye! After this, Lovey stayed at home.

The Warnes Bar at the Lymington Queen's Head Inn has secret cellars which were only discovered when there was renovation work going on at the site.

The Smugglers Road can still be seen from the present-day car park of the same name. This is a sunken road which heads across the heath land. It is thought it was cut so that smugglers could move their cargo unseen from the main road.

There is a story of one luckless Ringwood excise man in 1783 who, hearing that Burley was a hotbed for smugglers, took a number of his men and went to investigate. The diligent searchers seized a goodly amount of contraband and prepared to remove it. News of this sort travels fast in the New Forest and soon every smuggler in the area had arrived to confront the excise men, all of whom fled the scene except the officer from Ringwood. He stood his ground and got severely beaten for his pains. The contraband was recovered and people spoke of the event for years afterwards.

Another tale of 'recovering' smuggled property, which had been confiscated by the excise men came from Cranborne. Dan, possibly Dan Sims who died in 1826, was busy cutting turf when he was alerted to the fact that his hidden barrels had been found in his house by the excise man during a raid. Dan was not a man to take this lying down and so repaired for a quiet drink, sitting unobtrusively in his local, the Flower de Luce. Soon enough the excise man came in, bragging about the haul he had found. He told the assembled company that he had had all eleven kegs removed to his house. Dan filed the information away and left. He later went to the excise man's front door and painted a cross on it. Then he went away. Soon afterwards, at about midnight, a gang of men armed with a sledgehammer and a loaded pistol determinedly hacked the door down and took Dan's barrels back, riding off with them in a cart.

'Keystone under the hearth, Keystone under the horse's belly' is a local saying from Fordingbridge, a well-known smugglers haunt. This refers to the two most popular places for contraband to be hidden: under the hearth with a lamp lit on the top, or in the stable under the floor. The town was formerly called Forde, referring to the ford in the town, and smugglers would also sink kegs in the River Avon. Fordingbridge was on the smuggling route through the local villages of Redbrook, Stuckton and Frogham.

The Solent and Southampton Water were both patrolled and house-to-house searches also sometimes produced results. Wendy Boase tells of the ninety-year-old invalid living in Calshot who was happy to chat with excise men when they searched her house. She was unable to rise from her bed and they were too respectful of a sick elderly lady to move her. It did not occur to them that she might be lying in bed with smuggled goods and she was much more sprightly than she made out. They left her in peace. In fact, each time they were in the vicinity she strategically took to her bed secure in the knowledge that she could charm the usually taciturn men.

There are tales of smugglers fooling the excise men by reversing the shoes on their horses' feet and, in Netley Marsh, a smuggler had fake cargo delivered at Eling while the real contraband arrived further down the coast.

Smuggling was big business all over the country and Hampshire was no exception. The improvement of the coastguard service sounded the death knell for the early smugglers, who are now regarded with romantic nostalgia.

The Wayfarer's Dole

A custom stretching back to 1136 still exists in Winchester to this day. Any traveller can ask for the Wayfarer's Dole at the gatehouse of the Hospital of St Cross and will receive a horn of ale and a small square of bread.

In an age when travelling was frequently on foot and consequently slow, tiring and often hazardous, the donation of food and shelter for poor travellers was undertaken sometimes by charitable minded persons but more often by the Church, particularly before the Reformation. Travellers knew that they could go to monastic houses and request a Wayfarer's Dole to tide them over.

In 1136 Bishop Henry de Blois founded the Hospital of St Cross as an enduring site for thirteen poor men. Legend has it that he chose the site because a religious house had been laid waste by the Danes there and all that was left were its ruins. De Blois vowed to use the site for a new building, established to aid the poor. The word 'hospital' is used as a term for 'hospitality' and the site also incorporated a church. The Church of St Cross, although begun in the twelfth century, was not finished until the thirteenth and thus incorporates both the Norman and Early English styles of architecture. It was added to over the next few centuries when windows, glass, the nave vault and chancel woodwork, to name a few of the later additions, were included. The wooden cloister, with its low arches, is Tudor. The gardens are full of flowers and herbs and the whole is overlooked by nearby St Catherine's Hill.

Cardinal Beaufort added the Almshouse of Noble Poverty to the site in 1446, for higher-ranking men who had fallen on hard times through no fault of their own.

Both the hospital and the almshouse are now run under the same director. However, it is easy to distinguish the Blois Brethren, Henry de Blois' original poor men, as they wear black gowns and the silver cross of the Knights Hospitallers of St John. The Beaufort Brethren wear dark red gowns and have the cardinal's badge on their trencher hats. They all have free housing, a food allowance and receive pocket money.

Originally the hospital provided free meals for 100 poor people, which increased to 200 later. The dole was substantial. Each recipient received nearly 3lbs of coarse bread, a bowl of hearty soup, two eggs or meat or fish and three quarts of small beer, a weak brew. In addition, thirteen of those in direst need also received lodging and supper, a loaf of wheat bread, a gallon and a half of small beer and soup, and a three-course dinner every day. The Charter of Foundation sets out in some detail the conditions of the chosen thirteen, who must be 'feeble and so reduced in strength that they can scarcely, or not at all, support themselves without other aid'.

Over time the dole has been threatened by corruption or incompetence. The Master of the Hospital was in charge of the finances and intervention was necessary in the fifteenth century when William of Wykeham stepped in to regulate the hospital's revenues. A clause in the 1696 statute of the hospital stated that the master could claim any surplus after he had discharged his dues. This led to widespread abuse and caused the hospital much suffering in the eighteenth century. The Hon. Brownlow North (1741-1820) was appointed Bishop of Winchester in 1781 by his half-brother, Lord North, the Prime Minister. In 1807 he appointed his son, Francis, later the Earl of Guildford, as the Master of St Cross. He held this post for almost fifty years. His neglect of the hospital and the revelation of wholesale embezzlement was to cause a huge scandal when the Revd Harold Holloway told the press of it in 1855. The legal action that followed led to the earl's resignation and bankruptcy for the hospital.

Nowadays the hospital gives out its dole at the Porters Gate, mostly to tourists, hence the size of the portion. That the custom lives on in the twenty-first century is testament to the spirit of charity.

Virgins' Crowns

The Church of St Mary the Virgin, in the tiny village of Abbotts Ann, near Andover, which is strewn with thatched cottages, is remarkable both for its peaceful location beside open farmland and for the preservation of a long-held custom.

In 1710, Thomas 'Diamond' Pitt (1653-1726), ancestor of Prime Minister William Pitt (1708-1778), bought Abbotts Ann, with its Manor House and the old church, which was mentioned in the Domesday Book. Tim Tayler, Secretary of the St Mary the Virgin Parochial Church Council, the church management committee, says:

> St Mary the Virgin is one of very few Queen Anne churches which were built in this country. It is a Grade I listed building. The lord of the manor, 'Diamond' Pitt, who had been the Governor of Madras, built it in 1716. Pitt had acquired a very large diamond, which he sold to make his fortune. With part of the money he rebuilt this church. The original diamond is in the Louvre now, in Paris.

Inside the building, the stained-glass windows are remarkable. One was presented to the church by current and former pupils of the village school to thank outgoing rector, the Revd Hon. Samuel Best, for his years of service between 1831 and 1873. The windows smile down on the congregation and cast light on the Virgins' Crowns, which line the walls high up near the ceiling.

Many visitors to the church come looking for the Crowns. Also known as Maiden's Garlands, they were once commonly awarded to girl and women virgins throughout the country and they were also known in Europe. The custom, thought to be of medieval origin, has almost died out, but in Abbotts Ann it has survived and Virgins' Crowns are awarded to both male and female recipients. Tim Tayler says:

The practice of Virgins' Crowns, or Maidens Garlands, is a very old one. Whilst the practice largely died out in the eighteenth century in the Age of Reason, as it was thought to be a superstitious practice, it really took off here in the late eighteenth and during the nineteenth centuries. I have a suspicion that this was because at the beginning of the nineteenth century a Nonconformist blacksmith arrived in the village from Wiltshire, called Robert Tasker.

Tasker took over the village smithy in 1809, aged twenty-four:

He founded the Waterloo Ironworks in the Anna Valley. He was a very strict Nonconformist and a great philanthropist. He wouldn't work on Sunday and he did not like the established Church. He preferred to set up his own meeting house and so he fell out with the rector in a big way. He lost custom locally and there were threats on his life. Stones were thrown through windows and so forth. Eventually he overcame these difficulties and from about 1831 onwards, in conjunction with the new rector, Samuel Best, he helped to found the village school, which was one of the first co-educational village schools in the country, with a very forward thinking curriculum. But the previous rector, Thomas Burrough, had not got on with Tasker and I suspect that the Virgins' Crowns were started to encourage the village people to come to the established church and not go to Tasker's meeting house, but this is only a guess.

Guess or not, the Virgins' Crowns, which Shakespeare called 'virgin crants' in *Hamlet*, from the Germanic word for 'wreaths' or 'garlands', are still awarded to those who were born and who die in the Abbotts Ann parish and who were of good character; that is, who were churchgoing virgins.

The Crowns, which Gilbert White described as 'memorials of chastity' when writing of those he had seen in Selborne in 1789, were made originally from bent hazel, representing virgin wood, but latterly from pressed oak. They are very light weight, belying their more substantial appearance and are about 38cm high and 25cm wide. Manufactured entirely by hand by the bereaved family, they consist of the crown-like frame covered in small white paper rosettes which represent roses, a sign of purity. Hanging from the frame are five paper chaplets, or gloves, upon which the family write the name and age of their dear departed and meaningful verses from hymns or scriptures. The odd glove is supposedly a challenge to anyone who disputes the family's claims of purity and harks back to the medieval roots of the custom, the practice of throwing down a gauntlet being the traditional method of challenge amongst duelling knights. Tim continues:

When a person dies application to the church is made to award a Virgin's Crown. There is a story of a teenage boy in the 1960s who was killed in a motorcycle accident and he was not allowed to have one of these Crowns, apparently for reasons known. When the decision to award a Virgin's Crown is given, the Crown is made. It is brought into the church with the coffin for the funeral service. The Crown is hung up on a hook that is visible to all, at the front end of the gallery. Two girls dressed in white carry the Crown on a white wand or stick and they lead the coffin down to the churchyard for the interment, then the Crown is brought back for a period of time. If it does not fall down from the hook, that is supposed to signify that the person is as good as their family said that he or she was, and so it is put up on the wall.

The last Crown was awarded to Miss Lily Myra Annetts, who died in 1973, aged seventy-three. Her Crown is still intact and can be seen hanging with forty-seven others in the church, just along from that of a relative, William George Annetts, who died in 1919 aged fifteen. Each Crown hangs beneath an escutcheon bearing the name, age and date of funeral of the deceased. The Crown stays in place until it falls down with age. The oldest escutcheon is dated 1740 and was awarded to John Morrant. All that remains of the Crown is the top of the hanging material. Some are in a remarkably good state of preservation, browned to a velum-like appearance but virtually intact, despite being in situ for nearly two centuries.

The names of those awarded a Virgin's Crown have been embroidered onto the brightly coloured kneelers found inside the church.

Tim Tayler has the final word on this peek into the folklore of this part of Hampshire. 'The hardest part of the whole process in recent years is finding two teenage girls to dress up in white!'

Churching of Women

Birth and the beginning of life often seemed magical to people of yesteryear. But the ever-present danger, in the form of evil spirits, witches, fairies and ill omens, was never far away and babies and new mothers had to be guarded against their malevolence.

An echo of the New Testament's Purification of the Virgin (in the Book of Luke), the practice of Churching of Women, a pilgrimage to receive a blessing made by a new mother as soon as she was recovered from the ordeal of childbirth, was widespread. The mother had to have given birth to a legitimate baby, one born within wedlock, and the baby should not have been baptised outside the Roman

Catholic faith. The blessing, given by a priest in a church that celebrated Mass, was a thanksgiving for having survived the ordeal of giving birth, a grave consideration in an age when deaths in childbed were very common. The ceremony was performed even if the child was stillborn or had died before it could be baptised.

The woman would come veiled on the fortieth day after her confinement. It was considered unlucky for the new mother to go outside of her home before being churched as it was popularly believed that she would be kidnapped by the fairies, who delighted in carrying off un-churched mothers.

Gifts for Newborns

In many parts of the country, including Hampshire, children born at midnight or at twilight were thought to have second-sight. Those born in the 'chime-hours', generally thought to be when the bells were rung for night time monastic prayers, were said to have received the mixed blessing of being able to see ghosts and spirits which other people could not see. The seventh child of a seventh child was also considered to be gifted. Fathers passed their gifts onto sons, as did mothers to their daughters.

William Hone tells us that children will not thrive unless they are christened. He further instructs that unless they cry during the ceremony, they will not live long.

Sir Bevois of Southampton

The city of Southampton has several references to the legend of Sir Bevois (Bevis); his love Josian; Ascupart, the giant who became his page; and the lions who guarded Josian. Take a wander along Bevois Street, Josian Walk or Ascupart Street in Kingsland; drive along Bevois Valley Road in Bevois Valley; visit Bevois Park, Bevois Mount or Bevois Town; or have a look at the twin lions at the Bargate. It is quite obvious that the legend of Sir Bevois lives on in the town and the legendary characters have been claimed as the town's own. Indeed, part of the legend has it that Sir Bevois founded Southampton.

So, who was this Sir Bevois? Viktoria Turner, in her paper 'Legends, Lions, and Virgins: The Legend of Sir Bevois of Southampton' tells us that 'an open mind should be kept as to whether the original pre-Norman version of the legend was based on fact or not'. A useful website, This is Hampshire, goes for a stronger statement and pronounces that 'There was no real Sir Bevois', whilst Lawrence

Main speculates that the ancient ring-shaped earthwork at Bevisbury, near the Hampshire/Berkshire border, is actually the final resting place of the legendary figure. A trip to St Peter's Church in Curdridge will leave you in no two minds about Sir Bevois' reality. High up on the church's Victorian tower are gargoyles shaped to look like Sir Bevois in chain mail; in the act of drawing his sword; the beautiful Josian; Ascupart; Bevois' horse Arundel; and members of Bevois' family. They were all fashioned in 1894 and guard the 84ft-high structure.

We know quite a lot about Sir Bevois, and it is full of rich, heavily embroidered detail. Much of his story has been passed down from Anglo-Nordic romantic poetry dating from the twelfth century, which itself stemmed from an earlier lost Middle English version. Michael Drayton (1563-1631) also tells the story in his *Poly-Olbion* in 'Song II', published in 1612.

The tale is told of Sir Bevois, the son of Sir Guy of Hampton, now Southampton, and of an unnamed mother who was the daughter of the King of Scotland. Sir Guy had married his much younger bride in his later years and she promptly took a lover, who she later asked to murder her husband so that the two of them could marry and live happily ever after. Turner tells us that at the age of seven Sir Bevois is said to have 'cudgelled his step father almost to death'. Clearly her son was in the way of her happy new life and so his mother sold him into slavery.

The merchant whom Sir Bevois was sold to took him across the sea to Armenia and resold him to Ermyn, the Armenian king. It was while he was in Armenia that he escaped the king's clutches, fought his enemies and killed a boar, which had been creating panic and havoc for many long days. His mighty sword, Mortglay, was said to have magical properties and his horse, Hirondelle (or Arundel, from the French word for 'a swallow') are said to have aided him in his exploits and so have become part of the legend.

Ermyn's daughter was the beautiful Josian (Joisyan) and Sir Bevois fell in love with her on sight. The legend says that he was warned that he should not marry a woman who was not pure and his bride also had to be a king's daughter. Josian had been married to Yvor of Mombraunt for seven years but claimed that she was still a virgin. Sir Bevois believed her and carried her off. He left her sheltering in a cave with her servant Boniface. While he was away two lions pounced on the luckless Boniface and ate him. However, as Josian was both a king's daughter and virtuous, they were unable to harm her and so sat quietly on either side of the cave until the return of St Bevois, who recognised the danger they represented and so promptly slew them both.

Sir Bevois acquired his squire, Ascapart, described by Jim Brown as a 'savage giant', after being attacked by him on an Armenian seashore. Sir Bevois, himself no pygmy, was prevented from killing him when Josian stepped in and stopped him doing so, saying that Ascapart should serve Sir Bevois as a page instead. Turner tells us that in Copland's sixteenth-century translation of the tale, Sir Bevois says to his lady, 'Dame, he wyll us betraye'.

Sir Bevois and Ascapart were christened at Southampton Water and then Sir Bevois married his Josian. He had decided to come back to Southampton to avenge his father's death and reclaim his lands. In true grisly medieval style, he is said to have driven his mother to leap from the top of a high tower and then he boiled her liver in a giant cauldron to make dog meat.

Further adventures soon followed. One tells of Sir Bevois building Arundel Castle in Sussex, while another says that this was the Arundel Tower at the fortified Southampton Castle. Either way, Sir Bevois named the building he is supposed to have built after his horse, the mighty Hirondelle. That wandering minstrels frequently came from Arundel to Southampton may have had something to do with intertwining the two tales.

When Sir Bevois realised he was dying, he went to the top of the Arundel Tower and threw his magical sword, Mortglay, as far as he could. It ended up some two miles away and it is where the sword landed, supposedly in two pieces, which is where our hero is supposed to be buried, on the site of the house and gardens which the Earl of Peterborough built in the early eighteenth century, now known as Bevois Mount.

Legend is divided on the ending of the story. A popular version has it that after the death of the giant Ascapart, Sir Bevois and Josian died together in each other's arms. This romantic ending seems fitting for the devoted couple.

As a postscript, the statues of the lions at the Bargate, which have stood for more than 270 years, are now in a serious state of disrepair. One lost its tail in September 2018, when it fell off due to corrosion. Dr Andy Russel, Southampton's Archaeology Unit Manager, has highlighted the fact that the lions need 'serious treatment' to keep them guarding the Bargate. In 2020, the lions will be removed from their plinths to receive specialist treatment that will mean they will be a feature of Southampton into the future.

'Lost In the Dark Peal'

The endowment of a bell that could be rung between eight and nine o'clock at night as an aid to lost travellers was a useful charitable deed in an age with few roads, fewer still signposts and no lighting out in the countryside. A traveller lost in the rural surroundings of a village would hear the bell tolling and be guided towards the sound.

William Davis was one such traveller who owed much to the bells sounding out in this way. On the evening of 7 October 1754 he was lost in the countryside, not far from Twyford. He heard the bells from Twyford's church ring out and stopped his horse, realising he was going the wrong way. As he did so he peered through the darkness and realised with a jolt that he was on the very edge of a deep quarry. If the bells had not sounded at that precise moment, causing him to stop, he and his horse would have plunged to certain death. When he died he left £1 in his will for the provision of an annual peal of the Twyford bells on the anniversary of this event and a feast for the bell ringers.

Although the money ran out long ago, the annual peal still sounds and the feast still goes ahead. Old William would have been proud.

King Arthur's Round Table

The magnificent oak round table, 18ft in diameter, weighing 1,200lbs and seating twenty-four, is displayed on the wall in the Great Hall of Winchester Castle.

Thomas Malory (1405-1471), the colourful author of *Morte D'Arthur*, was convinced that Winchester Castle was Camelot and so it seems fitting that King Arthur Pendragon's Round Table be found here.

It was made in the fourteenth century and was repainted during the reign of Henry VIII, when it was used for a banquet to celebrate the Feast of Pentecost. The central Tudor Rose is telling, as it is a reminder to all in the land that the Tudor dynasty was supposed to be descended from the Pendragon line. The names of the Knights of the Round Table feature on the edge of the table.

The origins of Arthur's story are elusive. He is thought to be the brave Christian knight mentioned in the seventh century Welsh poem 'Y Godolin' by Aneirin Gwawdrydd. His victorious battles against the Saxon invaders are listed by Nennius in the eighth century, although he is thought to have used a certain amount of poetic license (Paul Halsall). William of Malmesbury, writing in the twelfth century, takes Arthur into the realms of myth and legend by claiming in his *History of the Kings of England* that his tomb is unknown and he will return; this is a popular theme with Welsh heroes. Geoffrey of Monmouth, writing just after William, supplies much of the background to the story we know today. Drawing on Welsh legends and his own imagination, it is through him that we learn that Arthur was the son of Uther Pendragon and was born in Tintagel Castle in Cornwall. He was crowned king at the age of fifteen at Silchester and Geoffrey also brings Morgan Le Fey and Merlin into the story for the first time. He tells us that Arthur and Modred, Arthur's nephew, battled and that Arthur was mortally wounded. He does not tell us that Arthur actually died, thus bringing his account into line with that of William of Malmesbury.

The Round Table is first mentioned in *Roman de Brut*, written by Robert Wace in 1155. He says that the table was round so as to seat all of Arthur's knights equally. Malory goes further by adding the detail that the table was a gift from Leodegrance, Guinevere's father, on her marriage to Arthur.

Mallory, writing whilst detained in gaol as a Lancastrian sympathiser, wrote 239 chapters in nine books on the life and death of Arthur and his knights. It was published as twenty-one books in 1485, fourteen years after Mallory's death.

Whatever the truth about Arthur, the Round Table at Winchester is a spectacular monument to an enduring legend.

St Mary's Parish Church, Kingsclere

The church at Kingsclere is unremarkable in most ways; that is until one looks up. It is then that the unusual weathervane is noticed.

So the story goes, in 1205 King John was staying at the hunting lodge King Henry II had built near Kingsclere. When a thick fog came down while he was returning from a day's hunting, he took refuge in the local inn in the village. The landlord was taken unawares and had not had time to prepare the room for his royal guest. King John spent an uncomfortable night, for he was not alone in the bed. In the morning he was considerably angry as bedbugs had feasted on him. He commissioned the likeness of one of the bugs to be made into a weathervane and for it to be set atop the parish church as a warning to others of the welcome they could expect in the village.

The question is, is this story true? As weathervanes were not invented until about a century after the supposed date of this event, it would seem that this story should perhaps be taken with a pinch of salt. As the now defunct *The Bedbug Recorder* published by the Kingsclere Heritage Association took pains to explain, the problem is that there have been so many refurbishments of the weathervane because the metal it was made of, wrought iron, was susceptible to the elements. Each modification altered its appearance.

The present weathervane replaced the Tudor one in 1751. It was repaired in 1826 and 1848, each time slightly altering the design. *The Bedbug Recorder* noted that a print dated 1820 showed that the weathervane at that time had only four legs and was squarer than the present version. It is not known if the current weathervane is an attempt at copying the earlier Tudor model, or if it was a new design for the time. All of which makes it very difficult to substantiate the bedbug story.

The cockerel is the most common form for a weathervane but in the Middle Ages there was an enthusiasm for real and imaginary beasts. Of these, the tortoise was the rather surprising favourite choice. This echoed *Aesop's Fables*, symbolising the need for patient work towards success. A fire is thought to have damaged the church tower at the beginning of the fifteenth century and it is speculated that the weathervane had to be replaced then. It is possible that this was in the shape of a tortoise.

There is also the possibility that the weathervane might have resembled that of the Wherwell Cockatrice, which adorned the church at Wherwell (see Chapter Five). This beast, with the head of a cock, the body of an eagle and the tail of a dragon, is similar to that on the church at Eastbourne, which has the body of a dragon draped with a Fleur de Lys.

The one truth seems to be that we do not know the origins of the Kingsclere Church weathervane. For the moment, clinging to the seemingly mythical King John's bedbug tale seems like a good idea.

The New Forest Shakers

One day Suffolk dressmaker Mary Ann Girling had a dream. She dreamt that she was the embodiment of the Second Coming of Christ and that she should lead her followers to Utopia. When she also found the stigmata marks on her hands and feet, they convinced her. It was quite a dream and would change her life forever.

Mrs Girling was the wife of an iron founder and machine fitter in Ipswich. They had married when she was just sixteen and they had two children. As a result of her dream, she left her family and moved to London as the guest of the Plumstead Peculiars, the strict religious sect founded by John Banyard in 1838, proclaiming that she could not die as she was engaged in God's work. She founded the Jumpers of Walworth sect in Battersea, where worship consisted of followers kissing and then dancing in circles until they fell unconscious to the floor. Huge crowds would gather to watch this spectacle and Mrs Girling's fame spread.

In January 1872 Mrs Girling, by now calling herself 'Mother', found her Utopia and moved her group, calling themselves the Children of God, to New Forest Lodge in the tiny parish of Hordle, in the New Forest. Her group slowly swelled in size until there were 164 followers. They made their own clothes, including a costume for the women modelled on bloomers, the long female underwear vaguely resembling voluminous trousers which, in staid Victorian England, were something worn but never mentioned, and definitely were not displayed in public. Whispers soon started to circulate in the village. The cult's members were also sworn to celibacy, each sex strictly segregated apart from meeting during the working day. At the time of the 1871 census, Hordle parish had a population of only 868 so it can be imagined just what an impact the group's arrival had in the area.

Worship at Hordle involved dancing, trances and fits. Their Sunday services were open to the public and led to the group being called 'Convolutionists' and a popular misconception was that they were connected to Shakers and the Quaker movement. Philip Hoare points out that although she was accused of witchcraft and hypnotising her followers, Mrs Girling nevertheless attracted some serious interest, in particular that of Andrew Thomas Turton Peterson. He was a judge who had spent much of his life in Calcutta, India, and now owned many local acres.

Peterson, in common with many of the local gentry, had lost staff to the sect. He was interested in mesmerism, as were many of the 'great and the good' of the day and studied the way that Girling's followers behaved. He conducted experiments in mesmerism and concluded that if he could mesmerise a person to follow his own will, this had implications as proof for the existence of the soul living outside the body. Peterson was inspired to build the folly at Sway, Peterson's Tower, allegedly after a séance during which Sir Christopher Wren is said to have given him the plans for the tower's design (see Chapter Seven).

Mrs Girling did not allow any form of outside work and so there was little money coming into the sect, apart from what new members brought with them when they arrived. In December 1873, the group could not meet their half-yearly £25 mortgage interest payment and a writ was issued in April 1874. Bailiffs duly arrived and seized goods, in the form of their horses and cattle, to pay the debt. The residue of the sale of these assets was not passed on to them, and by the next interest due date they were again unable to pay. Things were becoming desperate. Members began to leave and the rest lived off meagre rations, going longer and longer without food. On 15 December 1874 the Children of God were evicted unceremoniously from New Forest Lodge. They existed in a lane for weeks until they were able to rent a farm in Tiptoe, where they lived until 1886 when Mrs Girling surprised everyone, not least herself, by dying.

Forest Lodge is still standing and is now a nursing home.

A French Spy in Portsmouth

Smugglers, as we have seen, were cunning and could be merciless, but were not often traitorous. Thus it was a smuggler with a conscious who was responsible for the downfall of David Tyrie, a spy for the French in the 1780s.

Ian Fox gives a comprehensive account of Tyrie's misdeeds and eventual mistakes, which ultimately cost him his life, but it is by reading the newspaper coverage in the *Hampshire Chronicle* of the time, available in the public domain on the ancestry.com website, that one realises the real strength of feeling behind the bare facts.

Tyrie had been passing British secrets to the French for an undisclosed number of years and it is not known just how much damage his activities caused. He refused to tell anyone anything of his life and left a signed statement to this effect, which was dated 23 August 1782 and was written in Winchester Gaol just before his execution.

In November 1781 Tyrie, then working in the Navy Office in Portsmouth, approached James Mailstone, a well-connected old friend, with an offer Mailstone found hard to refuse. Tyrie said he could use his influence to procure Mailstone the contract to supply provisions for the East India line of ships. All Tyrie wanted in return was a little information now and again. He would pay well for details of all naval movements in and out of the port. He hastened to reassure his friend that everything was cleared through the authorities and so Mailstone earned an extra £30 over the next few months by supplying increasingly detailed information to Tyrie.

Captain Bowles was an unscrupulous sea captain who was quite happy to smuggle contraband or run secrets for Tyrie. He started picking up Mailstone's information directly from the informant and this luckless individual soon became more and more alarmed at what he was being asked to do. Mailstone started to falsify some of the information demanded from him.

When Bowles' ship was lost Tyrie needed a new courier and, in February 1782, he thought he had found one in Captain William James, a smuggler happy to earn £15 by running wine from France, ostensibly for the East India Co.'s ships. It was when Tyrie gave him a packet of envelopes to deliver to France on that first trip that Captain James wondered what was going on. After thinking long and hard, he opened the envelopes and read the contents. What he read had him going urgently to the government in London.

The letters contained details of ship movements and the stations of the nation's warships. It gave precise numbers and particulars of departures of the East and West India fleets, their destinations and the escorts they had. In short, the letters contained so much damaging information about British shipping, both military and civilian, that the French, if they had received it, would have been able to inflict major harm on Britain.

In the meantime, Tyrie's wife had been apprehended after delivering sensitive 'family documents' to a Mrs Hervey (for reasons undisclosed), who had opened them, understood the significance of the pages of ledger entries giving an account of the entire condition of the British Navy, which Tyrie had copied out, and promptly passed them on to the authorities. Days later, Tyrie himself was also arrested.

Sent to Winchester, he was interrogated but would not talk. He was brought before a special court convened at Winchester Castle in August 1782 and charged with high treason. The trial was swift, even though Tyrie rejected thirty-five jurors. On 2 September 1782 the *Hampshire Chronicle* noted his lawyer, 'Mr Counsellor Watson', gave an 'excellent Speech'. Unsurprisingly the jury found him guilty and he was condemned to the hideous death reserved for particularly heinous crimes, that of being hanged, drawn and quartered.

Fox notes Tyrie's attempts to avoid his horrible fate. Tyrie tried to commit suicide with a razor but the prison guards caught and overpowered him. He tried to organise his rescue on his transfer from one prison to another without success and then he was part of an ingenious mass breakout plot at the Winchester Jewry Street Gaol. The yard-thick walls of the dungeon were loosened painstakingly and a tunnel was dug, through which the prisoners hoped to pour. Sadly for them, and in particular for Tyrie, the tunnel was discovered and their hopes of escaping to France were dashed.

Justice caught up with David Tyrie on Saturday 24 August 1782. He was taken to Portsmouth, where he was dragged on a sledge to Southsea Common and through the crowds, who had turned out to witness what would be the last such execution in England. There was a slight delay when it was realised that the rope was missing and it was physically impossible to hang him. The *Hampshire Chronicle* says that throughout the preparations, as a rope and tackle had to be found, Tyrie maintained the 'most singular composure and magnanimity'. The newspaper reported that Tyrie showed concern for his still-living father and feared that the news of his son's crime would turn his hair grey and send him sorrowfully to his grave.

Death did not come swiftly to Tyrie. The *Hampshire Chronicle* tells us that he was hanged for twenty-two minutes and then laid out on the sledge. The sentence was carried out precisely: 'His head was severed from his body, his heart taken out and burnt, his privities cut off, and his body quartered'. He was then put into a coffin and immediately buried on the beach.

That was not the end though. As soon as the dignitaries had gone, the sailors in the crowd dug up the coffin, emptied Tyrie's body out and 'cut it in a thousand pieces, every one carrying away a piece of his body to shew their messmates on board'.

Interest was so intense in the case that a week later, when the execution was reported in the newspaper, not only had it been estimated that 100,000 people had turned up to witness the execution but the transcript of the trial was on sale at 1s a copy.

Highwaymen

Tales of highwaymen littered Hampshire's history for several centuries. Time and the Hollywood treatment have given us a romantic picture of these gentlemen, but there is little doubt that these determined thieves posed a real danger to the unsuspecting public. Highwaymen often targeted certain main roads, particularly after a fair when traders would be taking their profits home.

Captain Alexander Smith's entertaining 1926 work, comprehensively titled *A Complete History of the Lives and Robberies of the Most Notorious Highwaymen, Footpads, Shoplifts and Cheats of Both Sexes, Wherein their most Secret and Barbarous Murders, Unparalleled Robberies, Notorious Thefts, and Unheard-of Cheats are set in a true Light and exposed to Public View, for the Common Benefit of Mankind*, details the lives and careers of those who chose to utter those famous words, 'Stand and Deliver!' for personal gain.

Thomas Sympson, known as 'Old Mobb', was born and lived with his wife and extended family in Romsey. He had a successful career as a highwayman for over forty-five years. Smith tells us that Old Mobb once robbed the astrologer John Gadbury (1627-1704) on the Winchester to London road. Gadbury pleaded poverty, which Old Mobb was having none of, 'having no compassion on his pretending to be in need,' and proceeded to relieve him of £9, with much swearing and intimidation.

A lady travelling along on the stagecoach to Bath fared badly, being robbed of £40. While this was taking place another victim came along, so Old Mobb, not one to miss a chance, turned his attention to the newcomer. He robbed Cornelius Tilburgh, described by Smith as 'the mountbank [swindler] living in Lincoln Inn Fields', a travelling 'doctor' who sold 'cures' to the sick, of £25 and a gold medal, said to have been presented to him by King Charles II.

Old Mobb came to a predictable end. Caught committing a robbery in Westminster, he was tried on thirty-six indictments at the Old Bailey and was found guilty of thirty-two. He was hanged at Tyburn on Friday 30 May 1690.

Captain James Hind, originally from Chipping Norton in Oxfordshire, the son of a saddler, was apprenticed to a butcher, a position he found difficult. He ran away after two years and joined forces with Thomas Allen, a noted highwayman in his own right, who taught him all he knew. On the Petersfield to Portsmouth road one day, Hind stopped a 'gentleman's coach' in which 'gentlewomen' were travelling to a wedding. He robbed the bride of her dowry, £3,000 in gold, and escaped amidst a loud hue and cry.

Hind was a Royalist who liked to stop and rob Parliamentarians when the chance came along. He and Allen stopped Cromwell himself, but were overpowered and Allen was arrested and later hanged. Hind escaped and lived to rob a Parliamentarian, Sergeant Bradshaw, of both gold and silver.

His luck ran out after ten years or so of the highwayman's life and a friend betrayed him. He was found guilty of murder for the killing of a man in Knole in Berkshire and then of high treason. He met a grisly end, being hanged, drawn and quartered on 24 September 1652. He was just thirty-four years old.

Highway robbery was not confined to the seventeenth century. The *Salisbury and Winchester Journal* of 1827 details a 'Daring Highway Robbery' in its edition for Winchester, dated Saturday 22 September. The newspaper states that on the previous Wednesday evening, between the hours of 8–9 p.m., one Charles Tarver, who was a corn factor living in Romsey, was on his way home when:

> ... he was attacked about the middle of Pauncefoot Hill, within a mile of the town, by four footpads, one of whom seized his horse's bridle, another presented a horse pistol to his breast, at the same time demanding his property, and threatening to blow his brains out in case of resistance, while the two others pulled him from his horse.

These then were desperate men, determined to get what they could from the unlucky Mr Tarver. The newspaper carries on with its description of the robbery by telling its readers the highwaymen 'rifled his pockets of their contents' and stole:

> £230 in ten, five, and one pound notes of the Romsey, Southampton, Winchester, and other banks, including two five, and two one pound notes of the Yeovil bank, a yellow canvas bag in which were 12 and 2 half sovereigns, and some silver, a market or memorandum book, and various other articles.

After the robbery the victim eventually arrived in Romsey and raised the alarm. The thieves were not found, although the next day children discovered the bag that had carried the gold, which had been discarded just outside the town. The extensive newspaper report finishes with a description of the villains, who were armed with bludgeons as well as the pistol, and a reward of £35 was offered 'for the apprehension of the offenders'.

In the time before an effective police force, apprehending highwaymen and other law breakers was a difficult proposition and the villains knew it. The County Police Act, which gave Justices of the Peace the right to have a paid police force in the English counties, was still twelve years away when this last robbery took place. Coverage in a newspaper, in a time when much of the population could not read or afford to buy the publication, did not ensure the high level of awareness amongst the people that we have from media coverage of a crime today.

Murder in Boldre

The highly informative Southern Life website tells a grisly smuggling tale with a bit of a twist.

It would seem that seventeenth-century smuggler families were not adverse to a little murder and they did not mind who it was they murdered. A story from Boldre, a reputed smuggling haunt, is connected to the house now known as Baywater House, but formerly called Formosa.

An unnamed smuggler and his daughter once inhabited this house. It was remote and this made it attractive not just for storing contraband, but also as a quiet resting place for someone carrying secret documents who did not want it generally known he was in the area. This is the use it was put to when a young messenger arrived one night. He was carrying documents for James Scott, 1st Duke of Monmouth, whose rebellion against James II was to lead to a bloody end at the Battle of Sedgemoor in 1685.

The smuggler's daughter liked the look of the messenger, but liked the jewellery he wore even more. The only way to get it and keep it was to assassinate the messenger. This is just what she did, with the help of her lover who also had an eye for a pretty bauble. The luckless man's body was buried in the garden and the jewellery was divided between the pair. No one seemed to notice the man was missing and the guilty pair rested easily.

Centuries passed. In the twentieth century Mrs Gordon-Hamilton owned the house, which by now had been extended. She grew used to hearing the sounds of barrels rolling and tip-toed footsteps in the oldest part of the house and put the sounds she heard down to its use by smugglers years before. It was in 1920, when she had her photograph taken in the garden, that she was startled to find that it was not just the spirits of smugglers she was sharing her home with. The photograph showed a young man standing next to her, complete with curls fashionable in the seventeenth century. After showing the photograph to a friend, the friend dreamt that the young man wanted them to dig in the garden. Intrigued as to what they would find, they began to dig.

They found a secret chamber but it was empty and so, determined to get to the bottom of the story, Mrs Gordon-Hamilton called in a medium. It was through this person that the story of the murder that had occurred at the house came to light. Alas, the messenger's body was never found.

The Tigers

The Royal Hampshire Regiment was originally formed of the old Meredith's Regiment (named after the Adjutant General, Thomas Meredith), which was formed in 1702 and became the 37th Regiment of Foot in 1754. It then became the 67th Regiment of Foot in 1756, which eventually grew to become part of the North and South Hampshire's, and finally became the First and Second Battalions of the Hampshire Regiment in 1881.

1 August 1759 was the date of the Battle of Minden, a town on the banks of the River Weser in Hanover, Germany. The battle took place in the middle of the Seven Years War with France and Prince Ferdinand of Brunswick commanded the British forces. He noticed a group of enemy cavalry which, if not eliminated, would cause a lot of damage to his troops. He therefore gave the order to the six infantry regiments under his command that they were to advance 'by' the drum (Edwards). The 37th Foot was one of the regiments involved.

The order was received but it had become slightly confused in transit and so it was that the infantrymen advanced 'at' the drum and so sped across the battlefield in time with the drums. As they did so, they picked at the numerous wild roses growing on Minden Heath and pushed the blooms into their hats and coats, and also into their equipment, although by all accounts they kept in perfect formation as they did so.

Seeing what the British were doing amused the French, who sneered at the thought of infantrymen attacking mounted troops. The British ignored them and, when the French charged, calmly loaded their muskets and waited until they were almost on top of them. They then fired, bringing down rank upon rank of the enemy. In disarray the French who survived the slaughter retreated, only to be pounded by shellfire and further musketry.

It was customary for the Royal Hampshire Regiment to celebrate victory by wearing roses in their hats and to decorate their colours and drums with roses on the anniversary of the battle.

In 1826 the 67th Regiment was awarded its badge, the tiger, and with it the nickname 'The Tigers' for its long service in India. It went on to win four Victoria Crosses in China in 1860.

During the First World War, huge numbers of Hampshire men volunteered to join the Hampshires and soon there were thirty-six regiments in the county. Subsequently, the county was devastated by its heavy losses.

The Hampshire Regiment was granted the title 'Royal' in November 1946 in recognition of its gallant service in the Second World War, when it won another two Victoria Crosses.

In 1992 the Royal Hampshire Regiment merged with the Queens Regiment and became the Princess of Wales's Royal Regiment.

A Chat with Southampton's Town Crier

The Town Crier acted as master of ceremonies at major events and made guest appearances in support of local charities. The last Town Crier of Southampton was John Melody, a former teacher and a resident of Shirley. He died in-office in 2014 and has not been replaced. Speaking to the author in 2009, he talked about becoming the Town Crier:

> I started as Town Crier in the year 2004. There are no written records [about the Town Crier] until about the sixteenth century when there was a Town Crier appointed. There was a Town Crier until about the middle of the nineteenth century and then the Town Crier was sacked for not doing his job properly. There was a long lapse and then town crying started again around about 1980, so it has been continuous since that time.
>
> I was in the teaching profession and had been made redundant. I saw an advertisement saying that they wanted a Town Crier for Southampton and I thought, 'I can do that!' I just applied and I think seven of us were shortlisted. The actual contest was at the Bargate and they had the film crews there, as well as the newspaper reporters and photographers. We were given a script to present, which we had not prepared and had not seen before, and we had to do our own personal cry. Fred Dinage was there and he was recording the number of decibels that people were crying. I had the loudest voice and the clearest and I was appointed. I was really pleased.

What John modestly did not mention was the fact that his 104-decibel cry actually broke the recording device measuring the volume of each contestant's cries! He continued:

> I attend quite a number of events in a year. Some of them are for charities. The official ones as Town Crier for the city of Southampton are the ones

involving Mayor Making, Beating the Bounds and Court Leet. I do garden fêtes and this year [2009] I have done quite a number. One of the most memorable ones was Connaught Place in Wickham, which needs to raise a great deal of money for charity and to maintain the building. We raised about £8,000 in two and a half hours, so it was very good. I also did the garden fête for Cedar School and the children there are handicapped and many are in wheelchairs. It was a splendid occasion. Very often if there is a cruise ship I will go into Mayflower Park and do a welcome for it. I also go down to the Saints football ground and make announcements outside.

Sadly, John Melody has passed away since this interview. The author sends her condolences to John's family and friends. John could never be missed at an event. He was replendent in his black and gold tricorn hat, scarlet coat trimmed in gold braid, ruffled white shirt, black knee length trousers and long white stockings. His death ended a centuries-old tradition in the city.

The Office of Mayor

The *Salisbury and Winchester Journal* of 1827 devotes much of its Winchester report on Saturday 22 September to informing its readers of the election of the mayors of various Hampshire towns. Richard Littlehales, Esq., we are told, was elected on Monday 17 September 1827 to be the Town Mayor of Winchester and his election was celebrated with a sumptuous meal, which included turtle and venison, for over 200 persons at the George Inn.

Richard Sweeper, Esq., became the Town Mayor of Romsey on Friday 21 September. Mr Sweeper, it was noted, was one of the town's burgesses.

John Simmonds, Esq., the newspaper also mentions, was elected Mayor of Basingstoke in the same week.

The office of mayor was noteworthy and the election of new town mayors was news in the nineteenth century.

In Southampton the first mention of the mayor was in a letter reputed to date from 1217. Unlike today when each mayor is elected for one year, mayors then could stay in office for as long as they wished, provided they were fit for the job, and were originally appointed by the monarch. Later the outgoing mayor appointed a successor, but change came in 1835 when councillors began to elect the mayor.

The Southampton Archives Service states that the first Southampton mayor mentioned by name was Walter Fortin, who was mayor from around 1220 to 1234. Until the election of Lucia Marion Welch in 1927, the 704th

Mayor of Southampton, all the town's mayors were men, usually local businessmen. Councillor Peter Baillie became the 797th Mayor of Southampton in May 2019. Councillor Susan Blatchford, the 582nd Sheriff of Southampton, will succeed him.

The Southampton Town Mayor chaired the council meetings and the town courts, and managed such various items as the regulations over trade and industry, dispensing poor relief and ensuring that central government directions are carried out. The Town Mayor could perform marriages during the 1650s after the English Civil War. Since 1835 the Mayor's duties have been more ceremonial.

The Town Sergeant supports the mayor. Paul Potter was one of those called upon to assist as Southampton Town Sergeant. Now retired, he says of the office of mayor:

> It is all ceremonial today but years and years ago Mayors had a lot of power because they were appointed by the monarch. They collected revenue for the monarch through taxes from the town for things coming in through the port. The Town Sergeant was the Mayor's protector.

The Mayor wears a traditional red cloak on ceremonial occasions and the Town Sergeant carries a large mace-like object. Potter explains:

> The Mayor's Mace dates from 1675. Maces were originally instruments of war. They became decorative and were processed to show the importance of the person within the procession. This is the same reason for the red robe to a population who could not read or write; to show whom the important person was. It was purely a symbol.

BIBLIOGRAPHY

Books

Acorah, D., *Haunted Britain: Over 100 of the UK's Scariest Places to Visit* (HarperElement, an imprint of Harper Collins Publishers, 2006)

Alexander, M., *British Folklore, Myths and Legends* (George Weidenfeld and Nicolson Lits, 1982)

Alford, V. and Gallop, R., *The Traditional Dance* (Methuen, 1935)

Allen, R.R., *The Concise Oxford Dictionary of Current English* (Clarendon Press, Oxford, 1990)

Baker, B. et al, *The First 700 Years* (New Forest Printing, 1999)

Barfield, N., *Supermarine* (Chalford, 1996)

Barlow, F., *William Rufus* (University of California Press, 1983)

Barton, J., *Hampshire Headlines* (Countryside Books, 1993)

Beddington, W.G. and Christy, E.B. (Eds), *It Happened in Hampshire* (The Hampshire Federation of Women's Institutes, 1936, 1977 edition)

Black, M., *WI Calendar of Feasts* (WI Books, London, 1985)

Boase, W., *The Folklore of Hampshire and the Isle of Wight* (Batsford, London, 1976)

Brode, A., *The Hampshire Village Book* (Countryside Books, 1980)

Brown, J., *The Illustrated History of Southampton's Suburbs* (The Breedon Books Publishing Co. Ltd, 2004)

Browne, J.P., *Folksongs of Old Hampshire* (Milestones, Horndean, 1987)

Burbridge, B. and Prior, T., *Romsey Heritage Trail* (Test Valley Borough Council, Undated)

Burbridge, B., *Romsey Town Guide and Map 2008* (Local Authority Publishing Co. Ltd., Lower Dicker, 2008)

Burch, C.E.C., *Minstrels and Players in Southampton 1428-1635* (City of Southampton, 1969)

Cecil, D., *A Portrait of Jane Austen* (Penguin Books, London, 1978, 2000 edition)

Christian, R., *The Country Life Book of Old English Customs* (Country Life Ltd., London, 1966)

Edwards, T.J., *Military Customs* (Gale and Polden Ltd, 1950)

Evans, I.H., *Brewer's Dictionary of Phrase & Fable* (Cassell, London, 1870, 1990 edition)

Forman, J., *The Haunted South* (Robert Hale, 1978)

Fox, I., *Hampshire Tales of Mystery and Murder* (Countryside Books, 2001)

Esmond, R. and Triggs, A., *Portsmouth 'The Good Old Days'* (Halsgrove, 2002)

Hoare, P., *The Ghosts of Netley* (Hampshire County Council, 2004)

Hoare, P., *England's Lost Eden: Adventures in a Victorian Utopia* (Fourth Estate, 2005)

Hoare, P., *Spike Island* (Fourth Estate, 2001)

Hole, C., *English Folklore* (B.T. Batsford Ltd, London, 1940)

Howard, T., *Austen Country* (Grange Books, 1995)

Huxley, E., *Florence Nightingale* (Chancellor Press, 1975)

Ingram, J.H., *The Haunted Homes and Family Traditions of Great Britain* (W.H. Allen, 1890)

Jenkins, E., *Jane Austen* (Victor Gollancz Ltd, 1973)

Jones, R., *Haunted Castles of Britain and Ireland* (New Holland Publishers, 2003)

Kilby, P., *Southampton Through the Ages* (Computational Mechanics Publications, 1997)

Kingsclere Heritage Association, *The Bedbug Recorder* (2001)

King John's House & Tudor Cottage Trust Ltd, *The Story of King John's House and Tudor Cottage Romsey* (Test Valley Borough Council 1995, 2006 edition)

Long, R., *The Haunted Inns of Hampshire* (Power Publications, 1999)

Main, L., *Walks in Mysterious Hampshire* (Sigma Leisure, 1998)

Millson, C., *Tales of Old Hampshire* (Countryside Books, 1980)

Montagu, B., *The New Forest Embroidery* (New Forest Association, 1981)

Moor, Major E., *Bealing Bells* (John Loder, 1841)

Sandell, E.M., *Southampton Cavalcade* (G.F. Wilson & Co. Ltd, Southampton, 1953)

Shore, T.W., *History of Hampshire* (Elliot Stock, 1892, EP Publishing Edition 1976)

Smith, A., *A Complete History of the Lives and Robberies of the Most Notorious Highwaymen, Footpads, Shoplifts and Cheats of Both Sexes, Wherein their most Secret and Barbarous Murders, Unparalleled Robberies, Notorious Thefts, and Unheard-of Cheats are set in a true Light and exposed to Public View, for the Common Benefit of Mankind* (George Routledge & Sons, 1926)

Spence, J., *Becoming Jane Austen* (Hambledon & London, London, 2003)

Tate, P., *The New Forest 900 Years Later* (Macdonald and Jane's, 1979)

Turner, B.C., *A History of Hampshire* (Phillimore, Chichester 1963, 1978 edition)

Underwood, P., *Ghosts of Hampshire and the Isle of Wight* (Saint Michael's Abbey Press, Farnborough, 1983)

Underwood, P., *Nights in Haunted Houses* (Headline, 1994)

Vesey-Fitzgerald, B., *Portrait of the New Forest* (Robert Hale, 1966)

Warner, Revd Richard, *Topographical Remarks Relating to the South-Western Parts of Hampshire* (R. Blamire, Strand, London, 1793)

White, A.M., *Outlines of Legal History* (BiblioLife, LLC, 2009)

Whitlock, R., *In Search of Lost Gods: A Guide to British Folklore* (Phaidon, 1979)

Reports, Papers, Brochures and Articles

Hayes, I., 'Ghost of Itchell' (*Hampshire, The County Magazine*, September 1975)

Ivey, J., 'Our New Forest, a Living Register of Language and Traditions: Report on New Forest Traditions' (undated)

Rickard, C., 'HMS *Mercury*, Swift and Faithful, 1941-1993' (2006)

Turner, V., 'Legends, Lions, and Virgins: The Legend of Sir Bevois of Southampton' (published 2001 on www.southernlife.org.uk)

Author unknown, 'The Two Churches of Saint Peter Stockbridge' (Quality Business Services, 1995, second edition 1999)

Websites

1911 Encyclopaedia, http://www.1911encyclopedia.org/Henry_John_Temple,_3rd_viscount_
	Palmerston

Absolute astronomy, http://www.absoluteastronomy.com/topics/River_Avon,_Hampshire

Air Racing History, http://www.airracinghistory.freeola.com/Schneider.htm

Alresford, http://www.alresford.org/

Archive, http://www.archive.org/stream/festivalsholydayoourli/festivalsholydayoourli_djvu.txt

Archontology, http://www.archontology.org/nations/england/king_england/henry_young.php

Asiya, http://www.asiya.org/sabbats/lammas.html

Bartleby, http://www.bartleby.com/81/13227.html

BBC,
	http://news.bbc.co.uk/1/hi/special_report/86133.stm
	http://www.bbc.co.uk/southampton/features/ghosts/haunted_hotel.shtml
	http://www.bbc.co.uk/hampshire/content/articles/2005/03/22/newforestshakers_feature.
	shtml
	http://www.bbc.co.uk/hampshire/content/articles/2009/05/01/may_day_feature.shtml
	http://www.bbc.co.uk/radio4/history/inourtime/inourtime_20041021.shtml

Blu Pete, http://www.blupete.com/Literature/Biographies/Reformers/Cobbett.htm - TOC

Bookrags, http://www.bookrags.com/research/threshing-machine-woi/

Brittanica, http://www.utopia-britannica.org.uk/pages/HAMPS.htm

Britannia,
	http://www.britannia.com/history/docs/asintro2.html
	http://www.britannia.com/bios/swithun.html
	http://www.britannia.com/history/monarchs/mon35.html
	http://www.britannia.com/history/monarchs/mon26.html
	http://www.britannia.com/history/monarchs/mon25a.html
	http://www.britannia.com/bios/henofbls.html
	http://www.britannia.com/history/docs/magna2.html
	http://www.britannia.com/history/monarchs/mon37.html

British Dictionary of National Biography online, http://www.tim.ukpub.net/Murder/Alice.
	html

British History, http://www.british-history.ac.uk/report.aspx?compid=56511

British Postal Museum and Archive, http://postalheritage.org.uk/exhibitions/onlineexhi-
	bitions/vapurchasegrantfund/notices/swanwithtwonecks

Broadlands, http://www.broadlands.net/historyfs.htm

Church Times Archive, http://www.churchtimes.co.uk/content.asp?id=72407

Crediton, http://www.crediton.co.uk/tourism/boniface_crediton.html

Daily Echo,
	http://www.dailyecho.co.uk/news/3933737.Historic_Dolphin_Hotel_goes_into_
	administration_/
	http://www.dailyecho.co.uk/leisure/pubs/pubreviews/4089380.The_Red_Lion__High_
	Street__Southampton/

Damerham, http://www.damerham.net/html/history.html

Daughters of Wisdom, http://www.daughtersofwisdom.org.uk/gbi_province/history/index.
	htm

Development Trusts Association, http://www.dta.org.uk/ourlongandlivelytraditionUN-
	PUBLISHED/historycontentsummary/maryanngirling.htm

Dr John Crook, http://www.john-crook.com/

Duhaime, http://www.duhaime.org/LegalDictionary/C/CourtofPiePowder.aspx

Encyclopaedia Britannica Online,
    http://www.britannica.com/EBchecked/topic/103293/Cerdic
    http://www.britannica.com/EBchecked/topic/246394/grisaille
e-castles, http://www.ecastles.co.uk/merdon.html
EFDSS, http://library.efdss.org/archives/
Find Artricles, http://findarticles.com/p/articles/mi_6764/is_3_9/ai_n31202529/
FOCSLE, http://www.focsle.org.uk/SCoFF/gardiner.ht
Forest Tracks, http://www.forest-tracks.co.uk/paulmarshs/pages/mummers.html
Paul Halsall, http://www.fordham.edu/halsall/basis/nennius-full.html
Fordingbridge, http://www.fordingbridge.gov.uk/index.cfm?articleid=2308
Frederick Lee Bridell, http://www.frederickleebridell.co.uk/
Geograph, http://www.geograph.org.uk/photo/22591
Genaealogy,
    http://freepages.genealogy.rootsweb.ancestry.com/~dutillieul/ZOtherPapers/HCSep21782.html
    http://freepages.genealogy.rootsweb.ancestry.com/~dutillieul/ZOtherPapers/
    S&WJSep241827.html
Google Books, http://books.google.com
Grantham, http://www.grantham.karoo.net/paul/graves/russell.htm
Hampshire Chronicle, http://www.hampshirechronicle.co.uk/news/news_
    winchester/4646807.Ancestral_voices_heard_again/
Hampshire Constabulary,
    http://hampshireconstabularyhistory.org.uk/?page_id=1099
    http://hampshireconstabularyhistory.org.uk/?page_id=937
Hampshire County Council,
    http://www3.hants.gov.uk/hampshire-countryside/odiham-castle.htm
    http://www3.hants.gov.uk/culture-all/local-heroes/brusher-mills.htm
    http://www3.hants.gov.uk/guidedwalks.htm
    http://www3.hants.gov.uk/hampshire-countryside/odiham-castle.htm
    http://www.hants.gov.uk/hampshiretreasures/entries/v05p016e08.html
    http://www3.hants.gov.uk/logos/cx-logos-hog.htm
Hampshire Ghost Club, http://www.hampshireghostclub.net
Hampshire Net, http://www.thisishampshire.net/news/4566570.Historic_hotel_has_new_
    owner/
Hand Picked Hotels, http://www.handpickedhotels.co.uk/hotels/rhinefield-house/History/
Hants, http://www.hants.gov.uk/hampshiretreasures/vol05/page129.html
Historic UK, http://www.historic-uk.com/HistoryUK/England-History/SouthSeaBubble.
    htm
HMS Victory, http://www.hmsvictory.com
Holloway Pages, http://hollowaypages.com/jonson1692bartholmew.htm
Home Clara, http://home.clara.net/reedhome/winchester/interior.htm
Indigo Group, http://www.indigogroup.co.uk/edge/Mazes.htm
Justus Anglican, http://justus.anglican.org/resources/bio/123.html
JStor, http://www.jstor.org/pss/432707?cookieSet=1
Kingsclere, http://www.kingsclere.org.uk/
Landscaping, http://landscaping.about.com/od/plantsforshadyareas/p/foxglove_plants.htm
Lay Dominicans, http://www.30p.org/stlouis.php
Local History Initiative, http://www.lhi.org.uk/projects_directory/projects_by_region/south_
    east/hampshire/history_of_theatre_royal_winchester/brief_history_of.html
Lonang, http://www.lonang.com/exlibris/blackstone/bla-419.htm
Luminarium, http://www.luminarium.org/encyclopedia/alleyn.htm

Mariners 1, http://www.mariners-l.co.uk/UKRNMainBases.htm

Master Mummers, http://mastermummers.org/groupslist.php?p=6&ctrl=old&step=20&csNam
e=&otCode=G&format=summary&search=

Megalith,
http://www.megalithic.co.uk/article.php?sid=11608
http://www.megalithic.co.uk/article.php?sid=5912

Middle Ages, http://www.middle-ages.org.uk/minstrels.htm

National Archives, http://www.nationalarchives.gov.uk/education/politics/g5/

National Trust,
http://www.nationaltrust.org.uk/main/w-mottisfont
http://www.nationaltrust.org.uk/main/w-vh/w-visits/w-findaplace/w-
hintonampnergarden/w-hintonampnergarden-history.htm

Nelson society, http://www.nelson-society.com/

New Advent, http://www.newadvent.org/cathen/03761a.htm

New Forest Association, http://www.newforestassociation.org/New%Forest%20Embroidery.
pdf

New Forest Park, http://www.new-forest-national-park.com/new-forest-wildlife.html

Number 10, http://www.number10.gov.uk/history-and-tour/prime-ministers-in-history/
viscount-palmerston

Online literature, http://www.online-literature.com/austen/

Paranormal Tours, http://www.paranormaltours.com/event_in_detail.php?event=282

Quest for Ghosts, http://www.questforghosts.com/haunted-houses/hinton-ampner-garden.html

Render Plus, http://www.renderplus.com/hartgen/htm/scealdea.htm - name3552

Royal, http://www.royal.gov.uk/MonarchUK/Symbols/Greatsealoftherealm.aspx

Royal Naval Communications Association, http://www.rncca.com/PDF%20Docs/MercHist1.
pdf

Royal Naval Museum, http://www.royalnavalmuseum.org/info_sheet_trafnight.htm

SAPS, http://www-saps.plantsci.cam.ac.uk/trees/rosacan.htm

School of the Seasons, http://www.schooloftheseasons.com/lammas.html

Smugglers,
http://www.smuggling.co.uk/gazetteer_s_13.html
http://www.smuggling.co.uk/gazetteer_s_12.html

Stratfield Saye, http://www.stratfield-saye.co.uk/

Source Text, http://www.sourcetext.com/lawlibrary/underhill/01.htm

Southampton City Council, http://www.southampton.gov.uk/council-partners/council-
lorsrepresent/mayorsoffice/

Southern Life,
http://www.southernlife.org.uk/piepowder.htm
http://www.southernlife.org.uk/weyhill_fair.htm
http://www.southernlife.org.uk/folklor3.htm
http://www.southernlife.org.uk/brusher_mills.htm
http://www.southernlife.org.uk/andriots.htm
http://www.southernlife.org.uk/castles_forts.htm
http://www.southernlife.org.uk/netley_abbey.htm
http://www.southernlife.org.uk/bevois.htm
http://www.southernlife.org.uk/hants_regt.htm

Spartacus,
http://www.spartacus.schoolnet.co.uk/PRpalmerston.htm
http://www.spartacus.schoolnet.co.uk/PRcobbett.htm
http://www.spartacus.schoolnet.co.uk/PRhunt.htm

St Boniface, http://www.stboniface.org.uk/whowas.htm
St Cross, http://www.stcross.f2s.com/
The Gatehouse, http://homepage.mac.com/philipdavis/English sites/1281.html
The Morris Ring, http://www.themorrisring.org/more/cs.html
Think Quest, http://library.thinkquest.org/26602/entertainment.htm
This is Hampshire, http://archive.thisishampshire.net/2005/9/30/94631.html
Tour UK, http://www.touruk.co.uk/houses/househamp_broad.htm
Urban 75, http://www.urban75.org/mayday02/history.html
Victorian Web, http://www.victorianweb.org/history/pms/palmerst.html
Wikipedia,
    http://en.wikipedia.org/wiki/Court_of_Piepowder
    http://en.wikipedia.org/wiki/Horatio_Nelson,_1st_Viscount_Nelson
    http://en.wikipedia.org/wiki/Pope_Clement_I
    http://en.wikipedia.org/wiki/House_of_Wessex_family_tree
    http://en.wikipedia.org/wiki/Asser
    http://en.wikipedia.org/wiki/Napoleon_III_of_France
    http://en.wikipedia.org/wiki/Henry_V_of_England
    http://en.wikipedia.org/wiki/Lucy_Broadwood
    http://en.wikipedia.org/wiki/Cecil_Sharp
    http://en.wikipedia.org/wiki/Churching_of_women
    http://en.wikipedia.org/wiki/Orderic_Vitalis
    http://en.wikipedia.org/wiki/Walter_Tirel
    http://en.wikipedia.org/wiki/William_II_of_England
    http://en.wikipedia.org/wiki/Bread_and_circuses
    http://en.wikipedia.org/wiki/Siebe_Gorman
    http://en.wikipedia.org/wiki/William_Walker_(diver)
    http://en.wikipedia.org/wiki/Godwin,_Earl_of_Wessex
    http://en.wikipedia.org/wiki/Winchester_College_football
    http://en.wikipedia.org/wiki/Frederick_Lee_Bridell
    http://en.wikipedia.org/wiki/Jane_Austen
Winchester College, http://www.winchestercollege.co.uk/wincoll-football
Winchester Morris, http://www.winchester-morris-men.org.uk/history.htm
Winchester Walks, http://www.winchesterwalks.co.uk/html/st_catherines.html
Witching, http://witching.org/
Women's History, http://womenshistory.about.com/od/empressmatilda/a/matilda_timelin.htm
Verderers, http://www.verderers.org.uk/index.html

INDEX

Other titles published by The History Press

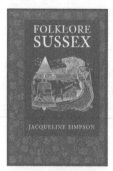

Folklore of Sussex
JACQUELINE SIMPSON

Sussex, though near London and nowadays extensively urbanised, has a rich heritage of traditional local stories, customs and beliefs. Among the many topics explored here are tales linked to landscape features and ancient churches which involve such colourful themes as lost bells, buried treasures, dragons, fairies and the devil. This book contains updated accounts of county customs and, alongside original line drawings, is illustrated with photographs and printed ephemera relating to Sussex lore.

978 0 7524 5100 8

Folklore of Kent
FRAN & GEOFF DOEL

Kent boasts a plethora of characterising traditions which include hop-growing, smuggling and saints. All this reflects the curious history and geography of the area. This book also covers topics such as seasonal customs including harvest traditions; drama; witchcraft, saints and holy wells; and the background and songs surrounding fruit and hop-growing. *Folklore of Kent* charts the traditional culture of a populous and culturally significant southern county.

978 0 7524 2628 0

Haunted Hampshire
RUPERT MATTHEWS

This well-researched book showcases almost 100 ghostly encounters from around Hampshire. The stories are arranged as a tour around Hampshire, guiding the reader on a journey through the New Forest, Winchester, Southampton, the edge of the Downs, the Test Valley and the hills around Overton. Exploring everything from pubs and churchyards to castles and ports, *Haunted Hampshire* will appeal to anyone interested in the supernatural history of the area.

978 0 7524 4862 6

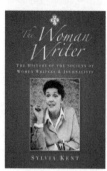

The Woman Writer
SYLVIA KENT

To celebrate the centenary of the birth of the Society of Women Writers and Journalist's much-loved President of twenty-two years, Joyce Grenfell, the Society's archivist, Sylvia Kent, reveals the long and fascinating history of the Society. Not only is the evolution of the Society fully explored, but also the lives of many of its members have been thoroughly researched to paint a vivid picture of how the Society has gone from strength to strength.

978 0 7509 5159 6

Visit our website and discover thousands of other History Press books.

www.thehistorypress.co.uk